GW00568190

Mo

Peter Hill was born in Hull in 1939 and educated at Hull Grammar School and the University of Wales. He intended to become a feature film director, but turned down an opportunity to join the film school at U.C.L.A. when he was offered a position as a producer for the B.B.C. Since 1969 he has worked in the Current Affairs Department there, primarily as an investigative producer.

For the past four years his work has been almost exclusively on the 'Rough Justice' series. This was originally his idea, and he has since become one of the few people in Britain – indeed, in the world – who work specifically on the investigation of such cases. He has written many articles and given lectures on the subject of miscarriages of justice, and is the co-author of *Rough Justice* (1983). Peter Hill lives in South London with his wife Anne, his son Julian and his daughter Laura.

Martin Young was born in Glasgow in 1947 and brought up in Edinburgh and London. He was educated at Dulwich College and at Gonville and Caius College, Cambridge. He first worked for television in the North-East of England and went on to become a reporter and presenter on B.B.C. television's 'Nationwide' and 'Tonight' programmes. More recently he has been reporting throughout the world for 'Newsnight' and 'Panorama'. He is currently working on the third series of 'Rough Justice', the programme which in 1984 won him the Broadcasting Press Guild Award for 'the most outstanding contribution to television in front of the cameras'.

Martin Young and his wife Susan live in an Oxfordshire farmhouse with their two children, Jonathan and Annabel.

Tom Sargant was born in 1905 and educated at Highgate School, gaining distinction as a classical scholar and an all-round athlete. Family circumstances prevented him from taking up a scholarship at Cambridge; instead, he entered his family firm and until 1955 worked in the non-ferrous metals industry. In 1942 his book *These Things Shall Be* prompted Sir Richard Acland to invite him to join the National Committee of his Christian Socialist movement, Common Wealth. After the 1945 General Election he joined the Labour Party and unsuccessfully contested South Hendon and West Lewisham.

In 1956 he became involved in sending observers to the Treason Trials in South Africa and Hungary. As a result, he became founding secretary of the law reform society, Justice, serving until his retirement in 1982. He has pioneered several important campaigns, including the Ombudsman and the Criminal Injuries Compensation Scheme, and has continued working with the 'Rough Justice' team since his retirement. He was appointed a J.P. in 1965, awarded the O.B.E. in 1966 and an Honorary Master of Laws degree by Queen's University, Belfast, in 1977.

Tom Sargant lives in Highgate with his wife Dorothy and has two married daughters.

MORE ROUGH JUSTICE

Peter Hill and Martin Young

with Tom Sargant

Foreword by Ludovic Kennedy

Penguin Books

Penguin Books Ltd, Harmondsworth, Middlesex, England
Viking Penguin Inc., 40 West 23rd Street, New York, New York 10010, U.S.A.
Penguin Books Australia Ltd, Ringwood, Victoria, Australia
Penguin Books Canada Ltd, 2801 John Street, Markham, Ontario, Canada L 3 R 1 B 4
Penguin Books (N.Z.) Ltd, 182–190 Wairau Road, Auckland 10, New Zealand

First published 1985

Made and printed in Great Britain by
Richard Clay (The Chaucer Press) Ltd, Bungay, Suffolk
Filmset in Monophoto Plantin by
Northumberland Press Ltd, Gateshead,
Tyne and Wear

Contents

Foreword

The re-investigation of the three murder cases in *More Rough Justice* is a further example of a remarkable partnership between the lawyers' organization, Justice,* and B.B.C. television; more specifically between Justice's former Secretary, Tom Sargant, and producer Peter Hill and presenter Martin Young.

The book also brings us up to date on the state of the three other cases from Tom Sargant's files which Young and Hill first filmed and later wrote about in the earlier book, *Rough Justice*. All three cases were reviewed with the result that one man (Jock Russell) had his life sentence quashed; another (John Walters) was unconditionally released from Broadmoor; while the McDonaghs, released on parole, have just had their convictions for murder referred back to the Court of Appeal.

This is gratifying news and says something about the influence of television publicity. All the more disappointing, therefore, to learn that the Home and Scottish Offices have done nothing to release or otherwise take steps to bring about the quashing of the convictions of the three people whose stories are told in this book. It is hard to see how any fair-minded person who saw on television or who reads here the painstaking and admirably objective reconstructions of the cases undertaken by Messrs Young and Hill can come to any other conclusion than that George Beattie (imprisoned for more than eleven years), Ernie Clarke (more than five) and Margaret Livesey (more than five) are anything but innocent.

That anyone can believe that the wretched Margaret Livesey first tied up her burly fourteen-year-old son Alan (presumably

* 93a Chancery Lane, London W.C.2. The organization works on a shoestring and has recently put out an appeal for £200,000.

6

with his permission), then tortured and stabbed him to death is beyond comprehension. As Lord Salmon has said, 'I can't see it at all.' Nor could the eminent forensic scientist, Professor James Cameron, who considered it a straight case of homosexual bondage. But to the Courts and the Home Office it all made perfect sense.

What is the main cause of miscarriages of justice in Britain today, and why are they now so common? After half a lifetime of studying them, I have not the slightest hesitation in saying that, in most cases, it is due to the actions taken or not taken, and the evidence in Court given or not given, by the C.I.D. This view is amply borne out by almost every single case in *Rough Justice* and *More Rough Justice*.

What often happens is this: a crime is committed and for days, perhaps weeks afterwards, there is no indication as to who the perpetrator might be. Then one small piece of circumstantial evidence (often quite beguiling, as in the case of Ernie Clarke) comes to light, which leads the C.I.D. to think that A may be the guilty party. Time goes by. There are no further leads or developments and policemen – many overworked, some none too bright, all feeling the need to obtain results – allow their belief in A's guilt to harden into a certainty. And sooner or later they cease to consider the possibility that A might be innocent.

But one small piece of circumstantial evidence is not enough for a conviction. Corroborative evidence must be found, and where it cannot be found, it can be, and sometimes is, invented. Equally, when evidence surfaces to suggest that A may be innocent or B must be guilty, it can be ignored in the deluded belief it must be mistaken. In this way the police consider that justice is being done.

What can be done to prevent the police continuing with these practices? There is, in my view, only one answer – radical in the extreme – and that is to relieve the police of the responsibility of investigating serious crime and turn the job over, as they do in France and elsewhere, to a highly trained *juge d'instruction* or judicial investigator. This official has the power to question or detain anyone he pleases and *directs* the police to assist him in his investigations.

This is known as the inquisitorial system (as opposed to the accusatorial system here) because whereas the minds of the British

C.I.D. are geared to seeking a suspect, the mind of the *juge d'instruction* is geared to seeking the truth. Had such an official conducted the primary investigations into the three cases in this book, those of Margaret Livesey, George Beattie and Ernie Clarke, it is unlikely they would ever have been arrested, let alone convicted: all three would be walking, as they should be, in freedom today.

It has been suggested that the forthcoming Public Prosecutor in England and the existing Procurator-Fiscal in Scotland provide adequate safeguards against police malpractices. But Fiscals are apt to accept police reports and recommendations too uncritically, and there is no reason to suppose that the English Public Prosecutor will be any different. Neither official has, or will have, anything like the powers vested in the French *juge d'instruction*.

When I was a boy, it used to be said (always by those quite ignorant of it) that English justice was the finest in the world. Today, in the light of the many miscarriages of justice that have occurred in recent years, that claim is no longer heard. Indeed, a reasonable case could now be made out for it being one of the worst in Europe. If we seriously want to reduce the number of miscarriages of justice to the sort of level at which they occur in France, then we should consider adopting at least some elements of the French system.

The two non-lawyers who have had more experience of miscarriages of justice in Britain than anyone else are Tom Sargant and myself (we can clock up almost fifty years between us), and we are united in our belief that the accusatory system and miscarriages of justice go hand in hand (for a summary of the numerous hazards that face a man wrongly accused under our system, and the inadequacies of the remedies available, see the book's last chapter).

Tom has said elsewhere that the English Bar will never countenance change because its deeply conservative practitioners have been brought up to revere the system and are therefore incapable of reforming it. If that is so (and it well may be), then it is up to Parliament to act.

Ludovic Kennedy

I

The Murder of Alan Livesey

It is possible to believe that a mother might murder her own son, but is it possible to believe that she would torture him first?

That is the central question in the case of Margaret Livesey, still serving life for a crime she almost certainly did not commit. If she is innocent, then she is the victim of a quite appalling double injustice – the loss of her son and the loss of her own liberty.

Margaret Livesey was forty-three years old in 1979. She had lived for six years in No. 41 The Crescent, Bamber Bridge, with her husband, Bob, and their three children, Derek, nineteen, Janet, eighteen, and Alan, fourteen. The Crescent is a quiet little cluster of ordinary houses, situated just a few miles from Preston in Lancashire. There's a touch of 'Coronation Street' about it – everyone knows everyone else's business. Gossip is free and it thrives. The biggest event that has ever happened in The Crescent, Bamber Bridge, took place on the evening of 22 February 1979. It was the start of Margaret Livesey's present and continuing nightmare ...

At 11.28 p.m. the police were called to her house. Her fourteen-year-old son, Alan, had been found murdered. He lay in a small pool of blood on the floor of the living room. He had been stabbed ten times. The story of exactly how and when he had been found was to be among the most vital evidence in the case.

As the police began their investigation they soon formed a picture of people's movements in The Crescent on the night of the murder. Mrs Livesey, they knew, had been out at a local pub until around closing time; Alan's father, Bob Livesey, had been at work on the night shift at the nearby British Leyland factory; so Alan had apparently been alone in the house. As the map shows, The

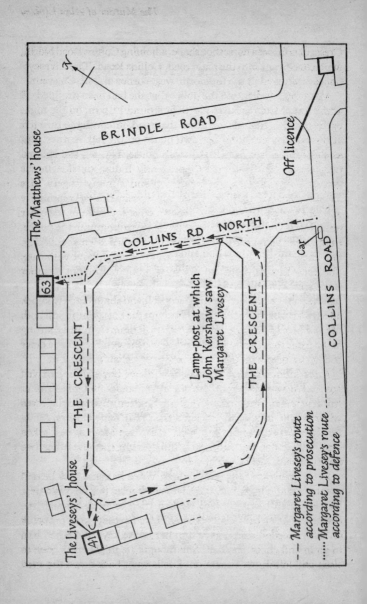

N

BRINDLE ROAD

The Matthews' house

Off licence

COLLINS RD NORTH

63

THE CRESCENT

Lamp-post at which
John Kershaw saw
Margaret Livesey

THE CRESCENT

Car

COLLINS ROAD

The Liveseys' house

41

--- Margaret Livesey's route
according to prosecution

.... Margaret Livesey's route
according to defence

Crescent is in fact a horseshoe shape, adjoining Collins Road North, which itself runs into the main road, Collins Road. The Liveseys' house is situated in the top north-west corner of The Crescent.

Margaret Livesey told the police that she had been dropped off at the top of Collins Road North at around 11 p.m. on the night of the murder. She walked down that road, intending to turn left at the bottom and go to her own house on the next corner. But as she approached Mrs Matthews's house, No. 63, she spotted two of the local youngsters, apparently hiding outside in the garden. They were Andrew Matthews and Tommy Rogers. Mrs Livesey, like everyone else in the tiny, gossip-ridden community of The Crescent, knew that these two boys and most of the other teenagers in the road had been getting into trouble with the police. Indeed, she was worried that her son Alan had been shoplifting. She knew he was already in trouble for messing about with cars. She knew that Andrew and Tommy should not be out together at all, and certainly not at 11 o'clock at night.

When she challenged them they ran off and she decided to knock on Mrs Matthews's door to tell her about the boys. She found both Mr and Mrs Matthews and Mrs Rogers, Tommy's mother, sitting in the front room having a drink. Mr Matthews offered her a cider and Mrs Livesey sat down on the arm of a chair to drink it.

A few minutes later the older Matthews boy, Leslie, arrived home. He was dispatched to see if he could find his brother Andrew and the Rogers boy, Tommy. He returned without them and was sent off to check a second time with Tony Rogers. Again Leslie returned without the boys. This time Mrs Livesey asked him to check on her son Alan. She thought that the other two might be with him in her house.

Leslie was away for a few minutes. When he came back he said that he could not get into the Liveseys' house, but he could hear the television blaring away. He had tried to peek through the curtains, but he could not see Alan. Mrs Livesey, now probably on to her second drink, gave him her house keys and asked him to go in and check on Alan. She thought he might have gone to sleep and left the television on. Leslie went back down the road to No. 41. The next few minutes are etched in his memory for ever. Even today, each time he recounts it, the story is almost word for word the same:

Leslie told us:

> So I went up, opened the door and pushed it open and I could smell a funny smell. I didn't know what it were, so I went into the front room, the telly were on full, then I realized what it were, it were gas.
>
> And Alan lay on the carpet in front of the fireplace, with his hands tied behind his back and all that. And I thought, they're messing about ... someone is going to jump out and start messing about. So, as I got down to him, I said 'Alan, are you alright?' And no answer at all. So I shook him about, turned him over. He were all wet and that. And there was a red sock round his neck. So, as I moved that away, I saw everything – cuts and bruises, cuts and gashes everywhere.
>
> And I just tried giving him the kiss of life and nought happened and there were blood spurting out of his throat. So I covered it up with my hand, tried again. And nothing happened. So, from there I just ran all the way down here and I said to Mrs Livesey, I sat in the corner of the room and said, 'Christ, he's dead.'

Leslie tried to persuade Mrs Livesey not to go to her house – but of course she did. Leslie remembers that vividly too: 'And as she went in, she looked in and said: "Oh, Alan, oh Alan." Then she knelt down, put his head in between her knees and she said something about, "I don't want him to die with his eyes open ..." So from there I ran to the phone box, phoned for the police.'

That phone call was logged by the Bamber Bridge Police at 11.28 p.m. That time remains the only reliable time check in the entire case. But from it, as we were later to discover, a great deal can be deduced.

The police arrived remarkably quickly – within about three minutes. The front room must have been a horrible sight. The dead boy lay on his back between the settee and the fireplace. Leslie had turned him over to give him the kiss of life, but the murderer had presumably left the boy face down on the carpet, with his hands tied behind his back. His clothing was rumpled up, his vest and jersey pushed up towards his chest. And that clothing was itself odd. Earlier in the evening – at about 6 o'clock – Alan had had a meal and then gone out to the off-licence with his mother. At that time he had been wearing trousers and a jumper. Now he was dressed in his best army cadet uniform and his best, almost new boots.

Before the police could do anything they had to clear away the gas. Whoever had killed the boy had turned all the gas taps on. Although Mrs Livesey had turned them off when she found Alan, the house was still full of gas. So the windows were thrown open and the cold February air came flooding into the house. Subsequently, this was to cause a problem for the pathologist. The temperature of a dead body can be one of the most useful factors in determining the time of death. But Alan Livesey's body had lain first in an unheated house (the gas taps had been turned off and turned on again unlit) and then had been subjected to the cold air, which was let in when the police arrived. By the time the body was properly examined, at 2.40 a.m., those conflicting temperatures would make determination of time of death even more hazardous than it is normally.

The wounds on Alan's body indicated a remarkable degree of malice and, in some cases, premeditation. There were ten stab wounds. Six of them had done real damage, penetrating the body to a depth of as much as 4 inches. The other wounds were more superficial, described as being rather like small nicks inflicted by the point of a knife. One of them was a cut just $\frac{1}{4}$ inch long across the top of Alan's right eyelid. It looked as if a knife had been placed carefully on the eyelid and then pressed just enough to break the skin.

The worst of the deep wounds were two 4-inch wounds in the neck, which had cut through the spine and transfixed the neck from front to back, and a $3\frac{1}{2}$-inch wound which had penetrated the boy's heart. A further wound penetrated the right lung to a depth of $2\frac{1}{2}$ inches. The pathologist noted that death came from shock, caused by multiple stab wounds. He said that great force would have been required to drive the weapon in and pull it out again.

But there were several other strange clues at the scene of the crime. Leslie Matthews had removed the red football socks from around Alan's neck. They had been punctured eleven times by the knife. It looked as if they must have been there around the boy's neck as he was attacked. The pathologist also found a piece of adipose tissue, human flesh, adhering to a sock, which further suggested that the boy had been stabbed in the neck through the socks.

There was little sign of a struggle. Curiously, too, there was not a lot of blood around the room. There was a pool of blood, which had soaked into the carpet around the boy's head and upper body, but there were no signs of blood splashes on the fireplace or the furniture. If the boy had been standing when first attacked, the pathologist would have expected to see some blood splashes.

To the police it must have seemed as if someone had sat astride Alan – hence the rumpled clothing – and teased and tortured him with the point of a knife before plunging it with great force into his neck and chest. Further reinforcing this growing theory was the elaborate way that the boy's wrists had been bound up with a tie. The knot went around both wrists and was tied in the middle, bringing the wrists together. Then each end was looped around each wrist individually and tied again. Finally the two ends were tied together between the wrists with a reef knot.

Also in the room – on the floor and on the settee – were two newspapers, one of which was the *Daily Mirror*. It was the edition of Wednesday, 21 February 1979. Page eleven was almost entirely given up to a graphic description of killings and torture in Northern Ireland, under the headline 'The Bloody Gang of Hate'. The article told the vicious tale of the so-called 'Shankill Butchers', a group of eight Protestant terrorists who between them killed and tortured nineteen people in Belfast within a seventeen-month period. In the Northern edition of the paper, the one that the Livesey family received, there was also a photograph of five lethal-looking knives that were the 'Butchers'' weapons. The *Daily Mail* and the *Daily Express* also carried similar reports and the same picture.

The police may already have thought that this was not such a straightforward affair. It did not look like a frenzied killing in a moment of extreme anger. It seemed altogether more bizarre, like a vicious game gone wrong.

The police had established fairly quickly the movements of the Livesey family and the Matthews boys on the night of the murder. Now, of course, they were interested in whether anyone had been seen entering or leaving the Liveseys' house while Mrs Livesey was at the pub and Mr Livesey was on his night shift. They heard that Alan was in the habit of having other boys in during the evening if he had been left alone at home.

And the police were lucky. A lad called Peter Nightingale came forward on the day after the murder. The night before, he told them, he had left his mates around 10 o'clock. He had walked down the area called 'the backs', the patch of rough ground behind the eastern side of The Crescent. He was going to climb over the fence into his sister's back garden. She is called Susan Warren and lives in the house next door to No. 41. As he put his leg over the fence, he recalled hearing a bolt being drawn back in the house next door. He realized that someone was coming out of the kitchen door, but he was surprised to see that there was no kitchen light on. He watched as the figure walked down the back garden path, hopped over the fence and disappeared on to the waste ground. From there the man could have walked off in a number of different directions. Nightingale's description was certainly helpful: five feet ten inches tall; whitish-blond hair which bounced as he walked, so was obviously quite long; an anorak. One of the remarkable things about the account was that it showed that Peter Nightingale, a simple lad who works in the local peanut factory, possesses an extremely good aural memory: he remembered the sound of a bolt being drawn on the back door; and he guessed the man was wearing an anorak because he heard the sound of the material rubbing against his arms as he walked down the garden path.

This looked like a promising lead. And more was to come. Peter Nightingale's sister, Susan Warren, who, you will recall, lived next door to the Liveseys', was also interviewed. Her house, No. 39, is actually physically joined to the Liveseys'. The front rooms share a common wall. So what had she heard through that wall on the night of the murder?

When she was first interviewed on 22 February, the day after the murder, she told the police that she had heard nothing from next door during the earlier part of the evening. She hadn't even heard the television. But as she was putting her youngest daughter, Tracy, to bed just before 10 o'clock, she heard a voice that she took to be Alan Livesey. She said that it sounded as if he was larking about with somebody. She was not surprised by this, as she knew Alan often had boys in when his mother and father were out, and the 'larking-about' noise was not uncommon.

She then went on to describe the noise she heard when the body was found; she heard Mrs Livesey shouting, 'He's bloody dead.' She seemed confused in her timing of these incidents, but it was clear from her descriptions that she *was* in fact talking about the moment when Leslie Matthews tried to get into the house and then, subsequently, when he returned with Margaret Livesey.

The police also interviewed Susan Warren's boyfriend. Ronnie Mason is the kind of solid, dependable type who naturally makes a good witness. In all that follows Ronnie Mason is one of the few people who have consistently told exactly the same story each time they have been interviewed. He too had heard the noise at around 9.55 p.m. He also timed it by the end of a television programme. He and Susan had just finished watching 'The Streets of San Francisco' and the adverts were on before 'News at Ten'. He described the noise as 'various shouts'. He too got the impression that Alan was just messing about with his mates. He also said that he had heard a noise when the body was discovered after 11 o'clock. Mason, who is slightly deaf, thought he heard Mrs Livesey shout, 'He's bloody dead.' A few minutes later he heard the police arrive.

With the evidence of Nightingale, Warren and Mason, the police now had a clear picture. The implication was that some friend of Alan's must have been in the house with him that night. There seemed to have been some sort of torture game, which had gone violently wrong. The two people next door had heard it and put it down to 'larking about'. Peter Nightingale had seen the murderer leaving the house. It is obvious that this was the general line the police were pursuing. They visited Alan's school, searching for people who might have been with him that night. They made inquiries about men who might have been hanging around the school. And they also went to the local army cadet headquarters. They even asked whether anyone who was involved with Alan might have homosexual tendencies. All this was in addition to the routine of a murder investigation: the extensive door-to-door inquiries; the search of the entire area for a knife which might have been the right size and shape to inflict the wounds; and the careful collection of all the clues at the scene of the crime.

So, given that the police were looking for a young man, five feet ten inches tall, longish, white-blond hair and homosexual tendencies, how did they come to focus all their attention on Alan's mother, Margaret?

Margaret Livesey became the prime suspect for the murder of her own son largely because of the evidence of her two next-door neighbours, Susan Warren and Christine Norris. Christine Norris was twenty-seven at the time, a capable, intelligent woman. She was unmarried but had two children whom she lived with at No. 43, on the right of the Liveseys' house and detached from it. Susan Warren was just a year older. She had separated from her husband and lived with her four children. As you will remember, her house, No. 39, adjoins Mrs Livesey's on the left-hand side.

Naturally, the police had interviewed Christine Norris after the murder. She told them that she had heard nothing at all on the night of the crime, except, of course, the noise of the police arriving after 11.30 p.m. She seemed to have so little to say that the police did not even bother to take a statement from her.

But four days after the murder, on Monday 26 February, Christine Norris went to talk to Susan Warren about the noises which may or may not have come from the Liveseys' house during the evening of the 22 February. As a result of that conversation a remarkable new piece of evidence now materialized from both women. Both of them now said that they had heard a violent argument between Alan and his mother at around 10.45 or 10.50 on the evening of the murder.

Christine Norris described her evening in great detail. She had waved her boyfriend off just before 10 o'clock and gone to bed. She is an avid reader, getting through two or three paperbacks a week. She read until 10.30 – she remembered all her timings from her digital bedroom clock. Before she drifted off to sleep, she heard Mrs Livesey shouting at Alan and Alan answering back. She was confident that it was their voices she had heard. She even claimed that she had heard Alan cry out, 'Help me!' She said that the 'Help!' was screamed out and the 'me' was quieter. She timed all this from 11.01 p.m. by the clock. In a long statement to the police on the Monday after the murder she also went into detail about the relationship between Alan and his mother as she had observed it during the preceding three years.

She recounted how Margaret Livesey would give her son 'irritable slaps' and how someone had once reported the Livesey family to the N.S.P.C.C. for alleged cruelty to Alan. An officer had come along and taken pictures of the boy. She alleged that Mrs Livesey would lock Alan in his bedroom for long periods and she had seen him sliding down the drainpipe to get out. All this was, of course, fairly damning stuff.

She admitted that she had not told all the truth to the two officers who had visited her after the murder, but she said she just did not want to get involved. It was, she said, only after she had talked to her mother and to Susan Warren that she had decided to come forward.

Susan Warren's first statement to the police on the day after the murder has already been described. She spoke of the 'larking-about' noise at around 10 o'clock and then the sound of the body being discovered. She made no mention of an argument nor of hearing Mrs Livesey say anything other than 'He's bloody dead!' – which was clearly when she discovered the body.

On the Sunday after the murder, the police interviewed Susan Warren again. This time she repeated her original story and specifically stated that after the 10 o'clock noise she had not heard another sound until the arrival of the police and ambulance people, which again was after the discovery of the body.

But now, after her conversation with Christine Norris, Susan Warren made two further, damning statements. On Monday 26 February she too said that she had heard an argument between Alan and his mother at about 10.45 or 10.50 p.m. And the following day, after the police had taken the lengthy statement from Christine Norris about the alleged cruelty to Alan, Susan Warren made a further statement saying that she had heard that Alan was a child 'not wanted'. She told the police that she had heard Alan's head being banged against the wall. She repeated the story about the N.S.P.C.C. officer being called to the house.

Armed with all this the police appear to have stopped any further inquiries about the man with the whitish-blond hair. All talk of homosexual murder and torture games seems to have been forgotten.

At 4 o'clock on Tuesday 27 February 1979, Detective Inspector Harry Marriner and Detective Sergeant Donald Biscomb interviewed Mrs Livesey, not this time as a witness, but as the chief suspect. They wanted, they said, to discuss some 'discrepancies' in her story.

Mrs Livesey agreed to help them all she could. She continued to insist that she had gone straight from the car that dropped her off at the top of Collins Road North to the Matthews' house. The police were alleging that she had gone straight to her own house; got into a violent argument with Alan; killed him; cleaned up the knife; turned on the gas taps; and then walked the long way around The Crescent before appearing again in Collins Road North and walking down to the Matthews' house. She admitted that she had been very worried about Alan. She had found six new batteries in the lining of his coat and she believed that he had stolen them. The police said that she had been arguing with Alan and that it had led to murder. Mrs Livesey replied that if they said she had done it, then she must have, but she could not remember. They took her through it step by step. At this stage she was clearly very confused. She was asking silly and illogical questions which indicated that she had not grasped the seriousness of what was being alleged. She asked the policemen what they thought her husband, Bob, would say about it. She asked them if they thought she could get a house on Clayton Brook, another council estate near by, because she could not go back to No. 41. She did not appear to realize that if she was found guilty she would be going to only one place – prison.

The interview took place over a period of nearly four hours. The police recorded the fact that Margaret Livesey began to cry. Then, they said, she confessed.

She said, according to the police, that when she came into the room Alan was lying on the carpet watching television. She saw that he was in his best army uniform and realized that he must have been out of the house. He denied it. The Detective Inspector asked her what she did then. She replied that *he* knew what she did, she stabbed him and stabbed him. She said she had used a kitchen knife that she normally used for peeling the potatoes. It had been lying on the settee. She said that after she had stabbed him she had covered his neck up with the socks so that she did not have to look at all the blood. Then she supposed that she must have tied him up to make it look as though somebody had broken in.

The police asked if she wanted to make a statement. She agreed. She wanted to get it all off her chest. She told them that she had not slept for three days.

She made her statement and signed her confession. Within a few days she withdrew it. She said that the police had convinced her, in her shocked, debilitated state, that she must have killed Alan. For a moment she had believed it herself. It was interesting to note that her confession failed to cover several important points. It did not account for the intricacy of the knots around the wrists; the fact that the stabbing appeared to have been made through the football socks; the gas being turned on; and, perhaps most significantly, the fact that the knife pricks on the body indicated torture.

Those facts did not concur with the kind of frenzied, domestic crime that, for a moment, Mrs Livesey believed she had perpetrated. None the less the confession was very damning evidence against her.

At the end of that interview session, at 7.45 p.m. on Tuesday 27 February 1979, Detective Sergeant Donald Biscomb formally cautioned and charged Margaret Livesey with murder. She replied:

> I only wish to say that I am sorry for what I did. I didn't mean it to happen. I wouldn't for the world have harmed my son intentionally. I was under pressure at the time and my mind must have snapped. I am sorry for the trouble I have cause (sic) the police, but I honestly did not realized (sic) I had done it until tonight.

The police now regarded the case against Livesey as almost complete. There was only one small embarrassment for them. Although they appeared to have lost interest in the man with the whitish-blond hair described by Peter Nightingale, they still had to account for Nightingale's evidence. All the young men in The Crescent who had in any way been involved with the events of the night of the murder had been questioned at length by the police. Among them was Raymond Nightingale, Peter's brother. He was first interviewed by Detective Inspector Marriner on 24 February, two days after the murder. But he was interviewed again on 3 March by Detective Constable Hardiker. He now said that after Mrs Livesey had been charged with murder, 'our Peter' came to him and told him that he had never seen anybody leaving the house where Alan died. He said he had told lies to the police because he was frightened.

On the same day, 3 March, Peter Nightingale was re-interviewed. He now said that the person he had described in his earlier statements did not exist. He said that he had not seen anyone in The Crescent around 10 o'clock on the night of the murder. He admitted that he had told his brother that he had lied to the police.

The man with the whitish-blond hair was eliminated, and the police now had a clear-cut case to bring to the trial. That trial began on 2 July 1979 at Preston Crown Court in Lancashire.

The Trial of Margaret Livesey

Margaret Livesey had, in fact, to endure *two* trials, both at Preston Crown Court. The first lasted until 11 July 1979. At that stage the jury had been out for almost two days. They had been instructed to reach a majority verdict. The foreman indicated that they would need more time. But then a close relative of one of the jurors was taken seriously ill and he was excused from the jury. A re-trial was called.

It is not, of course, possible to say what kind of verdict that first jury would have returned. They had heard the damning evidence of Mrs Livesey's confession, since withdrawn. They had heard equally damaging evidence from Christine Norris and Susan Warren about the irritable attitude of Mrs Livesey towards her son, Alan. But Mrs Livesey's defence counsel, Mr John Hugill, Q.C., had carefully highlighted the fact that neither woman had told the whole truth in their original conversations or statements to the police. During the course of his cross-examination he extracted admissions from both women that they had either withheld information or lied because they did not want to become involved. He also showed that on one area of timing Mrs Warren was mistaken. On the Monday (26 February) she had said that the 'argument' she heard between Alan and his mother had taken place at about 10.45 or 10.50 p.m. She repeated in Court that she remembered this time because it was near the end of a programme on I.T.V. called 'The City at Risk'. She remembered that the programme finished at 11 p.m. But Mr Hugill was able to show that it actually finished at 11.15 p.m. If she heard the noises of what she took to be an argument *after* 11 p.m., and even as late as 11.15 p.m., then perhaps what she had really heard were the voices of Leslie Matthews, and then Mrs Livesey, when they found the body. Christine Norris, however, was still adamant that what she had heard of Alan and his mother had happened between 10.30 p.m and 11.01, when she looked at the digital clock in her bedroom.

But whatever verdict the first jury might have returned, it is clear from their two days' deliberation that they were at least divided and uncertain about her guilt.

They had also heard Susan Warren's boyfriend, Ronnie Mason. He stuck to his conviction that the only sounds from the Liveseys' house that night had been the 'larking-about noise' at around 10 o'clock and Mrs Livesey's voice on finding her son dead. He heard no 'argument' in between. Mrs Warren had said nothing to him about an argument.

After Susan Warren's cross-examination and then re-examination by the prosecution counsel, Miss Joyanne Bracewell, the Judge, Mr Justice Talbot, intervened:

MR JUSTICE TALBOT: I would like to ask you this. I can understand, to some extent, though it is difficult to understand it fully; when somebody has been lying dead with a number of stab wounds, I can understand you not wanting to get involved. Do you understand?

SUSAN WARREN: Yes.

MR JUSTICE TALBOT: What I do not understand is why you – not wanting to get involved – made two statements which contained untruths. If you had said, 'I'm not going to say anything,' that is understandable, but why go and say something which is plainly untrue? Why does that prevent you from getting involved?

SUSAN WARREN: I do not know really.

MR JUSTICE TALBOT: No, I do not suppose you do. Very well, thank you.

The first jury had also heard the evidence of Peter Nightingale. He now reverted to his original story of the man with the whitish-blond hair. He said that he had retracted that statement because he was confused by the police and wanted to get out of their custody. He now asserted that he was quite sure he *had* seen and heard a man leaving the Livesey house shortly after 10 o'clock on the night of the murder.

We know the jury must have been divided. We can infer that they must have been confused by so many different versions of the truth from so many witnesses. But we cannot know what their verdict would have been.

A new trial was called. It was to take place just eight days later in the same Court in the same town. It was, on the face of it, an astonishing decision to re-try Mrs Livesey so soon in the same place. The Livesey murder is still a big story in the area today. At that time it was front-page headline news all the way. The *Lancashire Evening Post* had naturally reported the first trial in graphic detail:

2 July 1979: ARMY BOY 'STABBED TO DEATH IN RAGE'. This was a court report which began: 'An enraged mother stabbed her fourteen-year-old son to death after a violent argument, wrapped a football sock round his neck to hide the blood, and then tied his hands behind his back, it was claimed at Preston Crown Court today.'

4 July 1979: HORRIFYING WOUNDS OF STAB VICTIM ARMY CADET.

Perhaps the most dramatic report was published in the *Lancashire Evening Post* on Friday 5 July 1979. Alongside a photograph of Margaret Livesey, the paper proclaimed: WHY I ADMITTED KILLING MY SON ALAN. The report actually began: 'Murder suspect Margaret Livesey entered the witness box today to tell a High Court jury: "I never killed my son."

'Her voice trembling with emotion, the forty-three-year-old housewife said, "I didn't do it."' But the headline suggested guilt.

For a local paper reporting a major murder trial, this was all predictable enough and, of course, quite permissible within the law. The paper had no way of knowing that a second trial was to be called. But the fact remains that there must have been very few local people who had not been influenced by the headlines and graphic descriptions from the first trial.

Suffice it to say that, although the first jury had still not reached a decision after two days of deliberation, the second jury took less than five hours to return a guilty verdict. And they were unanimous.

The second trial seems to have followed very much the pattern of the first. Again, Peter Nightingale told his story of the man leaving the Liveseys' house at 10 o'clock. Again, Ronnie Mason recounted the tale of the 'larking-about noise', but denied that there had been any argument between Alan and his mother around 10.45 p.m. And again, Christine Norris and Susan Warren provided the main evidence against Mrs Livesey, apart from the alleged confession.

There was, however, a subtle difference between the cross-examination of both Miss Norris and Mrs Warren on the first occasion and that conducted by Mr Hugill, Q.C., at the second trial. It is clear that both witnesses were now prepared for the difficult questions, having, as it were, had a rehearsal just a week or so beforehand.

During the first trial, you may recall, Mr Hugill, Q.C., had cross-examined Mrs Warren about her statement of 26 February, in which she had finally told the police that she had heard an argument between Alan and his mother about 10.45 p.m. or 10.50 p.m. She had timed it because she believed it had happened towards the end of a television programme that she thought came to an end at 11 p.m. Mr Hugill had shown that it did not in fact end until 11.15 p.m. So, if she heard an argument it must have been after 11 p.m. It is possible that this mistake may have made an impression on the first jury. But in the second trial, no such impression could be created by the defence:

JOHN HUGILL, Q.C.: What time do you say you heard this argument between Mrs Livesey and Alan?
SUSAN WARREN: Between half past ten and eleven o'clock.

HUGILL: Was it nearer half past ten or nearer eleven o'clock?

WARREN: Eleven o'clock.

HUGILL: Did you originally say that it was about quarter to eleven?

WARREN: Quarter to, or ten to.

HUGILL: Was that after you had spoken to Mrs Norris?

WARREN: No.

None the less, despite the lessening of effect and the loss of the surprise effect of his original questions, Mr Hugill was still able to alert the jury to the conflicting statements that had been given: Mrs Warren had made five altogether. It was only in the fourth one that she told the story of the argument between Alan and his mother. Here Mr Hugill is asking her about her very first statement:

HUGILL: Would you look at that document. Is that the statement which you made on the twenty-third February?

WARREN: Yes.

HUGILL: At the top does it give your name and address and does it then say: 'This statement consisting of two pages each signed by me is true to the best of my knowledge and belief'?

WARREN: Yes.

HUGILL: '... And I make it knowing that, if it is tendered in evidence, I shall be liable to prosecution if I have wilfully stated in it anything which I know to be false or do not believe to be true'?

WARREN: Yes.

And a little later, in relation to the same statement of 23 February, after Mrs Warren had recounted details of the larking-about noise at 10 o'clock, and the sound of someone banging on the window or front door of the Liveseys' house about 10.30 p.m., Mr Hugill continued to check through her statement. He is still quoting from the statement of 23 February:

HUGILL: 'The next thing I heard was Mrs Livesey's voice: It would be about eleven ten p.m.' That is right, is it not?

WARREN: Yes.

HUGILL: 'I had not heard her enter the house at all. I thought I heard Mrs Livesey say, "He is bloody dead." I heard another voice which, at the time, I thought was Alan's.' Is that right?

WARREN: Yes.

HUGILL: So the voice which you heard saying, 'Oh, why?' you thought at the time was Alan's voice?

WARREN: At the time I did, yes.

HUGILL: It is easy to be mistaken about voices, is it not?

WARREN: Yes.

HUGILL: Then you say shortly afterwards the police arrived?

WARREN: Yes.

HUGILL: Is that statement true?

WARREN: Yes.

HUGILL: Then let me point out what it says, Mrs Warren. At the bottom of page three it says: 'The next thing I heard was about ten thirty p.m. when I thought someone was knocking on either the glass panel in the front door or on the window at number 41. The next thing I heard was Mrs Livesey's voice, it would be about eleven ten p.m. I had not heard her enter the house at all. I thought I heard Mrs Livesey say, "He's bloody dead." '

WARREN: Yes.

HUGILL: Is that true?

WARREN: Yes.

HUGILL: So you did not hear anything between ten thirty p.m. and Mrs Livesey calling out 'He's bloody dead'?

WARREN: I heard an argument.

HUGILL: That is why I asked you the question twice.

WARREN: Yes, but I missed it out.

HUGILL: You did not just miss it out; you said: 'The next thing I heard was Mrs Livesey's voice.' So that was untrue?

WARREN: Yes.

HUGILL: Indeed, if you go down a little further you will see you were asked by the police officers particularly, expressly, if you had heard a scream from the house next door, were you not?

WARREN: Yes.

HUGILL: You said: 'If anyone had screamed during the evening, I am certain I would have heard them.'

WARREN: Yes.

HUGILL: Of course, this statement was untrue in this regard?

WARREN: Yes.

HUGILL: Because, you say, Mrs Warren, you made another statement. You made a number of statements, did you not?

WARREN: Yes.

HUGILL: I think the next statement you made was on the twenty-fifth of February.

And after a brief intervention by the Judge, it was agreed that this was a statement made and signed by Mrs Warren:

HUGILL: Does that also begin: 'This statement is true to the best of my knowledge and belief?'

WARREN: Yes.

HUGILL: Is it true?

WARREN: No, because I have missed something off it.

HUGILL: You have missed something out. Not only have you missed something out but you have said that that *something* did not happen, have you not?

WARREN: Yes, because I did not want to get involved.

HUGILL: You did not want to get involved either. I see.

Christine Norris and Susan Warren fulfilled a further function for the prosecution case in the second trial, as they had in the first. As the two next-door neighbours they were both asked to describe the relationship between Alan and his mother. Christine Norris again described the irritable slaps that Mrs Livesey had been known to give Alan, and Mrs Warren described her conduct towards the boy as 'sometimes terrible'.

There were three other important areas of the case that the jury had to weigh up. First, did they believe that Margaret Livesey had given a confession while her mind was totally clear, or did they believe her when she said that she was still in shock after Alan's death? Had the police simply convinced her that she must have done it? Second, had she had enough time to kill Alan and do all the other acts associated with the murder before she reached the Matthews' house that night? And third, did the forensic evidence support her guilt?

In answer to the first point it is clear that the jury *were* convinced by the confession.

As far as timing is concerned, they were offered a tight but still plausible schedule, which must have satisfied them that Margaret Livesey could have carried out the crime. Yet the two people who were with her that night at the pub gave evidence that suggested she could not have reached the top of The Crescent until around 11 p.m. Frank Bamber, the man who drove her home, said that they had not left the pub car park until about 10.50 p.m. This was confirmed by Margaret's girlfriend, Marion Walker. She said she left them both in the car park at about 10.50 p.m., when Frank Bamber was busy scraping the ice from his windscreen. The police timed the journey at about four and a half minutes. So Margaret Livesey would have arrived at the top of Collins Road North, which runs into The Crescent, at a few minutes before 11 p.m., or even at 11. The barmaid at the pub, Diane Jones, said that the pub was empty at 10.45 p.m., apart from the staff. Even so, Mrs Livesey could not have arrived home much before 11. In order to believe her guilty the jury had to believe that: she walked from Frank Bamber's car to No. 41 The Crescent; picked a fight with Alan, tortured him and stabbed him ten times with great force; tied him up; washed the knife; turned on the gas taps; walked back the long way around The Crescent and down to Mrs Matthews's house. Mrs Matthews said that she had arrived some time around 11.10 p.m. The prosecution claimed that twelve minutes were 'missing' and that Mrs Livesey had killed Alan in that period. Could Mrs Livesey have done it all in that time? Again, the jury clearly thought that she could.

As far as the forensic evidence was concerned, the defence

thought that there were several areas that cast doubt on the prosecution case. Dr John Benstead, a Home Office pathologist, had examined the body at 2.40 a.m. on Friday 23 February. He estimated from body temperature that the boy had probably been killed about three to three and a half hours earlier – in other words, around 11 o'clock. Under cross-examination he confirmed that this could only be an estimate, an imprecise calculation.

He was also asked, under cross-examination, whether there were any deductions he could make from the state of digestion in the stomach of the dead boy.

DR BENSTEAD: The stomach did show little digestion, but in practice the records do show that digestion is very variable and it is not universally accepted.

HUGILL: So you could not say that it was three hours after a meal, or anything like that?

DR BENSTEAD: No.

HUGILL: It would appear to be fairly soon after a meal, though, would it?

DR BENSTEAD: I do not think one can state that.

The theme of torture does not appear to have been extensively pursued. In fact, in his examination-in-chief, Dr Benstead had said that the mixture of superficial nicks and deep stabbings was not surprising in a multiple stabbing like this. The jury also heard details of the knife which was presented as the murder weapon. It was a kitchen knife with a wooden handle. Its most distinguishing feature was a hole in the handle where the rivet nearest to the blade was missing. It was made clear that no traces of blood had been found on it. The jury were also treated to an elaborate description of the knot which had been found around Alan's hands. They must have been confused by the difficult evidence on how it was tied – indeed there was clearly some doubt about whether the lawyers themselves understood. However, no inferences were drawn from the knot's complexity and function. The jury were left only with the impression that it was complicated.

So the Judge came to his summing-up. He invited the jury to

make their own decisions about the weight they should attach to the evidence of Christine Norris, Susan Warren and Peter Nightingale, all of whom had told several versions of their stories. He noted that even Mrs Matthews, who in Court had said Mrs Livesey did not arrive at her house until about 11.10, had originally told the police that Mrs Livesey arrived at 11 p.m. With all the usual caveats that are delivered to an English jury, the Judge asked them to retire to consider their verdict.

Five hours later they returned to declare Margaret Livesey guilty of murder. Mr Justice Talbot passed the mandatory sentence: life imprisonment. Mrs Livesey's lawyers considered that there were not sufficient grounds for an appeal.

Margaret Livesey is still in prison today.

Re-investigation:
The Case of the Tortured
Teenager

Like all the 'Rough Justice' cases, Margaret Livesey's story was brought to our attention by Tom Sargant. Tom recounted the main facts of the case and put forward his reasons why Margaret could not have killed her son Alan. We were not supposed to be discussing new cases at all at the time: the next 'Rough Justice' series didn't even have a budget. We were actually taking further statements on the McDonagh case from the two principle witnesses, Sheila Eccleston and Clara Esty – as Tom will recount in a later chapter – but the Livesey case was hard to ignore.

Tom was taking up the case of someone who had confessed to murder. His years of experience have taught him not to jump too readily to the conclusion that just because someone confessed to a murder they did it. We were firmly of the opinion that Tom's experience led him to assume that because someone *had* confessed they most certainly had *not* committed the crime. He was also stressing the argument that the timings in the case proved that Margaret Livesey could not have murdered her son. Arguments about timings are another of his weaknesses. His abundant honesty leads him to believe that murderers take about the same time to do things as normal people do. Unfortunately, juries and the general public who sceptically watch our programmes tend to believe that murderers are superhuman beings who can run very fast without getting out of breath and commit murders in a few seconds; and then have a devilish cunning in disposing of the murder weapon where the average trained policeman cannot find it.

Tom has a phenomenal memory for case details; soon the many

anomalies in the case against Margaret Livesey were stacked up one after another. In the space of two hours he convinced us not only that Margaret had not killed her son, but that it was physically impossible for her to have done so. After we had heard his arguments the fears we had had about the confession and the timings argument seemed a long way away – and of little importance.

When 'Rough Justice II' was finally allocated a budget we went through the Margaret Livesey case again, this time with all the documents that could be made available to us by her solicitor. The belief that Tom had given us was reinforced by the details.

The statements of Peter Nightingale seemed to be of major importance. First he had said he had seen a man leaving the Liveseys' house just after 10 o'clock; then he had told the police that this was lies. Later he had gone back to his original story when a private detective employed by Mrs Livesey's solicitor had visited him. In Court he had stuck with his story that a man had left the house at this time. The jury must have either disbelieved him or thought this mystery man to be irrelevant to the truth about the murder. We believed that such a sighting could not be left unexplained. After all, both Susan Warren and her boyfriend Ronnie Mason had heard something going on in the Liveseys' house just before 10 o'clock. If there was a man there at around 10, he must have been the last person to see Alan alive before Mrs Livesey came home. He could perhaps tell us why Alan was in his cadet uniform. But did he exist? Only Peter Nightingale knew.

We looked carefully at Peter Nightingale's first statement to the police. He described how he had gone home that night by a short cut behind the houses at the side of The Crescent where the Liveseys' house was. Then, just as he was about to climb over the fence into his sister's back garden, his attention was drawn to the back door of the Liveseys' house. It was Thursday 22 February; it was about 10.10 p.m.; we knew from the Meteorological Office records that the weather was fine but cloudy; in other words, it was a dark night – and there are no street lights at the back of the houses where Peter Nightingale was standing. The reason he gave for his attention being drawn to the Liveseys' house convinced us that he was telling the truth. He said that he heard the bolt being pulled back – then the door being unlocked. Then someone walked out.

We know from research into the effects of television that about 80 per cent of the information received by the viewer comes from the picture; only 20 per cent comes from carefully written scripts. We know, too, from our reading of witness statements and the hundreds of interviews we have done that people tend to tell stories from their memory of visual images associated with the events. Only significant dialogue is ever quoted – and then it is usually wrongly quoted. So, we reasoned, if Peter Nightingale had been creating a lie in his first statement, he would almost certainly have begun with a visual image. The fact that he began with an aural memory pointed to the fact that he was telling the truth. Only if he had actually experienced the sound of the bolt being drawn in the dark would he have thought to begin his description of the scene with that fact. We did several tests of this theory on friends around the office. We described the scene in general, then asked them to cook up a lie about a man leaving the house. When we asked them why they looked towards the house they invariably said something about the light being switched on or off, or the curtains being drawn. No one ever began with the sound of the bolt.

Another small point interested us about Peter Nightingale's statements. Eight days later he made his second statement, saying that the man did not exist. He added that he was sorry and that he had told his brother it was all lies. On that same day Raymond Nightingale – Peter's brother – made a statement saying Peter had told him the story about the man leaving the Liveseys' house was all lies. Why, we wondered, was this statement by Raymond necessary? Indeed, which statement had come first? They had both been made on the same day. We reasoned that if Peter had walked into the police station and volunteered this information it needed no corroboration from Raymond, so Raymond's statement must have been made first. But there was nothing else in Raymond's statement on that day. Had he simply gone to the police and volunteered the information? We reasoned that he had not – because everyone in The Crescent knew by then who the killer was: Margaret Livesey had been charged with the murder four days earlier. But if the police had gone to the Nightingales', why had they gone to Raymond first? It seemed that they needed the statement out of Raymond before Peter would make his denial. In fact, when the private detective employed by Mrs Livesey's solicitor asked him about this, Peter Nightingale said:

> On the following Saturday afternoon the policeman came and took me back to the station at Bamber Bridge. When we got there he said, 'You know why we are here?' I said, 'No' and he told me, 'You saw no one coming out of the Liveseys' house that night, you've been telling us a pack of lies.' After about two or three hours I was told to make another statement saying that I had seen nobody leaving Livesey's house on my way home. I signed the statement even though it was untrue, but I wanted to get out and get home.

It had not been necessary to show him Raymond's statement. Of course Peter Nightingale returned to his original version of events when under oath in the Court. When asked about his retraction he said, 'They just kept asking me, "Why did you do it?" and that, and I kept telling them I didn't do it. I just got all confused. Then, with me being on my own at that time with nobody else around, I thought I was going to get blamed for it.'

At one stage it was to be suggested that it was actually Alan whom Peter had seen walking out of the back door of the Liveseys' house just after 10 o'clock. Peter replied quite specifically: 'From this man's appearance I would not connect him with anyone who lives in this area.'

But, in any case, it was not a suggestion that could be taken seriously. Peter knew Alan Livesey well. Alan's hair was neither blond, nor as long as that of the man who had left the house. Why should Alan leave by the back door as he did? He does not appear to have gone to any shop near by – everyone knew him and would have remembered him. He would have put the kitchen light on if he had been going out by the back door. But the man that Peter saw did not do so.

We were later to meet Peter Nightingale on several occasions. He always struck us as being an honest man, but we had difficulty in persuading him to appear before our cameras to repeat the story of the man leaving by the back door of the house, although he asserted it was the truth. He said that someone had told him he would be out of a job if he talked to us. That he eventually agreed to be interviewed seems to us to be proof of his sense of honour and truth.

In all, we believed Peter Nightingale's story about a man leaving the Liveseys' house at around 10.10 p.m. Coupled with the evidence from Susan Warren and Ronnie Mason of noises in the house at 9.55, it left a major hole in the story of what had happened there that night – a hole already being filled by our work on the forensic evidence.

When dealing with events that happened many years ago it is inevitable that the scientific facts collected at the scene at the time play a greater role in an investigation than witness evidence. 'Rough Justice' is always faced with interviewing witnesses about events that they would rather forget – or have indeed forgotten in detail. Some witnesses seem to place greater store in upholding the decision of the jury than in continuing the search for the truth. Others, no longer under the pressure of giving evidence in Court, remember things differently, making them less credible as witnesses. Witnesses inevitably tell their story the way they perceive it: as the years go by their own experience can mellow parts of the story and they post-rationalize until they see an untruth as the truth. It means that we can only rarely use witness testimony as key evidence in a case. But the scientific evidence remains unchanged and the interpretation of that evidence is even improved as more experience and information are gathered.

Our emphasis on the scientific evidence instead of on witness statements is often the reverse of the emphasis in the original investigation. This change of emphasis is well illustrated by the Livesey case.

The prosecution case against Margaret Livesey, which was believed by the jury, claimed that she killed her son, as her confession stated, at just after 11 p.m. She was supposed to have stabbed him with her kitchen knife first while he lay on the ground, then as he was standing up, then after he fell to the ground again. She was then said to have tied his hands behind him. We should emphasize straight away that the two forensic scientists who investigated this case were never as specific as this.

The Home Office pathologist, Dr John Benstead, said that death had occurred about three hours before his examination at 2.40 p.m. But he added that such estimates are imprecise and it could have been an hour or so earlier. He stated that the kitchen knife shown to him could have inflicted the wounds – but the forensic scientist, Dr Michael Harris, tested several knives from the Liveseys' house which could have caused the wounds. As for the particular kitchen knife produced as an exhibit, Dr Harris stated that there was nothing on it to connect it with the murder. He also stated that there were no blood splashes on any of the furniture around the body, though he admitted in Court that blood spurts could have been stopped by stabbing the boy through the football socks around his neck. At no time did either of these two forensic scientists produce any evidence which directly linked Margaret Livesey to the death of her son Alan.

The prosecution case presented a bizarre picture when we attempted to reconcile it with the evidence collected by the scientists and detectives. If she were guilty, then something such as this must have occurred:

She came into the house, took her coat off, and found Alan lying on the floor. She shouted at him (for about two minutes, according to the prosecution), but he didn't get to his feet. She picked up the kitchen knife from the settee, picked up the football socks from the clothes-horse and stabbed him through the socks. He got to his feet and she stabbed him again, he fell down and she stabbed him again several times but using light pressure on some of the stab thrusts while using very heavy pressure on others.

She must then have got up, taken Alan's tie from the clothes-horse, turned him over and tied his hands in a complicated knot. Then she took the knife into the kitchen and washed it under the tap. This washing was so thorough that no trace of blood was left in the dirt between the blade and the hilt or even in the hole in the handle where a rivet was missing and where bare unvarnished wood was exposed. (We presume here that Mrs Livesey, an ordinary working-class housewife, would know that an extra-ordinary amount of cleaning would be necessary to frustrate the scientists' tests for blood which are so sensitive that blood can be found where none can be seen by the human eye.) She would then have put her coat back on, turned the gas taps off, then on again, preparing to set up an alibi for herself. In all this she would have had to successfully avoid injury from kicks from Alan's boots – his best army boots with clean soles which had not once picked up any of the blood on the floor while he was standing up.

Such a hypothesis was arrived at by combining the known scientific facts and the assertions made by the prosecution from witness statements – primarily the confession by Mrs Livesey herself. It was one we simply could not believe, so we took the file to Professor James Cameron, Secretary-General of the British Academy of Forensic Sciences. He is one of the world's greatest pathologists and a specialist in child murders. When we went to him he had just arrived back from Australia, where he had been called to give expert evidence in the 'Dingo baby trial'. We spread the post mortem photographs of the Livesey case out before him and received a shock.

'Ah – a homosexual bondage case,' he said. We stared in astonishment. This thought had never crossed our minds, and the professor had seen only the pictures of Alan's body.

'No – it's a mother, killed her son,' we said.

Professor Cameron leaned back and smiled. He listened to our brief account of the case and agreed to look at it in detail for us.

But before we left we insisted that he should tell us why he had come to such a swift conclusion on merely seeing the pictures. He leafed through the photographs and found one of Alan's face. He pointed to the small nick on the right eyelid. It was described in the post mortem as 'a small and superficial nick, 0.2 inch'. 'I've seen many cases of mothers stabbing their kids,' he said, 'but I've never seen any of them inflict a wound like that one.' He went on to point out the ruffled clothing at Alan's stomach: he could have well been arching his back as his attacker sat astride him, pricking him with the knife ... and, of course, there was the complicated knot that tied his hands together behind his back.

It made much more sense if one constructed a scenario in which Alan willingly allowed his hands to be tied, and was then sat upon so that his legs were immobile and his boots useless as weapons. This would allow the murderer to prick Alan with the knife, and then kill him with several savage thrusts. The football socks could even have been placed across his mouth with one hand while the other hand wielded the knife. And, of course, there would be no blood splashes on the furniture, nor on Alan's boots, because he would never have been standing up. Nothing in that scenario conflicted with the scientific evidence.

We left the file with Professor Cameron so that he could study it in detail. It occurred to us that if we were looking for the murderer we would now head off to the places where the police had gone in the days before Margaret Livesey confessed: Alan's school and army headquarters.

But we were not looking for the murderer; we were trying to show that Margaret Livesey was innocent. Since the forensic evidence was now in the hands of Professor Cameron, we went to Bamber Bridge to talk to some of the witnesses. We received a severe shock. Most of the key witnesses would not talk to us. Peter Hill was thrown out of the Matthews' home with a threat that his legs would be broken if he came back. On another occasion when Mrs Matthews saw Tom Sargant get out of our car she ran off down the street to her sister's house and hid. A neighbour was later to tell the local paper that he threatened her with a piece of notepaper from the Tickled Trout – the local hotel where we were staying!

It soon became clear to us that The Crescent, Bamber Bridge, was one of the most gossip-ridden neighbourhoods which any of us had ever encountered. We remembered that there had been several anonymous letters circulated at the time of Mrs Livesey's trial. But we did not know that another wave of these letters had sprung up just before we had arrived in The Crescent for the first time. We only learned later that we had been accused of writing them! Perhaps that, more than anything, accounted for the record number of doors slammed in our faces in Bamber Bridge. The anonymous letter-writer took the part of Mrs Livesey and no doubt thought he or she was helping. But it meant that at the time when we were ready to talk to witnesses, we had to spend nearly six months earning the confidence of the neighbourhood.

Since we could not talk to the key witnesses directly, we talked to them through intermediaries. May Kershaw, a middle-aged spinster who had devoted her life to caring for her sick mother, had been a good friend of Margaret Livesey. Margaret had frequently helped May look after her mother during the last months of her terminal illness. May was now to repay the kindness. Not that she thought Margaret innocent – she had heard too much gossip for that. But she was impressed by our insistence that there was real doubt about the verdict. So she listened with an open mind and passed what she could remember of the arguments along the local grapevine. What was more important was the character reference that May gave us. To this day she remains uncommitted about Margaret Livesey's guilt or innocence because she is honest enough to admit she does not understand all the points of evidence. But *her* honesty recognized *our* honesty of approach. Soon we were hearing from May what the people of The Crescent were saying about us and what they thought about the case against Margaret Livesey.

We had another important source of information, Mr Mahas, an American who had come to Bamber Bridge many years ago and lived two doors away from the Liveseys. He was an avid reader and an amateur pathologist. He was intrigued when he heard that we were placing great emphasis on the forensic evidence in the case, so he invited us in for a cup of tea. We were surprised to see the range of books on his shelves, and more particularly, as he spoke, to learn that he knew of the work not only of eminent British pathologists such as Simpson and Cameron, but also of American pathologists whose names would mean nothing to most people in Britain.

Mr Mahas had heard nothing to cause him to think that Margaret Livesey was anything but guilty – until he met us. From the moment he heard that there was no evidence of blood splashes on the furniture around the body he began to have doubts. We were able to enter into a deep discussion of the case with him. Soon we became aware of one of the main reasons for the hostility in The Crescent: misinformation.

During our discussions Mr Mahas raised several points which were simply not in the evidence. He had heard things around the neighbourhood and read parts of the trial in the newspapers which had given him a totally false impression of the case. It was well known, for example, that Margaret Livesey had been investigated by the N.S.P.C.C. because she had beaten Alan black and blue, that she did it regularly and had even been known to knock his head against the wall to punish him. This was accepted as fact by everyone in The Crescent. It was completely the reverse of the truth.

It was true that someone had rung the N.S.P.C.C. and reported Mrs Livesey concerning her treatment of Alan, but the inspector who went to the house found no marks whatsoever on Alan to back up the allegations vehemently denied by Alan himself. In fact the N.S.P.C.C. inspector was impressed by Mr and Mrs Livesey and reported that they were caring parents.

Mrs Livesey's confession had been grossly mis-reported around the neighbourhood – as had the evidence of most of the witnesses. Their bitterness at being the targets of the gossips increased their reluctance to talk to us. When eventually they did, there were some who were reluctant to move from their fixed positions on the case in general – even though we showed them the evidence which disproved their points. One bitterly complained that it wasn't fair that we had the Court transcript with the evidence in it because it helped to prove our argument against his! That prejudice remains in The Crescent even today. Fortunately for us and for Margaret Livesey the key witnesses were not in this small band of bigots.

When we were at last invited into the houses of the key witnesses, the evidence which we filmed destroyed the prosecution case which had been based on their testimonies.

Remember that the prosecution argued that Mrs Livesey had arrived home earlier than she claimed. She had said she had arrived in The Crescent in the car of her friend Frank Bamber at 11 o'clock. Bamber's evidence that he arrived home soon after 11 p.m. had confirmed her story. But Christine Norris, the Liveseys' neighbour, told the Court that she had heard Margaret Livesey shouting in the house before 11.01. She was certain of that because she looked at her clock. In fact, you will remember, she admitted that she had told the police she had heard the shouting at about 10.45 p.m., though she couldn't be certain about that time. Susan Warren's final story to the Court was that she had heard shouting through the wall of her house, which joined the Liveseys' house, at a time between 10.30 and 11 p.m. – indeed at about 10.45 or 10.50.

What they told us in their filmed interviews was significantly different. Christine Norris stated now that the shouting had started at 11 o'clock by her clock. She denied having said it could have been at 10.45 p.m. In fact when we told her the time of the arrival of the police – 11.31 p.m. according to the police – she hedged even further. We asked her: 'So what you heard happened sometime between eleven' and she carried on: 'eleven and half past. But what exactly dead on the time I don't know.' Christine believes in her heart, we feel sure, that she heard shouting just after 11 p.m. But she admitted to us that the digital clock by which she timed her evidence was the one which she took downstairs every morning, and took upstairs every night. Since it was an electric clock which worked off the mains, it lost time every day as she took it off the mains to move it. No one had thought to check whether the clock was accurate or not, so it may well have been several minutes slow.

Susan Warren said in her interview with us that one noise she heard was 'a few minutes after eleven ... eleven ten ... five or ten minutes before the documentary on TV finished' (the documentary on I.T.V. finished at 11.15). But now, when it came to remembering any noise between 10.30 p.m. and 11 p.m., she couldn't remember. Her answers became so vague that she became almost incomprehensible, to a point at the end when she simply stopped talking. But this is how she began:

Q: So, Susan, you heard a noise at about five to ten, which you describe as a larking-about noise, which went on for a few minutes.
A: Yeah.
Q: What's the next thing you heard? And when do you think it was?
A: Mrs Livesey shouting – but that's after eleven o'clock. I can't remember the thing before.
Q: So the next thing you heard, some time after eleven o'clock was Mrs Livesey shouting.
A: Mm.
Q: What was she shouting, or what was happening?
A: Well I thought she shouted, 'He's bloody daft,' and then there was a lad who said something and then I heard her say, 'He's bloody dead.'

So both witnesses who had placed Mrs Livesey with Alan before 11 o'clock were now saying quite definitely that it was *after* 11 o'clock – and from what they were describing it was obvious that they had heard the voices of Leslie Matthews and Mrs Livesey when they found Alan's dead body.

The next question in this intricate reconstruction was the time at which Mrs Livesey arrived in The Crescent after leaving the pub. When they interviewed Mrs Livesey the police had accepted

11 p.m. There was some good evidence to back it up. Diana Jones, the manageress of the pub, said that Mrs Livesey's group of friends had been served with three half pints at 10.29 p.m. and that the pub was cleared by 10.45 p.m. Margaret Livesey's friend Marion Walker thought it was later than this and that they had left the pub at 10.50 p.m. She added that the three of them chatted outside about holidays for a few minutes. Frank Bamber, the other member of the party, agreed that they left the pub at 10.50 p.m. He remembered Marion Walker looking up at the clock and saying, 'It's ten to eleven.' (Pub clocks are notorious, however, for being five minutes fast.) He agreed that the two women chatted for a while. It was a frosty night and he had to scrape ice from his windscreen.

The police timed the journey from the pub to The Crescent as four and a half minutes. Even if Marion Walker and Frank Bamber were wrong about the time they left, Bamber and Margaret Livesey could not have set off before 10.45 p.m. So they could not have arrived in The Crescent until almost 10.50 – even by the most conservative of estimates. Frank Bamber thought that they actually arrived at about 11 o'clock. He remembered that Mrs Livesey finished off a cigarette before she got out of the car – though Margaret herself did not remember doing so. He remembered getting home at about 11.05 p.m., which would support his opinion because his home is four to five minutes away from The Crescent.

According to the prosecution, she now went straight home, killed Alan, then walked around The Crescent to make it look as if she was just arriving from the pub. She then went into the Matthews' house to set up her alibi.

So when did she arrive at the Matthews' house? This was the subject of some argument during the trial. When Mrs Matthews was first questioned she said that Mrs Livesey had knocked on her door just after 11 o'clock. At the trial she was less sure; she said that she had first seen Mrs Livesey that night at 'between ten past and a quarter past eleven'.

Leslie Matthews, her eighteen-year-old son, was another witness to this time. He said he had left the Withy Trees pub in the centre of Bamber Bridge at 10.55 p.m., had crossed the road and bought some chips in the shop there before walking home. The police timed this walk as seven minutes forty seconds. We do not know how long it took to buy the chips, but Leslie said at the trial that he arrived home at 11.15 or 11.20 p.m. At that time Mrs Livesey was already in the Matthews' house.

Andrew Matthews, the younger son, had been at a local disco with his friend Tommy Rogers. Andrew noticed the time by the clock at the Job Centre in the centre of Bamber Bridge, which is opposite the chip shop where Leslie bought his chips. Andrew says that the time was 10.55 p.m. Leslie was to follow the same route home. When Andrew and Tommy arrived home they crept under the front window of the Matthews' house to try to hear what was going on inside because Andrew had not been given permission to go to the disco and was hoping to sneak upstairs to bed without anyone noticing. As they did this, Mrs Livesey came up the street and called to them.

The final witness to the timing, Tony Rogers, Tommy's elder brother, was inside the Matthews' house at this time with his mother. He thought that Mrs Livesey arrived at 11.15 p.m. and that Leslie Matthews arrived about fifteen minutes later, at 11.30 p.m.

It was a very confusing collection of statements, but we could be sure that at least one of these estimates was quite wrong – that of Tony Rogers. He could not have seen Leslie Matthews arrive home at 11.30 p.m. because Leslie phoned the police to report Alan's murder at 11.28 p.m. The log of that phone call provided the one definite time in the entire case. Indeed, when we timed the trip from the Matthews' home to the Liveseys' home, some other estimates became incredible. The trip between the two houses took fifty-one seconds walking and between twenty and thirty seconds running. Between Mrs Livesey's arrival at the Matthews' home and Leslie's phone call to the police, Leslie did the following things:

1. He chatted to Mrs Livesey after he arrived home.
2. He went out into the streets, walking up and down to try to find his brother Andrew.
3. He went home and picked up Tony Rogers to help him find their two younger brothers.
4. He and Tony went to the Liveseys' house to see if they were there. They knocked on the door and searched around the back.
5. Leslie returned to the Matthews' home but stopped on the journey to chat to a friend of his, Mick Sheen.
6. After chatting to Mrs Livesey back in the Matthews' house, Leslie took the key of the Liveseys' house and went back to join Tony.
7. Leslie discovered the body and tried to give Alan the kiss of life.
8. He ran back and told the women in the Matthews' house that Alan was dead.
9. He ran with Mrs Livesey to the Liveseys' house where he waited while she tried to revive Alan. They opened the windows, turned the gas off and Leslie was sick.
10. Leslie ran to the phone box, a trip of at least a minute.

Our estimate of how long this would have taken was twenty-three minutes. This would mean that Leslie would have arrived home (where he would have seen Mrs Livesey), at 11.05 p.m. But we reckoned that even the most sceptical observer would grant that it *must* have taken eighteen minutes, meaning that Leslie must have arrived home at 11.10 p.m.

There was another line of reasoning to suggest that the earlier time was more probable: we remembered that Andrew Matthews and Tommy Rogers had left the employment centre in Bamber Bridge at 10.55 p.m. It would have taken them about eight minutes to get home – probably even less than this. Andrew should not have been out at all and the two boys were later than they should normally be. But they were only in The Crescent a few moments before Mrs Livesey appeared, which would therefore have been about 11.03 p.m.

Could these estimates be wrong? It seemed possible to us that

Leslie Matthews may have dawdled home with his chips and so arrived at around 11.15 p.m. or later, instead of around 11.05 p.m. But Andrew and Tommy wouldn't have dawdled. Moreover, it seemed almost impossible that the two sets of boys – Leslie and then Andrew with Tommy – could have *both* dawdled home that night – Leslie taking some twenty minutes instead of eight and Andrew and Tommy taking some seventeen minutes instead of eight. The coincidence was too much to be believed.

Taking into account all the evidence provided by the prosecution we reasoned that a fair estimate of Mrs Livesey's time of arrival at the Matthews' house was 11.05 p.m. It seemed from evidence in Court that she would have needed about ten minutes to kill Alan and then walk where she was supposed to have walked. Even with a conservative estimate of six or seven minutes for this, it did not seem likely.

But if Susan Warren and Christine Norris had heard a noise slightly earlier than they claimed, and if the estimate of 11.05 p.m. for the arrival of Mrs Livesey at the Matthews' house was slightly early, then it was just possible that Margaret Livesey could have committed the murder in the gap between 10.55 p.m. and 11.08 p.m. While we were pondering this and cursing the difficulty of dealing with timing evidence, a new witness turned up.

John Kershaw, the brother of May Kershaw who had kept us in touch with the neighbourhood, had left his girlfriend's house in Leyland that night at about 10.52 p.m. As he arrived home in The Crescent he noticed that the time was 11.01 p.m. Yet he had seen Margaret Livesey about halfway along The Crescent, walking in the direction of the Matthews' house. Kershaw was clear about his evidence. He had given it to the police at the time of the murder, but had not been called as a witness by the prosecution, nor had his evidence been called to the attention of the defence lawyers acting for Mrs Livesey.

By placing Margaret Livesey in The Crescent at 11.00 p.m. John Kershaw effectively cleared her of the murder. There was not enough time for her to have killed Alan either before or after 11 o'clock.

John Kershaw did not realize how important his evidence was because he, like everyone else in The Crescent, had never been given a full account of what everyone else had seen. We discovered that the more we talked about the case with the residents, the more they responded; they were beginning to realize that Margaret Livesey, far from being a murderess, was something more like a martyr.

Ordinary people are often particularly impressed with small details in a case, elements which they know a little about and to which they apply their common sense. Leslie Matthews, for example, was not particularly impressed with long explanations of the forensic case, but he was impressed with two small points. Mrs Livesey had given him the key to her house and asked him to check on Alan. When he had opened the door he had smelled gas. Later he had learned that all the gas taps in the house had been turned on. No one had ever doubted that the murderer had done this so that whoever discovered the body would also cause an explosion and destroy incriminating evidence. So why, we asked Leslie, had Margaret Livesey chosen him to go to check on Alan? Leslie was the only non-smoker in the Matthews' house that night. Since nothing in the Liveseys' house had been booby-trapped to cause an explosion, the murderer must have hoped that whoever found the body would either already be smoking, or would light a cigarette soon after entering the house. This was not the kind of evidence that would impress the Home Office – but it impressed Leslie Matthews.

So too did another minor point. Mrs Livesey had bent over Alan when she first saw his dead body that night. She had tried to close his eyes, saying to Leslie Matthews at her side that Alan wouldn't want to die with his eyes open. Leslie Matthews was not paying too much attention at this moment; he was feeling sick. But he remembered her attempt to close Alan's eyes. It is normal for rigor mortis to make the eyes rigid after an hour to an hour and a half. However, Mrs Livesey evidently couldn't shut Alan's eyes, for they remain open in the photographs taken by the police at the post mortem. If Mrs Livesey had killed Alan at around 11 o'clock, she should have been able to close his eyes at 11.20. This was once again evidence that we would not expect the Home Office to take seriously, but it appealed to the common sense of the residents in The Crescent.

Mrs Sadie Rogers, who lived next door to the Matthews, also applied common sense to her reasoning about what she had seen that night. She had been in the Matthews' house when Margaret Livesey had arrived at the door. This is what Sadie Rogers told us:

> Mrs Livesey sat on the arm of the chair. She had a drink, she crossed her leg over the other and said, 'Look at me,' and 'I've been out tonight.' She had a bandage on. Well, we didn't take much notice . . .
>
> Q: Where was the bandage?
> A: On her foot. I think it was her right foot, I'm not sure now. It was February and she had sandals on . . .
> Q: She drew attention to her legs? – she pointed out her bandage?
> A: Yes, and her sandals.
> Q: Would you have noticed if she'd had blood splashes on her?
> A: Why, yes.

According to Mrs Rogers, Margaret Livesey had been sitting only three feet away with her legs straight in front of Mrs Rogers's eyes. Not only did Sadie Rogers not notice any blood on the bandage, but Mrs Livesey apparently drew attention to the bandage. Was it possible for the bandage to be free of bloodstains? Had she taken the time to change the bandage? Was it an elaborate attempt to set up an alibi? Since Mrs Rogers had learned about all the elements of the timing in the case, her common sense told her that such a hypothesis was beyond the bounds of her belief.

However, we were interested in a different aspect of her evidence. Apparently Mrs Rogers had told the police all about the bandage in her statement. But that statement was never served on the defence. It seemed to us that it should have been.

When we had filmed interviews with all the key witnesses in

Bamber Bridge we felt that we already had a case that should release Margaret Livesey from prison.

Both Susan Warren and her boyfriend Ronnie Mason confirmed that they had heard 'larking-about' noises coming from the Liveseys' house at 9.55. Peter Nightingale confirmed that he had certainly seen a man leave the house at about 10.05. Witnesses to the timing showed that Margaret Livesey did not have enough time to commit the murder at 11 o'clock. John Kershaw's evidence had effectively destroyed whatever case there had been against her. If she had had blood on her after killing Alan, surely Sadie Rogers would have seen it.

We returned to London to interview Professor Cameron, who had been studying the forensic evidence, particularly the report of Dr Benstead, the pathologist on the case. Professor Cameron's conclusions were as follows:

> Dr Benstead's findings, taken at the scene at 2.40 a.m., from the temperature, from the presence of rigor mortis, the muscle stiffness after death, and the way in which the blood had pulled into the dependent parts, would suggest to me that probably death took place some five hours earlier, in other words in the region of probably 10.30 p.m. or 10 p.m. He correctly states that the presence of food in the stomach is difficult to be sure of as an aid to the estimation of time of death, yet his post mortem report states that there was little digestion of the stomach contents. We know for a fact that the deceased had a rather heavy meal at or about 6 o'clock of belly pork, carrots and both roast and boiled potatoes. Given that feature, and given Dr Benstead's findings, I would have estimated that that indicates something of approximately three to four hours after the last meal – which would place time of death between 9.30 p.m. and 10.30 p.m. Taking all these factors into consideration I would have thought that the time of death was probably in the region of 10 o'clock.
>
> Q: The knife which was alleged to have been the murder weapon was tested for traces of blood. You'll recall it had a rivet

missing near its blade, yet no blood was found. What's your reaction to that?

A: I would have doubted then that that was in fact the weapon that was used because had it gone in to the hilt. Obviously with the looseness of the hilt one would have anticipated trace evidence which could not have been washed away easily by the perpetrator. If there had been an attempt to wash away the blood, it would have tended to have remained within the handle of the knife along the edge of the non-cutting part of the knife.

If the exhibit in Court was not the murder weapon, we wondered where the real murder weapon could be. It was not in The Crescent – the police had made a very thorough search of the whole area. Margaret Livesey had certainly not left The Crescent.

Professor Cameron's conclusions – which in no way conflicted with those of Dr Benstead – added probability to the other side of the mystery, concerning the man seen by Peter Nightingale and the noises heard by Susan Warren and Ronnie Mason just before 10 o'clock. It seemed that the visitor to the Liveseys' house could well be the murderer.

We are not allowed to know whether the police collected any evidence at the scene of the crime that could point to the identification of the man. If fingerprints were found which could not be matched to anyone, they are not in evidence. If there were hairs or fibres on Alan's body as the evidence apparently suggested there should be, these are not in the evidence presented to the Court. But we did uncover one piece of evidence which we know was neither drawn to the notice of the defence nor fully followed up as might have been expected.

One of our routine methods of research is to study the photographs taken at the scene of the crime minutely, with the aid of a magnifying glass. In one of the photographs released to the defence in the case against Mrs Livesey we noticed a cigarette packet which had never been mentioned in any of the forensic reports. Indeed, it should not have been there at all if we were to believe the rest of the evidence about cigarettes in the case.

Evidence was given by the shopkeeper of the local off-licence, Mrs Dorothy Seed, that Margaret Livesey usually came into the shop every night with Alan. Mrs Livesey usually bought a couple of cans of cider for herself, then twenty cigarettes and some sweets for Alan.

Mrs Seed said that on the night of Alan's death there had obviously been friction between Mrs Livesey and Alan because she didn't buy Alan anything that night and as a consequence of this he was acting sullenly. It seemed to point to motive. And indeed, Mrs Seed was right; Alan had recently got into trouble with the police because he had been out joy-riding in a stolen car. Margaret Livesey was not pleased with her son's behaviour. But it seems in retrospect that the significant part of Mrs Seed's evidence is the fact that Margaret Livesey did not buy her son any cigarettes that night – and that he resented it. A packet of his favourite brand was found in the house – an unopened packet of twenty Players No. 6 in the pocket of his anorak. There was also a packet of Dunhill cigarettes in the room with eleven cigarettes in it – this was the brand normally smoked by both Mr and Mrs Livesey. Both these packs were mentioned in the forensic report presented to the Court and the defence lawyers.

But the third pack of cigarettes which we discovered in the photographs was never mentioned. It was an unopened pack of Benson and Hedges, lying on the carpet about two feet from Alan's head. No one has yet explained how that pack came to be there; no one in the house ever smoked Benson and Hedges.

In another of the photographs we could see several cigarette stubs. They were in an ashtray on a table near the body. These were not tested for saliva. If they had been, it is possible that we might have known the blood group of the person who dropped the pack of Benson and Hedges. This evidence is now unobtainable, but the fact remains that until someone finds an explanation for the pack of Benson and Hedges being in the house at all, we must assume that it belonged to someone else who was in the house that night; someone whose identity we do not know.

When one considers the impossibilities of the timing evidence presented against Mrs Livesey, the strength of the witness and forensic evidence that someone else was in the Liveseys' house at 10 o'clock and that Alan most likely died at that time, and the unrecorded evidence of the Benson and Hedges cigarettes, how can Mrs Livesey's confession be explained?

Throughout the investigation we had been discussing the case with Lord Salmon, a Law Lord and one of the judiciary's most senior and respected figures. He had always pointed out that there was nothing in Mrs Livesey's own hand which proved that she had ever made the confession. The only statement she had ever written was on the charge form. It is worth looking at again:

> I only wish to say that I am sorry for what I did. I didn't mean it to happen. I wouldn't for the world have harmed my son intentionally. I was under pressure at the time and my mind must have snapped. I am sorry for the trouble I have cause [sic] the police, but I honestly did not realized [sic] I had done it until tonight.

The third sentence of this statement seems to indicate that even at this point she did not remember killing Alan. But this statement was written after two other statements had been taken down. The first is contained in two statements written by the policemen interrogating her in which she is first said to have confessed to the murder. The second is in a statement allegedly written down by a policeman at her dictation.

Perhaps it is simply human nature to readily believe someone who confesses to a crime, no matter what the circumstances. But policemen are trained to be sceptical about confessions. They know better than anyone that many people will readily confess to a crime they did not commit. That is why the police always keep one part of their knowledge of the crime to themselves alone – 'special knowledge' that only the murderer can know.

Or nearly always; there is no 'special knowledge' in the confession of Margaret Livesey and the police do not appear to have kept anything particularly secret. They also appear to have thought little of the circumstances that Margaret Livesey found herself in when she made her alleged confession.

At the time of her son's murder she was regularly taking a drug called Prothiaden. It is an anti-depressant. Margaret had had a worrying time just a few months earlier when her daughter had had to get married because she was pregnant. Then Alan started to get into bad company. His latest escapade, joy-riding in the stolen car, would probably finish up in Court – or so his anxious mother feared.

Prothiaden is a relatively new drug. Although it has been extensively tested there are still certain aspects of it which will only be understood after years of experience in using it. Its manufacturers say that it should not be mixed with alcohol because they are not sure what the pharmacological effect might be. On the night of Alan's death Margaret Livesey had a glass of cider and four half pints of beer in the pub and at least two glasses of cider while sitting in the Matthews' house.

After she was taken away from the dead body of her son she was in a very agitated state. Witnesses say that one doctor gave her some sleeping pills and another gave her an injection. There is no firm evidence of what drugs or drink she took either on the night of the murder or during the five days before she made her confession, but if she took the Prothiaden alone she might have had the side effects of dizziness, sleepiness, palpitations, dryness of mouth and headaches. If she overdosed herself or drunk alcohol – which she might have done if her mouth was dry – then she could further have experienced sweating, nausea, blurring of vision and confusion of the mind. She might even have experienced abnormal cardiac rhythms.

She may also have felt guilty about Alan's death because she had left him alone in the house. She knew that her son was getting himself into bad company. Part of the tension between Alan and herself that night had arisen because she had arranged to meet Marion Walker in the pub but felt she ought to stay home to make sure Alan did not have any of his wayward friends in the house. Alan would not have died if she had stayed home, but he had persuaded her that he would behave himself while she was out.

The circumstances in which the alleged confession was made are therefore perhaps not those which the reader of such a confession might picture. She may well have been in a highly suggestible state, quite ready to accept that she had committed the murder but unable to remember having done so. If she had been over-dosing with Prothiaden she might know only too well that her memory had had several lapses over the previous few days.

The police approach to her in their interrogation was along the following lines:

1. Tell her what they believed had happened.
2. Ask her to fill in the details of their version of events.
3. When she said she could not remember the details, suggest to her that she was trying to shut it out of her mind.

Margaret Livesey's response to this questioning was as follows:

1. Accept that the police knew better than she what had happened.
2. Contradict them in their version of the details, but substitute another set of details in order that the police version was not wholly contradicted.

In spite of this compliance on her part, she got several points wrong and did not remember others which she might have been expected to recall.

She said that she placed the sock over Alan's neck after she had finished stabbing him. In fact there were two socks, both with stab cuts in them. One of the cuts had a piece of fatty tissue adjacent to it as if a knife had been pulled out of the flesh through the sock. It was also accepted by the scientists that the most likely reason why there were no blood splashes associated with the neck wounds was that the socks had been used to cover the neck while the stabbing took place.

She gave no account of the wound on Alan's eyelid which could only have been made by carefully controlled pressure if it were not to penetrate the eyeball. Alan's eyes were open in death but this wound showed that at some stage in the attack his eyes were closed for a significant period.

Her account had Alan facing towards the kitchen, whereas he was found on the floor with his feet extended in the opposite direction, as if he had been facing away from the kitchen.

She said that she had tied Alan's hands together after she had stabbed him, but there were no 'defence' marks on his arms, wrists or hands which are common when a stabbing attack is made in the circumstances she described.

There were no marks on her which might have been expected if she had attacked him while he was standing – he was wearing heavy army boots.

In her first statement she made no mention of the gas taps being turned on. Late in her second statement she said she must have turned them on. This was after she remembered that she had turned them off when she found Alan dead. She did not re-member where she had put the knife, nor how it came to be free of bloodstains. She claimed that she had tied Alan's hands so it would look as if someone had broken in – but she did nothing else to substantiate a break-in.

With this in mind, it is perhaps worth studying the main part of Mrs Livesey's confession. She was being interrogated by Detective Sergeant Biscomb and Detective Inspector Marriner.

BISCOMB: Margaret, you tried to get Andrew to go back to your house but he ran away, then Leslie went but couldn't get in so you gave him the key to get in and I think the reason for doing this is because you knew Alan was lying dead on the floor and you wanted someone else to find his body, isn't that right?

LIVESEY: *No I'm sorry, you're wrong, I wouldn't harm a hair on his bloody head, I wouldn't and everyone knows that.*

MARRINER: Let's talk about the neighbours hearing your voice at eleven o'clock.

LIVESEY: *I didn't go into that house from nine o'clock until I went in with Leslie at twenty minutes past eleven. While you're accusing me of this the real murderer is going free and it will happen to someone else.*

MARRINER: When these neighbours heard you shouting at Alan what was it that usually caused arguments between you?

LIVESEY: *He was always wanting something, it was want want want and he wouldn't do as he was told. Only last week I found a watch in the lining of his coat, then I found some brand new batteries.*

MARRINER: Did you think he'd been shoplifting?

LIVESEY: *Yes, he must have, he wouldn't buy six batteries.*

MARRINER: Did you get annoyed when he wore his uniform when it wasn't his night for the cadets?

LIVESEY: *Yes, he wasn't supposed to wear it unless he was going to the cadets.*

MARRINER: Well, let's forget about going to the Matthews', and I'll tell you what I think has happened. You were dropped off in Collins Road North after leaving the pub, now did you chat in the car before you got out?

LIVESEY: *No, I went straight home.*

MARRINER: That's right, you got out of the car and walked straight to your house. So from leaving the pub you would get home about eleven o'clock.

LIVESEY: *I didn't say I went straight home.*

MARRINER: You did say that and that is when the neighbours heard you shouting at Alan.

BISCOMB: Come on, Margaret, tell us what really happened, you had an argument with Alan before you went out and obviously something happened when you got home that sparked it off again.

[She then started to cry.]

MARRINER: Right, Margaret, as I was saying before, you arrived home at eleven o'clock and something was said that started you and Alan arguing again and unfortunately it ended as it did.

LIVESEY: *Well if you say that I've done it, then I must have, but I can't remember.*

BISCOMB: You will remember, you are just trying to shut it out of your mind. Just try and relax and it will come back to you.

LIVESEY: *But what will Bob say, what will people think?*

BISCOMB: That is something you'll just have to face eventually.

LIVESEY: *I'm not going back to that house, no way, I can't go back there. Will I be able to get a house on Clayton Brook? Oh God, what will Derek think of me?*

MARRINER: Right, Margaret, let's take it slowly from the time you arrived in The Crescent. You went straight home, did you go in the back door or the front?

LIVESEY: *The back, I think, because I went to the outside toilet.*

MARRINER: Then what did you do, did you take your coat off and hang it up or what?

LIVESEY: *Took it off, I just threw it over the back of the chair.*

MARRINER: Then what happened?

LIVESEY: *I can't remember, I can't remember.*
[She then started sobbing.]

MARRINER: You've arrived home, you've been to the toilet, taken your coat off and Alan is standing there in his uniform, is that what annoyed you?

LIVESEY: *He was lying on the floor watching the television.*

MARRINER: What started the argument?

LIVESEY: *As soon as I saw him in his uniform I thought he'd been out. But he just kept on denying it and denying it.*

BISCOMB: What did you do then?

LIVESEY: *Well you know what I did then, I stabbed him and stabbed him.*

BISCOMB: What did you stab him with, was it that ornamental knife or letter opener on the fireplace?

LIVESEY: *No, it was a little kitchen knife.*

BISCOMB: Did you go into the kitchen to get the knife or did Alan have it?

LIVESEY: *No it was on the settee, I must have left it there after peeling spuds. I usually peel the spuds in the front room.*

BISCOMB: What happened after you started stabbing him?

LIVESEY: *He fell to the floor, I stabbed him again then I turned him over, I didn't want to look at him, it was the blood, I covered his neck with a sock.*

BISCOMB: Why did you tie him up?

LIVESEY: *I don't really know. I just took his tie off the maiden and tied his hands together. I suppose I was hoping they'd think somebody had broken in, I don't know. Forgive me Alan, I didn't mean to do it son.*

BISCOMB: You are now under arrest for the murder of Alan. Is there anything else you want to tell us Margaret?

LIVESEY: *What else can I say?*

When faced with such a confession it is easy to overlook the suggestions made to Margaret Livesey in the questions of the two policemen. It is easy to overlook the possibility that, because of the drugs she took, she was in a highly suggestible state of mind. It is difficult to remember all the rest of the evidence in the case which points to the conclusion not only that Margaret Livesey did not kill her son Alan but that she could not have killed him because he died at around 10 o'clock – while she was a mile and a half away in the pub.

But if she had not confessed, the police would have no doubt carried on looking for a fair-haired man, five feet, ten inches tall, with homosexual tendencies. The man who left the Liveseys' house just after 10 o'clock. The man who was seen by Peter Nightingale, who was heard through the wall by Susan Warren and Ronnie Mason. The man who seems to have left a packet of Benson and Hedges cigarettes by the body of the boy he had just killed. The man who took the bloody murder weapon away with him to where the police could not find it.

When we came to film an interview with Lord Salmon for the programme, he surprised us by not placing some of the more hard legal evidence in the forefront of his argument. In the end he simply called on his common sense. He said:

> I can understand women sometimes getting provoked and dashing a son's head off. But what I find so hard in this particular case is that in the first instance she goes and tortures the boy. It's obvious that he must have been terrified and she'd been making him terrified by the slightest of knife cuts. She then

committed six most vicious and frightful blows with the knife going through the chest, through the throat and the heart. It's most fantastic that a woman of her age could have done this to her son . . . I can't see it at all.

It was the same common sense which had first given us a title for the film. The wounds on the body were plainly torture. A mother like Margaret Livesey would not torture her son. So the original title of the film remained: 'The Case of the Tortured Teenager'.

2

The Murder of Eileen McDougall

The approach to the River Tyne from the North Sea takes ships through the claws of the Groyne Pier into a wide and deep stretch of river. On their starboard side they look across to Tynemouth and North Shields; a statue of Admiral Collingwood stares protectively down upon them, as does the coastguard station. On the port side is South Shields, a smattering of amusement arcades, some little boats and cold beaches. As the river narrows again on its way up towards the shipyards, a row of drab petrol storage tanks come into view. A big blue sign on one of the tanks announces: VELVA. Today the depot is 'static'. It is simply used to store large quantities of petrol for long periods of time. But until the early seventies, ships would regularly tie up alongside the Velva Liquids jetty and discharge cargoes of petrol and chemicals into the giant storage tanks. With the regular change of contents in the tanks came a regular need for cleaning. It must be an unenviable task. Tank cleaners have to work in the sludge and the muck which clings to the base of the structures. Usually there is only a thin shaft of light coming from the small hatchway through which they clamber in. And in many tanks the fumes are unpleasant and dangerous. This is particularly so with tanks that have housed petrol or fuel oil.

Tank No. 1 at Velva can store nearly a million gallons of fuel oil. It is an enormous structure of steel plates riveted together in the last century, like the upturned hull of an old iron ship.

On Sunday 24 June 1979 tank No. 1 was standing empty. It was due to be cleaned. A small hatch about three feet in diameter had been removed from the bottom of the tank. At about 3 o'clock that afternoon Mick Mallenby and his mate, Eddie Dawson, pulled themselves through the hatch to start cleaning the tank. Billy Knott stayed outside as 'hatch man'. His job was to pass in the tools to the two cleaners. He ducked his head inside the opening and peered around, waiting for his eyes to become accustomed to the black interior. He saw what he thought was a plastic bag.

He called to Mick, 'What's in that plastic bag?'

Mick waded through the sludge on the bottom of the tank and picked the bag up.

A human torso fell out.

Mick Mallenby dropped the bag, and the two tank cleaners scrambled to get out into the fresh air once more. As far as Mallenby could see there were no legs and no head on the body. He said it was black in colour and appeared to be that of a child about twelve years old.

Acting Inspector Ian Duncan arrived to investigate shortly after 3 o'clock. Eddie Dawson was brave enough to enter the tank for a second time and show Inspector Duncan the torso. Then they searched further. On the other side of the tank they found a smaller parcel; it was wrapped in a canvas material and tied up with a piece of rope. Inspector Duncan undid the knot. He saw the top of a human head inside, with collar-length dark hair.

He then had trouble with his breathing apparatus and had to leave the tank. There was, in fact, nothing else to be found in that grim interior. Indeed, the legs of the body were never found. The torso had been severed around the waist and at the neck.

Two days later Dr Harischandra Ranasinghe, a doctor of Sri Lankan origin who is now the Home Office pathologist for the north-east of England, made a preliminary investigation of the two packages of human remains.

It must have seemed to him and to the police that the job of identification would be impossible. Virtually the only certainty about the case at the beginning was that it *was* murder – but of whom, and by whom? It must have seemed to them that these questions were unanswerable.

There was a further complication. The remains were, of course, deeply impregnated with petrol and would clearly remain toxic for a considerable time. Dr Ranasinghe's examinations had to take place in the open air and his post mortem had to be conducted five days after the body was found. He and his assistant wore full protective clothing and breathing apparatus to avoid the petrol and lead concentrations emanating from the body.

Against all expectations, the post mortem and the attendant examinations were to yield a remarkable amount of information. It was, said Dr Ranasinghe, the body of a young woman. From the X-rays of various bones he could fix her age at between sixteen and twenty and nearer to sixteen. He estimated her height at about five feet, three inches. He said that the original colour of the hair was auburn and it was shoulder length. He noted that she had once fractured her right collarbone, but the fracture was now healed. She had had her appendix out. The X-rays also revealed a small ear-ring in her hair.

He gave the cause of death as 'bleeding and concussion from a head injury with lacerations of the scalp and depressed fractures of the skull'. In all he noted six serious head injuries. He concluded that they could have been caused by a blunt object like a steel hammer with a restricted striking surface $1\frac{1}{2}$ inches in diameter.

The body, he said, had been cut up with a sharp knife. There was no evidence of bleeding associated with the cuts. This suggested that the dismemberment had occurred after death. In addition to the neck and waistline cuts, there appeared to have been an attempt to cut the torso vertically along the breastbone.

It was more than the police could have expected. But Dr Ranasinghe could not guess how long the body had been in the tank. Normally the state of decomposition of a body in an atmosphere which included oxygen would have given some indication. But, of course, this body had been immersed in petrol which had acted as a kind of preservative. No oxygen had been able to penetrate the petrol, so little corrosion of the bodily tissues had taken place.

But the vital clues to the identity of the torso came from the teeth. Mr Derek Jackson, B.D.S., from the Dental School at Newcastle University, was called to examine the mouth, teeth and jaws of the body on the same day as the post mortem. He discovered a significant abnormality in several of the girl's teeth. Two of her teeth had six cusps on their biting surfaces rather than the conventional four or five. In several other teeth he found three cusp formations where the vast majority of us have two cusps. He found that the wisdom teeth had not yet appeared. And he discovered that the teeth contained a very high fluoride content.

This latter was a very significant piece of information indeed. He concurred with Dr Ranasinghe that the teeth development suggested the girl was aged between sixteen and twenty-one and probably between sixteen and eighteen. Given that she was comparatively young he was able to say that the high fluoride content could only have been achieved if she had been brought up in an area which had provided a high fluoride water supply for a considerable time. The only area in the north-east region consistent with that would be the South Shields/Hebburn/Jarrow/Sunderland area.

Since the discovery of the torso the police had been investigating the missing persons files. But without any idea of where the girl had come from, or when she had been dropped into the tank, the task would have been impossible. But now they knew two very important facts. They were looking for a young girl around the age of sixteen and she had almost certainly lived locally. They could concentrate their search.

Very soon they came up with a name from the missing persons files. She was, or had been, Eileen McDougall.

She had gone missing in January 1970. She had been barely seventeen years old. She was five feet, four inches tall. In 1964 her records showed that she had fractured her right collarbone. Her appendix had been removed in 1969.

Eileen McDougall had five sisters and a brother. They were all examined by Mr Jackson. He found that every one of them had some evidence of the same unusual additional cusps on their teeth. It was so unusual that Mr Jackson concluded his report with this observation: 'In more than twenty-five years of clinical practice I cannot recall another example of such teeth.'

Common sense now dictated that the body was that of Eileen McDougall. But there was to be one further, extraordinary clue. By careful forensic work, Dr Ranasinghe had managed to extract the skin of a finger from one of the hands. The police managed to find an old school report of Eileen's on which she had left an inky fingerprint. They found eight points of comparison on the ridge structures of that fingerprint. A Court of Law would normally demand eighteen points of comparison, but it was none the less convincing evidence that all the other indicators were correct. The body in the tank was Eileen McDougall.

The police knew that Eileen had last been seen in the South Shields area in January of 1970. Was it possible that her body could have lain in tank No. 1 for almost nine and a half years? Considering the preservative qualities of the petrol in the tank, Dr Ranasinghe thought that it *was* possible. The police now found themselves investigating a trail that had gone cold almost a decade beforehand.

Where to start? There were only three possible leads: the clues on the body itself; the nature of the girl's life prior to her disappearance; and the scene of the crime, Velva Liquids.

First, the body itself had clearly been carried up to the top of tank No. 1 and dropped through the front hatch. This is a circular lid about two feet across. Even today it can be lifted easily with one hand. The other hatches are secured by dozens of bolts. There is no ladder on the side of tank 1. In order to reach the top of No. 1 tank you have to climb up the side ladders on an adjacent tank, walk across the roof, over a cat walk and on to No. 1 tank.

The police concluded from this that the murderer must have been very familiar with the Velva Liquids site. They also assumed that whoever had dropped the body into No. 1 tank must have known that it was not scheduled to be cleaned in the near future. They do not appear to have considered that the murderer may have been acting in a panic and may simply have been lucky in his choice of hiding place.

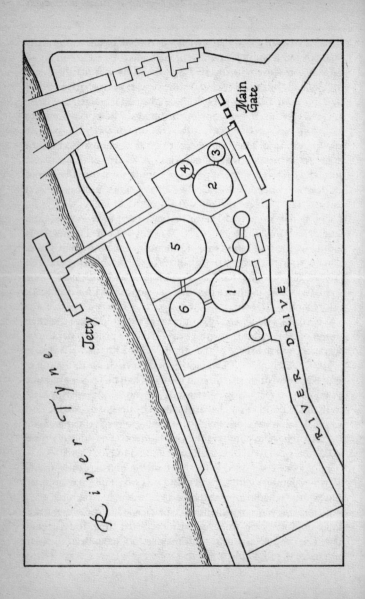

The forensic scientists were able to say, again from their examination of the girl's bone structure, that she had been killed sometime between 1970 and 1973. They told the police that she must have been dumped into the tank within four days of her death.

The appalling injuries that the girl had sustained appeared to link her even more closely with the storage depot. The hammer blows to her head could have come from an 'engineer's hammer'. This is the kind of hammer with a flat end on one side of the head and a semi-circular end on the other. Several of them were found on the Velva site. You will recall that the tank cleaners had discovered the torso in a plastic bag and the policeman had found the head in a canvas bag, tied up with cord. It transpired that both bags could have come from the site. The cord was particularly interesting. It was a material called 'gland packing', which was used on the site. Both the canvas and the gland packing could also have come from any of the ships docking at Velva Liquids.

Dr Ranasinghe had found various pieces of stone or coke embedded in parts of the flesh. On examination it was decided that these could have come from the 'bund' or coke barrier which surrounds Velva Liquids. It was even possible that Eileen McDougall's body had been cut up on the site. If so there would have been a lot of blood in evidence. But the investigation was taking place almost ten years after the murder. There was no way of knowing for sure where the girl had been murdered or dismembered. Equally, the police knew from the pathologist that the girl had been hit with the hammer while she was in an upright position. Here again there would have been a lot of bleeding. But, nine and a half years on, that was of little help to them.

The police turned their attention to the McDougall family and the life that Eileen had led before her disappearance. This proved to be an all too familiar story.

Eileen was one of a family of seven brought up in a council house on the Whiteleas council estate in South Shields. Her home life had obviously not been happy. Her father was away a great deal, working as a tank cleaner. As her older sisters and brother grew up they seemed to have seized the first possible opportunity to get away from the family home and set up on their own. In 1969 Eileen's older sister, Elizabeth, left home and found herself a flat at the other end of South Shields in an area called Lawe Top. It overlooks the mouth of the Tyne and the Velva Liquids site. Eileen herself was already in trouble. She was a bright, good-looking girl with a rather attractive snub nose, shoulder-length hair and a ready smile. But at school she began to rebel. First of all she was placed on report and then suspended. She had run away from home several times. Then in 1969 she was caught stealing a handbag and put on probation.

It seems clear that at this time, in 1969, the young girl was breaking away from her family, finding new friends – and new boyfriends in particular. She often visited her sister's flat and she must have met dozens of young people like herself, also enjoying their first burst of freedom away from the family home. This was, after all, the end of the sixties. Young people had asserted all manner of new freedoms in the decade.

Elizabeth, her older sister, was sharing her flat with two other girls, Mary Bell and Ann Sutherland. They had found themselves a babysitting job in the town. They were looking after three little children in a town house in Anderson Street, near the centre of South Shields. The children's parents were separated and their father looked after them when he was not at work. His name was Ernie Clarke. His work was at Velva Liquids.

This must have seemed to the police like the first major break they had had since the discovery of the identity of the body. It may well have obscured the significance of other facts they learned about Eileen. In particular, they might otherwise have wondered where Eileen was living during December of 1969. She disappeared for about two weeks. They might have wondered about a number of unanswered questions about her behaviour in December 1969 and January 1970.

As it was the police looked at the coincidence of the babysitting job, Clarke's obvious involvement with Eileen's sister and with Velva Liquids and thought to themselves, 'We have our man!'

And if that seems a slightly sensational and overblown way of putting it, it is in fact a direct quote from a contemporary account of the police investigation, written by one of the policemen on the case.

So who was Ernie Clarke? Ernest Adolphus Clarke, a West Indian born in St Kitts, came to England in 1963 and almost immediately found work as a pipe-fitter with a firm called Tubecraft Ltd. They were working on an oil installation in South Shields. Clarke has always been a good worker and he impressed the people at Tubecraft. But that company was soon taken over by Velva Liquids. The first manager of Velva, Douglas Moon, was also impressed by Clarke and offered him a job. He worked for Velva for four years between 1966 and January 1970.

The police were interested in the fact that Clarke had left the site on 31 January 1970, just a couple of weeks after Eileen McDougall had disappeared. Had his guilt forced him to quit? Well, Clarke's own version of events and, more important, the letters at the time, seem to show that his sacking was not engineered. None the less, his leaving Velva so soon was a strong point for the prosecution. One of his workmates, a man called Ronnie Embleton, was about to be promoted to chargehand. Clarke believed that the wrong man was being given the job and he was foolish enough to say so. He even wrote to Douglas Moon, suggesting that he should have promoted Brian Fenwick in place of Embleton. Mr Moon saw this as insubordination – this is a shore installation run very much on merchant navy lines – and wrote to Clarke terminating his employment.

Even then, Clarke did not leave the area. He stayed on in South Shields for nine months, trying to find work. Towards the end of 1970 he moved to Hull and *did* find a job. He was still living in Hull when the police approached him in July 1979. He readily admitted that he had known Eileen McDougall. He told the police that her older sister, Elizabeth, had been a babysitter for him, and that Eileen had occasionally come to his house with her. The police asked him about his preferences in women. He boasted to them that he liked white women between the ages of sixteen and twenty-one. He volunteered that he had had two girlfriends in South Shields, Liz and Ann. The police asked: 'Did you have sex with them?' and Clarke said: 'Yes, man, many times.' He confirmed later that these two were Elizabeth McDougall and her friend, Ann Sutherland, the couple who babysat for him. But Clarke strongly denied having sex with Eileen. For that matter, all of this might just have been showing off to the police; if it was, it would prove to be extremely injudicious. However, there is no evidence that Clarke had sexual relations with either of the girls who came to do the babysitting and both of them have always denied it. The police certainly never established more than the fact that Clarke knew Eileen and that she had come to his flat once or twice, always in the company of the other babysitters.

The police took Clarke back to South Shields police station. They investigated his past. He had a good reputation. He had only ever been in trouble with the police once when he was charged with the theft of a Post Office bank book. He had been fined £50. He had no other convictions of any sort.

He had been working in the Hull fish meal factory until March 1979, when he had been made redundant. But just before his arrest in July of that year he had found himself another job and was waiting for it to start. He was never, of course, going to take up that position. For the police were rapidly forming a circumstantial case against him. He was, they reasoned, the only man to admit knowing Eileen who also worked at Velva Liquids. If he was the murderer, when had he killed her and dumped her on the site?

The police now knew a good deal about Eileen's last few weeks before her disappearance. They still did not know where she had been staying for a couple of weeks in December, but they did know that she had gone to Maidstone in Kent around Christmas. She had been staying with her brother Billy and his wife, Marie.

Billy was another McDougall child who could not wait to leave home. His relationship with his father was a violent and unhappy one. At the age of sixteen he joined the Royal Engineers and was posted to Maidstone after his basic training. On a spell of duty in Gibraltar he met and married Marie. She seems to have enjoyed having Eileen to stay over the Christmas and New Year period. She helped the young girl with her clothes and even gave her some of her own dresses. According to Billy, Eileen had a job in early January, working in a brewery. She began to stay out until midnight almost every night. Then she suddenly gave up the job, and Billy, who was worrying about what she was doing in the evenings, suggested that she ought to think about going back to South Shields. He remembers her as an easy-going girl and says that she accepted his suggestion quite happily.

He took her back on the train to South Shields on Friday, 16 January 1970. Eileen was carrying some extra clothes in two plastic carrier bags.

Billy and Eileen parted outside the Ship and Royal, a pub in the centre of South Shields. Billy did not know where she was going. Wherever it was, it cannot have been far from the town centre. For, within half an hour, Eileen was in a different pub, the Douglas Vaults, in a different dress and without the two carrier bags. There can be little doubt about the change of clothes, because the new dress was quite startling. It was see-through and made of lace. It revealed her bra and panties underneath.

Elizabeth McDougall remembered seeing Eileen on that Friday in the Douglas Vaults and then subsequently at Latino's night club later in the evening. Eileen went home to a boyfriend's house until 2 in the morning but she did not spend the night there. Once again no one knows where she slept.

On 17 January, she was still in the area. Her mother thought that it was that Saturday, 17 January, when she ran into Eileen in Woolworth's in the main street of South Shields. Eileen still had not been home. The last place that Eileen had been seen alive was H.S. Edward Street at the home of a boyfriend called Graham Aitken. The circumstances were certainly dramatic.

She arrived at his door at 2.30 in the morning. Outside it was freezing cold. She was wearing a T-shirt and jeans. She said she had been thrown out, although she did not say where from. Graham took her in and they went to bed together. At 7 o'clock the following morning Graham's father came into his room and caught the two of them in bed. She gathered up her T-shirt and jeans, still wet from the night before and fled into the early Sunday morning. As far as we know, no one except the murderer ever saw her again.

So what theory were the police able to construct about Clarke's involvement in these events? First, they believed that Clarke's familiarity with the scene of the crime and his knowledge of Eileen was too great a coincidence. They were sure that he was involved in her death. This was the circumstantial case they were busy assembling:

They believed that Eileen had changed her dress at Clarke's house that day, the Friday. They no doubt thought that she had slept there on the Friday night. Perhaps there had been a violent row between Ernie Clarke and Eileen McDougall on the Saturday night and he had thrown her out. When she left H.S. Edward Street on the Sunday morning perhaps she had gone back to see Clarke. A further row had developed and he had killed her, dumping her body later that morning.

The duty log at Velva Liquids showed that Clarke was working there from 7 o'clock in the morning, just as Eileen was being chased out of H.S. Edward Street, until 2 o'clock in the afternoon, when his workmate Ronnie Embleton took over. This theory, for which there is no evidence whatsoever, would have involved Eileen going to the Velva site – almost half an hour's walk from Aitken's house – and Ernie Clarke killing her there during the morning. Then, the theory continues, he would either dump her body in the tank in daylight, before Embleton arrived, or alternatively, hide it on the site and return to dump it later.

Even the police, in their enthusiasm to solve this apparently insoluble crime, must have realized that this theory was most unlikely. They had failed to establish anything more than a casual acquaintance between Clark and Eileen. He had never tried to deny that he knew her. He had no history of violent behaviour and no motive for harming the girl. There was nothing to connect her with him or his flat at the time she disappeared. According to the timing of events she might even have been killed after he left South Shields.

It is doubtful if the police would have taken so weak a case to Court, and extremely unlikely that a jury would have convicted Clarke. But Ernie Clarke, already unlucky to have become involved, was to be deeply implicated by new evidence. It came to light on 13 July 1979, the day after the police had travelled to Hull and arrested him.

After his arrest the police concentrated on trying to establish a sexual link between Clarke and Eileen McDougall. But he consistently denied it, protesting that she was under age and he would not have touched her. But the new evidence changed the line of questioning. It came from Ronnie Embleton, the workmate whose promotion to chargehand had led indirectly to Clarke being sacked. Embleton recalled some strange events from nine and a half years beforehand. He felt it his duty to tell the police.

He began by recounting the details of the letter that Ernie Clarke had sent to the terminal manager about Embleton's promotion. Another of the workmates, Dennis McManus, had shown a copy of the letter to him. Then he said that he thought Clarke was a bit of a character. He alleged that Clarke had brought pornographic pictures into work with him. They were supposed to depict his wife with other women. He also claimed that on two or three occasions he had seen young girls, aged between fifteen and seventeen, near the depot gates. He suggested that Clarke knew them.

All this was unsubstantiated gossip. But then Embleton went on to detail some of the odd things that he claimed he had seen Clarke doing on the Velva site. On the eastern edge of the site there is a small storage tank, No. 4. Embleton said that he had been walking through the site when he had seen Clarke underneath the tank. The tank itself stands about five feet off the ground, supported on three brick walls. This leaves two channels underneath the tank running from east to west, and open at each end. Embleton said that he had seen Clarke adding bricks to the western end of the left-hand channel. He could not remember whether he was using cement or not. On another, separate occasion he said he had walked around tank 4 and caught Clarke opening a valve on the underside of the tank and apparently flooding the channel underneath. Tank 4 at that time was being used to store a kind of chemical which has to be kept warm if it is to remain liquid. When it cools it sets with the consistency of candle wax. Embleton repeated his story to us when we interviewed him:

> I went over to tank four and Ernie was in the process of just shutting this valve off and I were come behind him. He was on his knees, sort of thing, and I says – I looked at the channel, I could see, you know, that he had flooded it through – I said: 'What have you done that for, Ernie?' and hardly audible he said, 'Oh, that's nothing man.' I just knew that I wasn't wanted so I just diddled off, and I just never thought no more of it at the time, you know, and when the case came up I got to thinking and I thought, I had better go and report it.

Embleton had more to report. He was fairly sure that these two separate incidents had occurred shortly before Clarke was sacked. This, of course, put them around the time that Eileen had disappeared.

Four months later Embleton made another statement. This time he said that he remembered an incident when he had dug a trench. This, he said, had also happened just before Clarke was dismissed. The trench was six feet long by two feet wide by three feet deep. He was intending to bury rubbish in it. When he got back to the works the next day he discovered that Clarke had filled it in for him. He thought this was a bit out of character for Ernie Clarke. The police never proved that this trench contained anything other than rubbish, or that it had anything to do with the girl's death.

But under tank 4 they *did* find tons of a congealed waxen chemical – five tons of a chemical called stearyl alcohol. The police dug it all out and melted it down. They must have hoped that they would find the legs of the body, but all they found was the remains of two garments inside – a piece of gabardine material which seemed to be part of a pair of jeans and a girl's blue jumper. The jumper was twenty feet inside the left-hand channel and about a foot beneath the surface. It had been slit along both arms and up the back as if with a sharp knife. The police said it looked as if it had been cut off a dead body. It was heavily impregnated with the stearyl alcohol substance.

The police put it on to a dummy about the size of Eileen. It fitted. They asked her family and friends if it was Eileen's. No one could confirm this, but they did say that it *was* the kind of thing that she would have been wearing at the end of the sixties. Although there was no direct link with the dead girl and, most importantly, no forensic evidence of blood on the jumper or anywhere else, the police now believed that they had a strong case against Ernest Clarke. With Embleton's incriminating evidence of Clarke's strange behaviour under tank 4, with the jumper, dramatically cut up as if by a sharp knife, and the fact that Clarke knew the girl and worked at the site, they were now sure that they had the right man.

Almost a year after the discovery of Eileen's body, on 4 June 1980, Ernie Clarke came to trial at Newcastle upon Tyne Crown Court. He still vehemently professed his innocence.

The Trial of Ernie Clarke

The trial lasted from 4 June to 12 June and included a visit to the Velva Liquids site by the Judge, the jury and the defendant.

There were several factors which must have weighed heavily against Clarke, not least one piece of evidence stressed in the prosecution's opening remarks. Mr Walsh, Q.C., the prosecuting counsel, told the jury that he planned to lay before them a jigsaw of facts. Only at the end, he asserted, would they see the entire picture. But, in addition to this 'jigsaw', Mr Walsh said that there was an admission by Ernie Clarke. He told the Court that while Clarke had been on remand in Durham jail he had admitted the crime to a fellow prisoner, Alan Daglish. Daglish would tell the Court that Clarke had said to him. 'I did it, but they'll never prove it after ten years.' According to Clarke's solicitor this was a very dramatic moment in the opening of the trial. The Court received news of this admission 'in a deathly hush'.

The following day the local paper carried reports of the trial under the headline I DID IT. It was only then that Clarke's solicitor, Mr Duffy, was alerted by a colleague to the fact that Mr Daglish had a history of mental problems and was doubtless a totally unreliable witness. Mr Duffy obtained Mr Daglish's mental record. The defence counsel, Humphrey Potts, Q.C., approached the prosecution and asked whether there was something that Mr Walsh had omitted to tell him about Mr Daglish. Mr Walsh, in all good faith, said, 'No, nothing.' He checked with the police, who must have had access to Mr Daglish's mental record. They told Mr Walsh that there was nothing else he needed to know about Mr Daglish. At this point Mr Potts felt constrained to tell his opposite number what he knew. Mr Walsh checked with the police once more, no doubt in more forceful terms this time. He now discovered the truth and agreed that Mr Daglish's evidence must be withdrawn. Accordingly a statement was read out in Court saying that Mr Daglish was inclined to invent things which were not true and that his word was unreliable. His evidence was duly discounted.

In his summing-up Mr Justice Caulfield said: 'There is not a grain of evidence regarding any admission by the defendant, and the conversation, which was opened by Mr Walsh, with a prisoner whom we now know was very seriously mentally affected, does not exist. It is not before you. Disregard it utterly and completely.' This was a fair and just reference to the whole unfortunate incident, but, as we discussed in the first series of 'Rough Justice', it is a refined kind of mental gymnastics to ignore evidence so dramatically stated during a trial. In spite of this reference, the idea that Clarke might have 'confessed' may have stayed in the jury's collective mind.

One further factor which may have served to incriminate Clarke was not so dramatic but it was certainly salacious if the jury should choose to take it seriously. It was revealed in Court that Clarke had claimed that he had had sex with both Elizabeth McDougall and Ann Sutherland. The Judge pointed out in his summing-up that this had been firmly denied by both girls. He reminded the jury that Mr Potts, the defence counsel, had said to Elizabeth: 'I suggest to you that you did have intercourse with Clarke,' and that Elizabeth had replied: 'And I suggest to you that I did not.'

None the less, the image of Ernie Clarke as an older man interfering with younger girls can have done his case no good. What effect racial prejudice might have played in this particular context is impossible to judge. Suffice it to say that Clarke's black skin is unlikely to have been an advantage when the all-white jury were being invited to consider his possible relationships with white girls.

The jury were asked to decide if Clarke had murdered Eileen

between the 17th day of January 1970 and the 24th day of January 1970. In the exact manner of trials for serious offences it was necessary to establish:

1. that the victim *had* been murdered.
2. that the victim *was* Eileen McDougall.
3. that she *had* died between those dates.

The Judge was certainly impressed by the hard work of the pathologist, Dr Ranasinghe, and Mr Jackson, the dental expert, in determining the identity of the body. The jury must have been equally impressed. So there was no doubt that the girl had been murdered and virtually no room for doubt that she was Eileen McDougall. The Judge pointed out to the jury that it could have been possible for Eileen to die much later than 24 January 1970. But he also said that she would very possibly have been seen after that time around South Shields. The balance of probability was that she had died sometime around 18 January, the Sunday – the day she had left Graham Aitken's bed at 7 o'clock in the morning.

The police, as we have already seen, were convinced that whoever had murdered Eileen had an intimate knowledge of the Velva site. It was strongly put to the jury that only a Velva workman like Clarke would have known that tank No. 1 was not due for cleaning in the foreseeable future, and that there was a complicated route up to the roof of tank No. 1 from the adjacent tanks. In his summing-up the Judge, Mr Justice Caulfield, put the question like this, a question he described as possibly one of the most important in the case:

> You might ask yourselves in your room tomorrow: Who would choose tank one? Having seen the route to tank one [the jury had been shown it on the previous day at Velva], which has to be achieved by a platform and over tanks and by a walkway a short way to another tank, and having yourselves seen the area which, of course, is not exactly like this lovely model in front of you [indicating]. I mean, there are no pipes to clamber in that model as you had yesterday. Who would choose tank one as a place of concealment and, you may think, complete conceal-

ment? You might think that it would hardly be a stranger to Velva, but you might think it could be a stranger to Velva, who could have lived in the area and knew the site. But what about the head? What about Eileen McDougall's head? There is no dispute that it was found wrapped in canvas which, according to the foreman, Fenwick, is normally seen on the Velva site and that canvas packing which housed the head of Eileen was tied with a substance described as gland packing . . . and that gland packing, the evidence says, was used at the site . . .

The Judge went on to warn that these substances could also have come from ships that tied up at the Velva jetty. He also focused on the other employees at Velva at the time, excluding them from possible involvement in her murder. So just what weight should the jury attach to the undeniable – and undenied – fact that Ernie Clarke knew Eileen McDougall? Her brother, Billy McDougall, told the Court that he had visited Clarke after October 1969 and that Eileen had been with him. But Mr Justice Caulfield continued:

Do be careful, though; an acquaintanceship with Eileen McDougall away in 1969, or early 1970, even knowledge of Eileen, in no way connects the defendant, Clarke, with guilt. Many people in South Shields knew Eileen and some men, certainly two, on the evidence, knew her sexually, to put it in not too rough a way. There is nothing, you may think, absolutely nothing indicative of guilt in being an acquaintance of Eileen if it be the fact that Clarke is the only person at Velva who knew Eileen, that may well be your view. You may conclude that by reason of the ignorance of Moon [the manager], of Fenwick and McManus and Embleton [the operatives], of Eileen, that these people whom I have just mentioned, Moon, Fenwick, McManus and Embleton, can be excluded and excluded with ease as potential killers of Eileen . . .

Then the Judge returned to the theme of 'special knowledge' of the site:

Of course, the killer of Eileen could have been a stranger at Velva as regards employment, yet having knowledge of the site, its tanks, its access, but you might say to yourselves: Would a stranger have used the canvas to cover the head and the gland packing to tie the canvas? You decide.

So far the jury had the two circumstantial facts alone. Clarke had knowledge of the site where Eileen's body was found and he knew the girl. Neither of these facts could have been regarded as anything more than coincidence. And the controversy over whether or not there had been a sexual relationship between Clarke and his two babysitters, Elizabeth and Ann, was unresolved, unprovable and, in any case, of no real value in estimating whether or not he had known Eileen casually or intimately.

By far the most significant evidence was Ronald Embleton's. On Monday 9 June 1980 Mr Walsh, Q.C., conducted the examination-in-chief of Ronald Embleton. He brought Embleton up to the point where he had seen Ernie Clarke under tank 4:

WALSH: What did you see there or happening when you got there?

EMBLETON: He was just in the process of shutting the valve off. He had flooded that chamber there practically top of that wall. [Embleton was referring to photographs of tank 4 submitted as Court exhibits.]

WALSH: He flooded the chamber there?

EMBLETON: Yes.

WALSH: With what?

EMBLETON: This wax – we used to call it stearyl – which had to be kept hot to run. When it got cold it stayed just like white candle wax.

WALSH: How full was this channel when you saw it?

EMBLETON: It was practically to the top of the small wall that is just in the valve . . .

And, a few moments later, Mr Walsh went on to the other incident:

WALSH: Did you see something else at some other time?

EMBLETON: Yes sir.
WALSH: In connection with that tank four?
EMBLETON: Yes, sir.
WALSH: What was that?
EMBLETON: He was bricking the front of it up.

There was a delay while the Judge and the jury found the relevant photograph. It showed the western end of the two channels under tank 4, two 'entrances' as Embleton called them:

WALSH: Now, you tell us, what about bricks?
EMBLETON: He was bricking these two small entrances up here with the bricks and mortar . . .

Embleton could not remember which of the two incidents, the flooding and the bricking-up, had happened first. Mr Walsh continued:

WALSH: At the time it happened were you able to see any reason for bricking up the wall?
EMBLETON: No sir, none whatsoever.
WALSH: Or any reason for filling the channel with wax?
EMBLETON: No, no reason at all.
WALSH: Did you speak to Ernie Clarke about it at all or not?
EMBLETON: Just when I came up behind him I just asked him what he was doing, why he had done that and just sort of replied in a muffled voice, 'That's nothing, man.'.

Embleton went on to outline the story of the trench that he had dug and which Clarke had filled in for him unbidden. The three incidents were certainly suspicious and there was no reason to suppose that Embleton was lying or being malicious. Embleton said that he could not be at all sure about the timing of these incidents, but he did feel that they had been near the time that Clarke had left Velva Liquids, in other words near January 1970, when Eileen disappeared. The implication, quite starkly, was that Clarke had gone to elaborate lengths to hide the jumper that he had cut from Eileen's body in a flood of wax under tank 4. But if that was the case he would need to have carried out this manoeuvre between the time of Eileen's disappearance on 18 January and his own dismissal on 27 January. Douglas Moon, the Velva manager, gave evidence about why he had sacked Clarke. Clarke had not 'engineered' it.

During his cross-examination of Ronald Embleton, Mr Potts, Q.C. for the defence, pointed out that in order for these incidents to have happened at the substantive time Embleton and Clarke would have needed to be on shift at the same time, or their shifts would have needed to overlap. He referred Ronnie Embleton to exhibit 33, which was the time book from Velva Liquids. It gave the following shift pattern for Embleton and Clarke in the relevant period:

	Clarke	*Embleton*
18 January	7 a.m.–2 p.m.	2 p.m.–10 p.m.
19 January	6 a.m.–2 p.m.	3 p.m.–11 p.m.
20 January	6 a.m.–2 p.m.	3 p.m.–11 p.m.
21 January	6 a.m.–2 p.m.	3 p.m.–11 p.m.
22 January	6 a.m.–2 p.m.	3 p.m.–11 p.m.
23 January	6 a.m.–2 p.m.	3 p.m.–11 p.m.
24 January	} neither man at work	
25 January		
26 January	8 a.m.–4.30 p.m.	Not at work.
27 January	8 a.m.–4.30 p.m.	Not at work.

In cross-examination it rapidly became clear that the only opportunity Embleton could have had to overlap with Clarke would have been on Sunday 18 January, the day that Eileen actually disappeared. Even if one assumes that Embleton came early on to the site, as he was accustomed to do; even if one assumes that Clarke was prepared to hide the incriminating clothes in broad daylight while other workmates were on the site, you are still left with the fact that Embleton remembers *two* incidents, *two* separate events during that period. Mr Potts was able to show that at most only one could have happened in the time, and even that was hedged around with considerable doubt.

Having carefully taken Embleton through the duty log, pointing out that the shift times of Clarke and himself never coincided during the relevant period, he reached 23 January:

POTTS: And again, Friday the twenty-third the same applies: Clarke finishes at two. You do not start till three, I think, and I will be corrected if I am wrong?

EMBLETON: Yes.

POTTS: There was no further occasion before Mr Clarke stopped working for Velva Liquids that you were working indeed on the same day at all – if you look at the bottom row, that is right is it not? On the Saturday you were not at work on the twenty-fourth; neither was Clarke. On Sunday the twenty-fifth neither were at work. Clarke was at work on Monday the twenty-sixth, but you were not. He was at work on Tuesday the twenty-seventh and you were not, Mr Embleton, that is right is it not?

EMBLETON: Yes sir.

POTTS: It really comes to this: if either of these incidents that you describe concerning the flooding of the channel and the bricking up of the channel took place, they took place before the eighteenth of January, did they not?

EMBLETON: Yes.

POTTS: That must be right

EMBLETON: That must be right.

In his summing-up the Judge reviewed the various statements and actions by Clarke which the police had presented as incriminating. He went into more detail about the claim by Clarke that he had had sex with Elizabeth McDougall and Ann Sutherland. Both the girls had denied it. Clarke had been asked in Court:

Q: Did you have sex with Eileen?

CLARKE: No; not under age. I never fancy her ...

Q: Did you have intercourse with Eileen?

CLARKE: Never.

Q: Did Eileen come to your house alone?

CLARKE: No, never. She have no reason.

The judge also quoted from later police interviews with Clarke: At 6.35 p.m. on Thursday 12 July 1979, Detective Superintendent James Anderson interviewed Clarke. The main thread of his questioning at that time (prior to the Embleton revelations), was still about whether the relationship between Clarke and Eileen had been sexual. Chief Superintendent Anderson began by reminding Clarke that he was still under caution and then went on: 'From our inquiries, you are the only person who knew or had any connection with Eileen McDougall.'

Clarke replied, 'You are telling me that I am the only one at Velva that had any connection with Eileen . . . I am a worried man now.'

The police had quoted this as a potentially damaging admission. This is what Mr Justice Caulfield had to say about it:

'Now, that is not an admission. He *would* be worried. You would be worried if you were being questioned in respect of a crime which had been committed if, though you were there, you had not committed it.'

The Judge continued to dissect the same interview, quoting Chief Superintendent Anderson's comments:

'It appears strange to me,' Anderson had said, 'that the last time you remember seeing Eileen was at Latino's night club and the last time she was seen alive was at that night club in January 1970.' (In fact, as we know, she was seen subsequently by Graham Aitken and by his father.)

'Now, in fairness to the defendant,' Mr Justice Caulfield continued, 'there is not the slightest evidence that the defendant was at the night club at any material time between January the eighteenth and that other time.'

He continued to quote from the Anderson interview:

CLARKE: Do you want me to tell you that I'd kill her?

ANDERSON: Well, did you?

CLARKE: No, definitely not. Nothing like that is on my conscience. You are not going to tie me up. I will never admit. I would rather go to the gallows than go to prison for a long time.

ANDERSON: I am searching for the truth.

CLARKE: Don't kid me that there is any evidence after nine years.

The Judge commented, 'Well, you decide whether there is any evidence.'

On Sunday 15 July, after the police had found the girl's blue jumper and the piece of gabardine, Chief Superintendent Anderson interviewed Clarke once more. The Judge reminded the jury of that encounter: '. . . later on Sunday fifteenth July the police excavated under tank four. They had sifted the wax. They had obtained the exhibits which I have mentioned earlier.' He quoted further from the Anderson interview:

ANDERSON: Items of what appear to be women's clothing have been recovered from the channel under tank four, which you were seen flooding with chemical. The clothing appears to have been cut as if it had been removed from a dead body. Have you anything to say about that?

[He bowed his head, say the police, put his hands to his face and wept. The murder was put to him and he denied it.]

CLARKE: You are wrong. I never kill anyone.

[. . . and he had nothing to say; to the charge he replied, 'Not guilty.']

The Judge had already pointed out to the jury that when, previously, Clarke had admitted to being worried by one of the police accusations, that was hardly surprising – any of us would have been similarly worried. He might with equal justification have pointed out that if, indeed, Clarke did break down and weep at the news of the fresh evidence, that too was hardly surprising. *If* Clarke was innocent, then he must have known that the facts against him were (a) wrong and (b) purely circumstantial. If he suddenly learned that the police had found a substantive piece of evidence which appeared to implicate him directly in the girl's death, then no wonder he wept. But this was left to the jury's own imagination.

The jury retired at 11.43 a.m. on Thursday 12 July 1980. Much of the above was insubstantial. They must have known that the sex question was basically unresolved. Clarke's pronouncements did nothing to support his guilt and quite a lot to support his innocence. So they were left with three 'facts' to consider.

1. Clarke knew the girl. He never denied it.
2. Clarke worked at the place where her body was found.
3. Clarke had been seen doing something odd under tank 4, if they believed Embleton. On investigation, the underside of tank 4 had yielded up a jumper which appeared to have been cut from a dead body and could have fitted Eileen McDougall.

There is little doubt in the above list as to which is the significant clue. Certainly the jury did not deliberate for long. They returned to the Court at 5.15 p.m.

CLERK OF THE COURT: Members of the jury, have you reached a verdict upon which you are all agreed?

FOREMAN OF THE JURY: Yes.

CLERK: Members of the jury, do you find the defendant, Ernest Adolphus Clarke, guilty or not guilty of murder?

FOREMAN: Guilty.

CLERK: You find him guilty. That is the verdict of you all?

FOREMAN: Yes.

HIS LORDSHIP: Will you stand please? Ernest Clarke, this jury has convicted you of murder of a girl called Eileen McDougall. The sentence of the Court is fixed by law, as no doubt you know, and therefore I do not need to justify it, nor need I comment and the sentence of the Court is that you will be a prisoner for life.

Ernie Clarke is still in prison today.

Re-investigation:
The Case of the
Confused Chemicals

One of the reasons for the success of 'Rough Justice' lies in our approach to the re-investigation. Before we take up any particular line of investigation we spend a lot of time assembling all the available data on the case. Somewhere there are always some forgotten documents – not perhaps important in themselves – to cast a different aspect on the other documents that everyone else has been studying. We then draw up every conceivable line of investigation and apply it to the case papers. We often draw a blank. But occasionally we come up with something that no one else has thought about.

The case of Ernie Clarke certainly seemed impossible to us. It must have seemed impossible to the police when they first began looking for the murderer of Eileen McDougall. But they found a suspect and the jury found him guilty. The evidence against him was largely undeniable. Clarke readily volunteered that he knew Eileen – there was no point in investigating whether that was untrue. There was no question as to whether he had worked on the site. There seemed to be no reason why Clarke's workmate Ronnie Embleton should lie about the suspicious goings-on under tank No. 4 – he had pointed to the spot and – lo and behold – the jumper had been found there. It was cut up, the experts said, as if off a dead body.

We actually sent the case back to Justice because we thought that there was nothing in it for us to investigate. There were no scene-of-crime photographs – no one knew where the girl had been killed. There were none of the usual forensic clues – no fibres, hairs, fingerprints. There was no chance of proving an alibi. The records showed where Clarke had been – he had been on the site when the girl apparently vanished. Not only were there no new leads – there was no chance of them.

Tom Sargant sent the case back to us. He had a theory that perhaps a sailor had done the crime. Perhaps we could find which ships had visited the area, perhaps we could discover that there had been other disappearances near where one of these ships had berthed ... something along those lines. The truth was he genuinely believed Ernie Clarke to be innocent and also believed that he should, at the very least, never have been found guilty on the evidence. He posed the questions which had troubled us too – where were the legs and why were they not in the tank?

We never found the answers to these questions, but we read the case again. We did our usual routine of getting our hands on every available piece of paper. Then we read ... and read ... and read. It takes four and a half hours just to read the documents in the Clarke case, never mind digest the contents. And with each reading our doubts about the feasibility of the research increased. We checked through Clarke's movements. The police were right. We checked Eileen McDougall's movements in Maidstone. The police had been right all along, although their evidence had not conclusively proved it. We checked with the boy who had last seen her. He confirmed what he had said in Court. And then we checked the chemicals, the stearyl and lauryl alcohols. And then the case against Ernie Clarke was destroyed.

It began with a routine check through the exhibits officer's report. This is the deposition in which all the samples of evidence taken at the scene of the crime are logged. From it we learn who first found a certain piece of evidence, where he found it, when he checked it into the exhibits officer's care and where it subsequently went. By doing this we can not only deduce how the picture of the crime was being put together by the detectives on the case, but we can also see where certain exhibits were sent so that we can look up what checks and tests were made upon them. We can sometimes see that certain pieces of evidence seemed quite important at one stage of the investigation but subsequently became overlooked after a suspect was arrested. For example, a knife appeared in the evidence in the Clarke case. It was given to the exhibits officer on 12 July – by an officer who had just returned from interviewing Clarke in Hull. On 23 July this knife was given to a Detective Sergeant who had it for two days. We do not know what he did with it because he omitted these two days from his statement. But we can surmise from the exhibits officer's report that it did not go to the forensic laboratory and it did not go to the pathologist's office. After it was returned from this trip it never appeared in evidence again. Was that because it had no relevance to Ernie Clarke as a suspect, or because it was not relevant to the circumstances surrounding the death of Eileen McDougall? We shall never know. Our guess is that the police picked it up in Clarke's home in Hull in the vain hope that it might prove to be the murder weapon. The jury may well have surmised that none of Clarke's kitchen knives were checked. The exhibits officer's report tells a different story.

It was while searching through this report that we noticed that there was no reference to samples of wax taken from under tank No. 4 at Velva Liquids. Samples had certainly been taken because four of them appeared in Court as exhibits. So we checked in the scientist's report. There we found six samples listed. We checked back to the exhibits officer's report – and found a supplementary page after the main report. It concerned wax samples taken from under tank No. 4 – but there were only four samples, not six. They were the four which had appeared as exhibits.

We began to sense that there was something wrong. The two samples which were missing from the exhibits officer's report were clearly in the scientist's report – first as being both from under tank No. 4, and further as 'sample 93: wax from the right channel' and 'sample 94: wax from the left channel'. The exhibits of wax produced in Court, the other four samples, were *not* listed as being from either one channel or the other. Why, we wondered, had the two earlier samples, 93 and 94, which were better identified, gone missing? They were nowhere to be found in the exhibits officer's report and they did not appear in Court as exhibits.

The jumper, Exhibit 28, which had been used in Court to convict Clarke, had come from the left-hand channel under tank No. 4. According to the scientists it was saturated in stearyl alcohol. This was the same substance as sample 94, listed as coming from the left-hand channel in the scientist's report, but omitted from the exhibits officer's report and not presented in Court. The scientific report would have strengthened the prosecution argument that the jumper had come from the channel where, Ronnie Embleton claimed, Clarke had added bricks to the top of the wall – and poured the wax out in suspicious circumstances. Why then was this evidence not presented to the Court?

Was it, we wondered, because the presence of the substance stearyl alcohol weakened the prosecution case? The Judge had never drawn the jury's attention to the *two* kinds of wax that had been in tank No. 4 during the years 1969 and 1970. Although we did not have the full transcript of the trial, we guessed that there had been little, if any, mention in the prosecution's case of two chemicals. The Judge would certainly have mentioned them if there had been.

We looked through all the depositions concerning the chemicals that had been in tank No. 4. The four samples presented to the Court were 99 A, B, C, and D. 99A and 99D were predominantly lauryl alcohol. 99B and 99C were predominantly stearyl alcohol. Although these two substances may look very alike, they are chemically quite different. The manager from Lennigs, the company who actually owned the chemicals that had been stored at Velva Liquids, had no records of when stearyl and lauryl alcohol had been stored there. Working entirely from memory, he thought that he had been sending lauryl alcohol to Velva from 1969 to August 1972.

The foreman at Velva Liquids, Brian Fenwick, thought that tank 4 had held lauryl alcohol from February 1968 until September 1968, when stearyl alcohol had been put in it. He too was working from memory.

But Douglas Moon, the general manager at Velva Liquids, had stated that tank 4 had been used for the storage of stearyl alcohol from September 1968 until August 1969. It had then been used for storing lauryl alcohol until September 1972. What interested us about Mr Moon's deposition was the paragraph following this information. He said that he felt he could produce the records of the contents of tank No. 4. This was quite remarkable – because the trial and investigation took place in 1979. The records he was referring to were nine years old.

Mr Moon's dates were exact and seemed to come from the documents about tank No. 4; yet these documents had not appeared in Court before the jury. Was it that Mr Moon had been wrong – that the records did not exist? Or did the police actually have them, but not consider them to be relevant to the case against Clarke?

When we inquired, we discovered that Mr Moon had died since the trial. But luckily for us – and for Ernie Clarke – his wife had been present when he had made his deposition. She had been his secretary at the time and still worked at Velva. Mrs Moon confirmed that her husband had indeed had the documents before him when he had made his statements to the police.

Why then had these documents not appeared as part of the evidence against Clarke? Mr Moon's testimony showed that at the time that Eileen McDougall had vanished tank No. 4 had contained lauryl alcohol – yet the jumper that had appeared in evidence against him had been immersed in stearyl alcohol. Did the police think that this would perhaps only cloud the issues before the jury? The defence lawyers never knew that the records of tank No. 4's contents in 1969 still existed. But the police knew.

Our suspicions about the presentation of the evidence concerning the jumper were now fully roused. We devoted our attention to two lines of investigation. Firstly we had to find out everything we could about the two alcohols. Secondly we had to find the records for tank No. 4.

Dr Patrick Toseland, consultant biochemist at Guy's Hospital and a senior toxicologist, agreed to take an interest in the case. Not only did he read the original reports but he went up to South Shields to investigate for himself. There he surprised us all by discovering the original exhibits in the case. They had all been returned to Velva after the trial because they were actually owned by Velva Liquids. But no one had known what to do with them because Velva's site is a bonded area and there was no procedure for getting rid of police exhibits! Rather than commit an unlawful act, the management had simply left the black polythene bags where the police had dumped them. They still had the official seals on them, which Dr Toseland readily recognized. Soon he had in his possession the blue jumper, Exhibit 28, the samples of wax presented in Court, and the two samples 93 and 94 which had never been mentioned in the trial.

While Doctor Toseland did his tests on the samples of wax he had collected, we looked for documentation on the contents of tank No. 4. At first it seemed so easy. Just as the police had returned the exhibits, they had also returned the documents. Or at least so it seemed. Almost straight away we discovered a pile of old papers in the boilerhouse which contained the records for the contents of every tank at Velva between 1968 and 1975 – except the records for tank No. 4. We carried on searching through tea chests full of documents. There were three ways of proving what had been in tank No. 4. First, if we were lucky enough to find them, were the tank records which Velva had made out. But we could also consult the records of the Port of Tyne Authority, which listed which ships delivered what to where. We could also find the answer in the records of Lennigs, the actual owners of the chemicals. They sent letters to Velva telling them when to expect or make a delivery. They also periodically negotiated the price of storing the chemicals.

First of all we discovered from the Port of Tyne Authority that there had been no stearyl alcohol shipped to Velva Liquids between 8 March and 13 December 1969. We also discovered that a shipment of lauryl alcohol had been made to Velva on 12

December of that year. This could only have gone to tank No. 4 because tank No. 3 contained ethylene glycol at that time – and *only tanks 3 and 4 were equipped with the heaters needed for storing lauryl alcohol*. A look at the Velva shipping book for that date confirmed this – the shipment had gone to tank No. 4.

Next we found a series of letters from Lennigs, the owners of the alcohols, in which they were negotiating a price for the storage of lauryl alcohol in a new tank. These letters referred specifically to tank No. 4 and were dated at a time when tank 3 was already being used for the storage of lauryl alcohol. They could therefore only have been negotiating over the use of tank No. 4. In November of that year they sent a letter which referred to a shipment of lauryl alcohol. Tank No. 3 had already been storing ethylene glycol since October 1969. Once again the shipment referred to can only have gone into tank 4.

As this evidence mounted that tank No. 4 had contained lauryl alcohol when Eileen McDougall had vanished, we became increasingly suspicious about the disappearance of the records for this tank. Finally we took a shot in the dark and asked Velva Liquids to request the return of these documents from the police. Since it seemed that all the documents had been returned with the exhibits, there was no evidence to suggest that the police still held them. But in fact they did. They were sent by return of post.

The records of tank No. 4 showed clearly that it had been used for the storage of stearyl alcohol up to April 1969. The tank had then lain fallow until August 1969, when 3,500 gallons of lauryl alcohol was poured into it. This had stayed there until at least the end of 1970.

Our other records showed us that there was no stearyl alchol anywhere else on the Velva site in January 1970. In fact we have since established that there was never any stearyl alcohol on the Velva site after August 1969. Stearyl alcohol becomes liquid only at 55 degrees centigrade. How then did any stearyl alcohol get into the blue jumper if it was taken off Eileen McDougall's dead body in January 1970? Plainly the jumper had been placed under tank

No. 4 while the stearyl alcohol had been liquid. That could only have been before August 1969.

Why did Clarke's defence lawyers miss this simple point? First, they did not know that the records for tank No. 4 even existed. Mr Moon did not present them to the Court, and they were not presented as exhibits. Since the prosecution is supposed to present 'best evidence', there is no reason to suspect that better evidence about the contents of tank No. 4 existed in the police files.

But the confusion about this point was not helped by the list – prepared by the prosecution – of the witnesses they expected to call and what they expected to prove. In this list the prosecution called Dr Brian Wilson, a development chemist working for the owners of the alcohol, and Andrew Fyall, an assistant purchasing manager for the same company. They were listed to give 'details of contents of tank 4 during material times'. These gentlemen did not have access to the records of tank No. 4 – they only knew that stearyl and lauryl alcohol were sent to the Velva site. They did not even have the records on that information. According to this same list of prosecution witnesses, Mr Moon, who actually knew what was in tank 4 at the material times, was only called to describe 'the Velva complex and the employment of the accused'. In fact, when giving evidence in Court, Mr Moon spoke about the contents of tank No. 4, stating that it contained stearyl alcohol until August 1969. But the prosecution did not ask him to produce his records. In such circumstances how could it have crossed the minds of the defence lawyers that the best way of proving what was in tank No. 4 was to question Mr Moon on the records and to request the appropriate records from the police?

When one looks at the situation from the point of view of the jury at the trial the question of the two chemicals in tank No. 4 becomes even more covered in confusion. Although the two chemicals had been briefly described during the trial, the Judge made no reference whatsoever in his summing-up to the fact that there were two chemicals in tank No. 4. According to him it is all 'wax' – whether it is the stearyl alcohol in the jumper or the lauryl alcohol in samples 99A and 99D.

From such confused happenings are born miscarriages of justice. The key samples, Nos. 93 and 94, which were the most specific pieces of evidence taken from beneath tank 4, were left out of the exhibits officer's report for some reason. They were subsequently left off the exhibits list, so the attention of the Court was never drawn to their existence. Men who knew little of the contents of tank 4 were called to testify to the contents of the tank, yet the man who was capable of producing the best evidence of the contents was not asked to do so.

Prosecution counsel did not raise the question of the records when he questioned Mr Moon, and defence counsel failed to realize the hidden significance of the one sentence in Mr Moon's pre-trial deposition which hinted that the records might exist. Everyone in Court seems to have felt it was no use asking whether records from almost a decade before might still be available. No one mentioned that the police held these records in their files.

Any official inquiry today would no doubt point out the fault of the defence in missing the significance of two lines in hundreds of pages of evidence. But surely the fault lies more in our system of justice which has no means by which to ensure that such happenings – which have the result that only parts of the truth, not the whole truth, are brought before the Court – do not occur.

While we were obtaining the records of tank No. 4 we remembered a paragraph of the scientific report on the jumper. Dr Alan Young of the Home Office forensic laboratory at Wetherby had said that it was not possible to draw any conclusion as to when it had been deposited in the wax. We believed he had said this because he had not known that there was no liquefied stearyl alcohol on the site after August 1969. Although he had obviously been asked to put a timing on when the jumper had been deposited in the wax, he had not been given an important part of the data necessary for such a calculation. Mr Moon mentioned the records of tank No. 4 some four and a half months before Dr Young made his report. Was this just another unfortunate accident that resulted in a Home Office scientist unwittingly giving incorrect evidence to the Court?

Meanwhile Dr Toseland had been examining the exhibits in London. His report closed up any loophole that there might have been in the proof that the jumper had nothing to do with Eileen McDougall. His findings were:

> The jumper was immersed in stearyl alcohol. There is no evidence of gross contamination with lauryl alcohol. These findings indicate that the jumper had been in intimate contact with commercial stearyl alcohol and that it could not have been soaked in liquid lauryl (or whatever) and pushed into a melted layer of stearyl. The alcohols are not interchangeable. They will remain very stable, even over the time scale involved in this case and they are not transmutable into one another.

When we showed Dr Toseland the rest of the case against Clarke and the records of tank No. 4, he said:

> The jumper could only have been in the channel at the time stearyl alcohol was poured on to it. Wherever this jumper came from, it appears to me to have nothing to do with the death of this girl, considering the relative times of the lauryl and stearyl components in tank No. 4. This is one of the planks of evidence against Clarke, and I think this demonstrates that this plank is removed.

Because the trial of Ernie Clarke took place nine and a half years after Eileen McDougall disappeared, it was natural for the defence lawyers to assume that the proof of this particular plank was lost. Most companies throw their records away after seven years. In fact the proof lay in the police files. What would the effect have been on the jury – indeed on the Judge's summing-up – if that plank had been removed from the case during the trial? Would he have sent the jumper into the jury room as he did, to lie before the jury as they discussed the case? Would Clarke have lost his appeal if the proof had emerged from the police files after the trial? The police sent back everything that belonged to Velva Liquids *except the records of tank No. 4.*

Within a week of obtaining the above evidence on the jumper

we had a shrewd idea of what the jumper actually was and where it had come from. Velva Liquids is a dirty place; the men are constantly getting their hands oily. To clean themselves they use rags or 'industrial wipers', which Velva buys from a company called John Cowies in South Shields. Cowies in turn buys its supplies from a company called Beaumont's in Dewsbury, which collects rags from jumble sales and rag shops, cuts them up and sells them as 'industrial wipers'. In a very telling piece of television filming we showed Beaumont's most experienced rag-cutter, Ivy Woods.

Ivy did not know why we were filming her. She thought we were making a film about the rag business. When we gave her some jumpers like the one found under tank No. 4, she cut them up as she has been cutting them up for twenty-three years. They all came out of her machine cut in the same way as the jumper which had helped to send Ernie Clarke to jail. The jumper which the Judge had sent into the jury room because it was relevant to the case against Clarke was actually an 'industrial wiper' – a rag.

When we showed the evidence to Ronnie Embleton, Clarke's workmate who had first raised the question of tank No. 4, he was shocked to the core. After our interview with him he was off work sick for three days. We did not doubt his evidence that he had once seen Clarke turning the tap on under tank No. 4. Nor did we doubt that he had seen Clarke apparently bricking up a part of the wall under the tank. We did not doubt his sincerity when he said that he honestly thought that these two actions had happened at about the time of Eileen McDougall's disappearance. He did not question the authenticity of the records that proved him wrong.

He said: I was shocked because in all honesty I thought the police had found a lot more than was actually found under there. In all honesty I couldn't say when the incidents of the bricking up and running off of wax happened. It's within that period of time ... but if there hadn't been stearyl in there for nine months – I honestly thought it was shorter, you know. Time plays funny things with your memory.

We had a lot of sympathy for Ronnie Embleton. The police had asked him to remember small insignificant details from nine years before. They had then placed him in the witness box, and he had become a key witness. Without records no one could expect to give more than guesses in such a situation. Embleton's honest attempt to help had sent Clarke to prison. But Embleton had always had a sneaking suspicion he had been wrong. As we left he said, 'You know, I always thought the sun was shining when I saw Ernie running off the wax. It was a warm day.' The temperature in South Shields on 19 January 1970 was 45 degrees Fahrenheit.

We now felt we had found enough to win Clarke a reference from the Home Secretary to the Appeal Court. Not only had we proved that the main evidence against Clarke – the jumper – should never have been in the case against him at all, but we had won support for this position from a former Attorney-General and a former Judge in the Appeal Court whom we had been consulting throughout our investigation.

Nevertheless, we carried on the investigation into the death of Eileen McDougall because we felt it was not enough to prove that Clarke should not have been found guilty. We felt we should endeavour to show that he was indeed innocent. Just as we had thought that it was an impossible task to prove murder against anyone after nine years, so now we thought it impossible to prove Clarke's innocence after fourteen years. But we gave it a try.

There were two ways of proving Clarke's innocence. Firstly we could put together all the documentary records of the time and construct a scenario which showed that Clarke could not have murdered Eileen McDougall. Since no one knew when she had died this would prove to be very difficult. Secondly we could attempt to prove that someone else had done the crime. We put most of our efforts into this second line of attack, but embarked on the first: we looked at all the available evidence which might prove that Clarke could not be guilty. The medical evidence showed that Eileen could have died as late as 1973, but the police had thought that Eileen must have died before Thursday 22

January 1970. This was because that was the day her mother began to look around South Shields for her, the day Eileen was officially reported missing. They further believed that Eileen must have been murdered on Sunday 18 January because she was a well-known girl who could not have wandered around South Shields without meeting a friend somewhere. Since she had not been seen since the Sunday morning, the police assumed she died on that Sunday. We agreed with them – it was the most logical assumption to make.

We therefore tried to construct a scenario for that Sunday in which Clarke murdered Eileen. It became such an incredible hypothesis in the end that only the most prejudiced would believe it. It went like this:

Eileen left the house in H.S. Edward Street at about 7 a.m. If she had gone to Clarke's house that morning it would have taken about thirty minutes for her to walk there.

Clarke was on duty at Velva Liquids at 7 a.m. that morning until 2 p.m., when Ronnie Embleton took over from him. He set the boiler going at 7.30 a.m. according to his entry in the boiler book. So Clarke should have left for work half an hour before Eileen arrived at his house – unless he was late for work. Perhaps he had waited for her, gone in to work late and faked the entry in the boiler book.

Eileen had told her boyfriend Graham Aitken that she had been 'thrown out'. If Clarke had thrown her out, would he have expected her back – at 7 a.m.? As for going to work late, Clarke's foreman Harry Peterson had spoken to him about bad time-keeping and had been making spot checks on Clarke when he was on solo duty because Peterson suspected Clarke of stealing petrol from the Velva site. So Clarke is unlikely to have been late for work that morning. If he had faked the entry in the boiler book Embleton may have spotted this when he came on duty, because if the boiler had been fired later than Clarke's entry in the book the temperature in the tanks would have been unusually high when Embleton checked it later.

So, assuming that Clarke was at work when Eileen arrived at

his home, there are two alternatives: (a) she had a key to the house, and (b) she did not have a key.

If she had had a key she would have gone into the house, then, most likely, changed her wet clothes and gone to sleep. She had been thrown out at about 1 a.m. the previous night, had had some five hours' sleep and was still wet. In this scenario she would never have left the house alive. But Eileen was not killed at Clarke's house. The police ripped it apart and found nothing. Moreover, the pathological evidence showed that her body had been cut up on rough ground – there is no rough ground at Clarke's house where he could have done this. He had no car in which to transport her body whole.

Let us assume then that Eileen had *no* key. She would have tried to wake Clarke's children, who would then have been asleep on the third floor. It would be about 7.45 a.m. or earlier. Clarke's next-door neighbour Mrs Orr had been taking a more than passing interest in his visitors ever since his estranged wife had thumped on the door in early December 1969 shouting, 'He's got a brothel up there.' Mrs Orr had thought this highly unlikely, but she had noticed the 'young lasses' who babysat for Clarke while he was at work. If Eileen hammered on the door that Sunday morning to wake the children, Mrs Orr heard nothing.

If Eileen did not get into Clarke's house, then she must have gone down to the Velva site: she would probably have arrived just before 8 o'clock. At this time Clarke was firing the boiler, so she would have had to shout for him and wait at the gates. No one saw her there. But assuming that she did get in, she would have wanted to warm herself, sit down and have a cup of tea. She could only have done this in the site office. Sometime after this we must assume that Clarke picked up a hammer which happened to be lying around and attacked her from behind while she was either standing or sitting. Then he would have had to cut her up. The knife would need to be very sharp because whoever murdered her split her straight up the breastbone. And it would have been done on rough ground – as the scalloping effect on her torso indicated.

There is no rough ground on the Velva site which is not open to public view either from the river or the top of the hill behind the site. However, assuming that Clarke did this, then he would have the problem of covering up about five pints of blood that had spilled from the body. This he could no doubt wash away. But could he have washed away the smell of the blood so thoroughly that Ronnie Embleton would not notice it at 2 p.m. when he came on duty?

Let us assume that he could. After killing her, cutting up her body and disposing of the blood, Clarke would then have to dispose of the parts of the body. We do not know where the legs went, but we know that the head and upper torso went into the top of tank No. 1. Did Clarke now do this? He would have been an absolute fool if he had. By then it would be well past 9 a.m. – probably past 10 a.m. Tank No. 1 is overlooked directly from the pavement along the hill at the back of the site. At the top of that hill is the lookout for the Tyne river pilots. They keep a watch on the river throughout the day. Also on the top of the hill is a bus terminus and three pubs as well as many houses. People walk along the top on a Sunday morning to look out to sea and across the river to North Shields.

Perhaps Clarke could have got away with dropping the head and torso into the tank, with all these potential spectators, but he would be a fool to try. And so far in this scenario he's managed to do several things which show he is not a fool.

So, if he decided to hide the body and return during the night to dispose of it, where did he hide it? Frankly, there is nowhere in the storage compound where Clarke could have hidden the body to ensure that it would not be discovered by Embleton when he came to work in the afternoon. Clarke did not bury the body, because the torso has no evidence of burial on it. Let us assume, however, that he managed to find a place where Embleton would not stumble across the body. We then move on to the Sunday night when Clarke returns to dispose of it. Once again, would Clarke have put the torso into tank No. 1? Hardly. He would probably have tried to get it off the site because there was a security guard on duty. If that guard had seen Clarke on the site he would have known him at once – not only because Clarke was known to the guard, but because Clarke was almost the only Negro in South Shields.

There is nothing to show that Clarke saw Eileen McDougall at all on that fateful morning. We found the above hypothesis to be absolutely incredible. The evidence found on Eileen's body simply did not match the probabilities.

But if Clarke had not killed Eileen, then who did? We worked hard on tracing Eileen's movements from the end of November 1969 until the day she died. What we discovered showed that Ernie Clarke's defence lawyers had once again been misled because 'best evidence' had not been presented in the Court. Once again a document lying in the police files would have told the Court far more about the truth than the documents which appeared before the jury. Indeed, the evidence it contained would have impeached one of the witnesses for the prosecution.

The key question that needed to be answered in solving Eileen McDougall's murder was very simple. Where had she been on the Saturday evening before she arrived in H.S. Edward Street at 2 o'clock in the morning? Wherever she had been, she had been 'thrown out', in her own words. Wherever she had been was probably also the place where her clothes were. When she had left her boyfriend's house at 7 o'clock on the Sunday morning she had still been wet after the rain of the night before. The temperature was just above freezing. It would be reasonable to assume that she went back to wherever her clothes were.

No one ever came forward to tell the police where Eileen McDougall had slept in South Shields after she returned from Maidstone on the morning of Friday 16 January 1970. No one – not even her sisters, whom she saw during her last days – even asked her where she was sleeping. Yet we realized from evidence we had acquired quite early in our investigation that Eileen seemed to know of a place where she could sleep when she got back to South Shields.

She had not discussed the matter with her brother Billy on the long journey by train from Maidstone and had happily left him to join some of his old friends in the Ship and Royal pub in the centre of South Shields while she went off towards another pub, the Douglas Vaults, where she would expect to find her sister Elizabeth. During the rest of the afternoon and evening she saw her sisters Elizabeth, Linda and Leslie; she talked at length with a friend, Mary Bell, in the late afternoon; then she met several friends during the evening at a night club. None of these people remembered Eileen asking for a bed for the night.

When we spoke to Marie McDougall, the divorced wife of Eileen's brother Billy, we discovered another significant point. Marie remembered that Eileen had had few clothes in Maidstone, so she had gone through her own wardrobe and given some clothes to her. Among these was a red and black tweed skirt and jacket – probably too conventional for Eileen's tastes – but this was the suit that Marie remembered Eileen had worn when she had left Maidstone early on the morning of Friday 16 January. When Eileen arrived in the Douglas Vaults to see her sister in the afternoon of that same day she was wearing a brown tweed coat and a see-through dress. Not only had she changed into these clothes after leaving her brother Billy, but Marie McDougall could remember neither the tweed coat nor the see-through dress being in Maidstone. The tweed coat was particularly interesting because Eileen carried what little clothing she had in two carrier bags. The coat would not have fitted into a carrier bag – yet she had not been wearing it when she left Maidstone. Even the carrier bags vanished before Eileen arrived at the Douglas Vaults. None of the witnesses there remembered them.

We checked the railway timetables for January 1970 and estimated that Eileen had had about half an hour in which to find somewhere to change, pick up the tweed coat and see-through dress and leave the carrier bags. She must have gone to somewhere in the centre of South Shields. Moreover, that place must have been where Eileen had stayed in December before she had gone down to Maidstone, because her tweed coat and see-through dress were there. We later learned that she may have borrowed the dress on that Friday, but the tweed coat was actually her sister Elizabeth's lent to Eileen some weeks before.

It would have been logical enough to assume that Eileen McDougall had returned in January to the house she had left in December. But we had now established a real link between December and January through her clothing. As we investigated further into her life during December and November 1969 we discovered that Eileen had been visiting a place somewhere in the centre of South Shields for several weeks before she went to Maidstone. We realized also that evidence of this had been collected during the police investigation but had not been brought to the attention either of the jury at Clarke's trial, or of Clarke's lawyers. The question of Eileen's movements during December seems to have been left unnecessarily vague.

Eileen's mother, Mrs Agnes McDougall, made a statement to the police – which was handed over to the defence – in which she said that Eileen had come home from work one Friday night in December, had a meal, then left home saying she was going to a dance. According to Mrs McDougall, she then went out and never returned. Mrs McDougall's memory was faulty. In fact it was on Saturday 13 December that Eileen left home for good. She had been to Latino's night club in the centre of South Shields the night before and had missed the last bus home. She claimed she had stayed that night with her sister Elizabeth, who was living in Eastbourne Grove near the town centre. When Eileen returned home on the Saturday afternoon, Mrs McDougall told her to pack her bags and go. Mrs McDougall had done a little checking on her daughters. She had already been to the flat in Eastbourne Grove that morning and been told that Eileen had not been there the previous night.

This is a somewhat different picture of the home life of the McDougall family from that which emerged in Court. It comes from a document which lay in the police files throughout their investigation. In that same document is evidence that Eileen's brother Billy was searching for her in the centre of South Shields just before Christmas 1969. We did not know where she was, but he must have located her because Eileen left for Maidstone with him in late December. There is nothing of this in the statement Billy made to the police, which was subsequently handed to Clarke's lawyers. Perhaps that was because the information was not relevant to the case against Clarke. But that in itself would mean that she had not been staying at Clarke's house, which is about a quarter of a mile away from Eastbourne Grove where Elizabeth's flat had been: if Billy had found Eileen at Clarke's house the information would certainly have been relevant in the case against Clarke.

Mrs McDougall seemed to think that Eileen had gone to stay with a friend of hers on a housing estate a couple of miles away from her home. She seems to imply in her statements to the police that she did not know the exact address. In fact we discovered the house in question and heard that Mrs McDougall had been there during December asking after Eileen. The tenant, Mr John Howes, remembered Eileen staying with his daughter for about ten days. Eileen was then working at Plesseys in the centre of South Shields and Mr Howes would drive her down to work in the morning with another woman who lived just down the street and who also worked at Plesseys. He remembered, too, why he had taken Eileen back home: he discovered that she had not been going into Plesseys after he had dropped her off each morning. Her wages were being docked for non-attendance and she could not pay for her keep. Mr Howes was quite certain that he had taken Eileen home – but Mrs McDougall could not remember Eileen coming home.

What particularly interested us in all this was that Eileen seems to have had a place to go to in the centre of South Shields, just as she later did in mid-January. While she was staying with the Howes family there was heavy snow – not the sort of weather for a young girl to be wandering the streets in. If she had spent her time in pubs or cafés, someone would have recognized her. So if she wasn't going into Plesseys, as Mr Howes told us, then she was spending her days somewhere else – in the centre of town.

This naturally drew our attention to Elizabeth's flat in East-bourne Grove, which is very close to the centre of town. The more so because Elizabeth never mentioned this flat in any of her long and comprehensive statements to the police. We found this strange because we had met Elizabeth and had formed the opinion that she was essentially an honest person. Yet from documents which were in the possession of the police at the time of the trial we can deduce that Elizabeth had a flat at No. 6 Eastbourne Grove from about the beginning of December 1969 until just before Christmas.

Eastbourne Grove no longer existed when we went to find Elizabeth's former landlord. It had all been knocked down to make way for a new development. Tracing people who lived there in 1969 took us all over South Shields. What we discovered surprised us. Eileen had never been seen at No. 6 Eastbourne Grove, but she had been seen on several occasions in a different flat – No 11a Eastbourne Grove. This was a basement flat which appears to have been something of a hippy commune. Several girls – now respectable married women – told us how the door had been always open at this house; how sometimes up to thirty young people would be found sleeping on the floor there; and, more importantly to us, how they remembered Eileen McDougall being there. One stated in her filmed interview with us: 'Everybody used to go, everybody who was into drugs or anything. That was the only place in Shields where people could go for a smoke.'

We asked her if she had seen Eileen there.

'Yes, Eileen came with Mary Bell. I remember there were three girls; Mary Bell, Eileen, and there was this other girl, but I can't remember her name.'

It was possible that this girl might have been confusing Eileen with Elizabeth, but the girl's sister was in no doubt. She knew Eileen and had seen her in the hippy commune. She herself had had a nasty experience in the commune. One night she had been there to babysit for the woman who was the official tenant.

Somebody came to the door. He didn't actually knock because the person that came knew that there was no lock on the door. He came in and told me that the lady I was babysitting for had said he could come and wait for her return. So I let him in. I was putting the baby to bed and this man lit the fire. I remember hearing him walk towards me and then I just felt a thud on my head, on the back of my head. I went down and he started kicking and punching me in the face.

The man who assaulted this girl was never brought to trial for the offence. But he is currently serving a life sentence for murder.

None of this research proved in any way that Clarke had not killed Eileen McDougall or that someone else had. But it did reveal for the first time that Eileen had lived at least on the fringes of a dangerous environment. It was an aspect of the case which Clarke's defence lawyer could not explore because only the police knew that Elizabeth had had a flat in Eastbourne Grove in December 1969 when Eileen was thrown out of the family home. The police neither told the defence of the existence of the documents which held this information nor did they hand them over. We presume they thought the information was not relevant to the case against Clarke.

The relevance it has to Clarke's case is this: Eileen had a place where she could sleep somewhere in the centre of South Shields, not only when she came back there from Maidstone in January 1970 but also in December 1969. We do not know where she spent the night of Friday 12 December – though she said she had stayed in Elizabeth's flat in Eastbourne Grove. We do not know where she spent the night of Saturday 20 December and succeeding nights until Billy drove her to Maidstone. (There is some confusion over when this was. Billy said in Court that he spent Christmas in Maidstone with Eileen; his mother agreed with him. But in a report written in 1970 Mrs McDougall said that he went to Maidstone the weekend after Christmas and this is supported by statements from Billy's ex-wife, who remembers spending Christmas in Newcastle that year with Billy's sister Jean.) We do not know where Eileen spent the night of 16 January, but we know that wherever it was, she could gain entry there at 2 o'clock in the morning. We can assume that the place she slept that night was the same place she had slept on the missing nights in December, because she appears to have left clothes and carrier bags there and picked up some of her own clothing which she had not had in Maidstone. We can also suggest very strongly that the place where she stayed in December was *not* Clarke's house – because her sister Elizabeth and her friend Ann Sutherland were still baby-sitting for Clarke until Christmas. He gave them both Christmas presents – blue handbags. Eileen's brother Billy even went with Elizabeth to Clarke's house when he was on his Christmas leave – at the time when he was looking all over South Shields for Eileen because she had gone missing.

What effect this evidence would have had on the minds of the jury can only be conjectured. They did not have the privilege of hearing it.

There were several minor points in the Clarke case that needed to be cleared up. We found most of them to be of little importance. The material that Eileen's body had been wrapped in was a form of canvas that was found on ships the world over as well as on the Velva site. Pieces of it had been left around the site, so anyone could have used it. Similarly, anyone could have got into the site. Security was much more lax in 1970 than it was nine years later at the time of the trial. As for the hammer which was used to kill Eileen, it was perhaps the most common type of hammer in Britain. We went to the local hardware store in South Shields and bought six different hammers that could have inflicted the wounds on her head.

But one last aspect of the case still seemed important to us and demanded an explanation. If Clarke had not killed Eileen, why then was her body dumped on the Velva site at all? This, we felt, may well have been the question that had ultimately prompted the jury to find Clarke guilty.

We collected all the information we could on the tides in the

River Tyne, the habits of the people of South Shields, even the habits of the fish in the river and came to this conclusion:

Almost everyone in South Shields knows that the river is at its deepest and the tide at its strongest on the southern side, just at the point where Lawe Top – the hill behind Velva Liquids – falls to the seashore. Fishermen – and there are many in South Shields – know that the best fishing is to be had from the end of the Velva Liquids jetty which juts out into the river at this point. The Velva jetty has breakwaters under it which slow the waters to the seaward side of it near the river bank. At this point on the river bank there is an open space which has been used as an informal car park since before the war. If anyone wanted to dispose of Eileen McDougall's body from the boot of a car into the deepest and fastest waters available in South Shields, he would drive to this car park late one night, take her body out of the boot in sections and drop it off the end of the Velva jetty. It was high tide at 1 a.m. on the night Eileen vanished. The water off the jetty would be 40 feet deep. We speculated that the murderer may have already made one such trip with the legs, and was about to go out on to the jetty again with her head and torso when he was disturbed by a party of fishermen who had come to sneak out on to the Velva jetty – as they commonly did. Trapped inside the Velva site, unable to go out on to the jetty, he would then head for the point which was farthest away from the jetty and dispose of the rest of the body there. This place would be tank No. 1, where Eileen's body was eventually found.

Such would be the actions of the murderer – unless he worked on the site. Because if, like Clarke, he had authority at Velva, he would have ordered the fishermen off the jetty – and disposed of the rest of the body there.

If this chapter has seemed to be full of speculation, that is because speculation is inevitable during the investigation of a crime that took place fourteen years ago. But the main points that should be borne in mind about the trial of Ernie Clarke are not speculation.

A significant part of the evidence presented against him in

Court – the blue jumper – has now been proved to have had no connection with the dead girl at all. Important evidence about this jumper did not reach the hands of the defence because the prosecution in this case departed from the accepted rules of presenting 'best evidence' and thus it was difficult for the defence to appreciate the full significance of Mr Moon's deposition either at the trial or on appeal.

Evidence about the movements of Eileen McDougall in December 1969 was also kept from the Court. Prosecution witnesses were allowed to make statements in Court which could have been impeached by reliable evidence in police files – documents which the defence could not know still existed. This evidence also was not available at the time of Clarke's appeal.

3

The Murder of
Margaret McLaughlin

People outside journalism are often surprised that we hardly ever meet the subject of our 'Rough Justice' investigations. In English prisons the inmates are only allowed visitors to whom they are related, or whom they have known prior to their imprisonment. Journalists are certainly not allowed inside. Because all the subjects of our first programmes have now been released as a result of the television series and subsequent submissions to the Home Office, we have now met Jock Russell, Michael and Patrick McDonagh and John Walters. Meeting them for the first time was a strange experience, because we both felt that we already knew them well; in one sense we knew more about their cases than they did themselves. For the character of each individual shines out from his circumstances, home life and all the myriad details exposed by a criminal investigation and trial. After the second series of programmes we felt that we understood the sad, disappointed life of Margaret Livesey, her son a worry to her, her husband permanently on the night shift, and her occasional sorties to the local pub to meet friends. We thought we knew a lot about Ernest Adolphus Clarke, the hard-working, proud West Indian bringing up his three children on his own. But the character who emerged most clearly was the subject of our third investigation, George Beattie.

In Scotland they have a phrase for a lad like George – 'a big saftie'. In more formal terms he was described medically as emotionally immature and of slightly below average intellect. He was just nineteen at the time he was accused of murder. He is still remembered around the Lanarkshire village of Carluke as a simple boy who would offer to carry the old people's shopping bags for them, or to 'run a message' for his mother. In The Crescent, Bamber Bridge, we encountered a great deal of unexplained bias and bitterness against Mrs Livesey; in Carluke we found no one who really believed that 'the big saftie', George Beattie, the lad whose passion was train-spotting at the local station, could possibly have found it in him to kill, and to kill brutally.

Yet a Scottish jury – or at least a majority of them – believed that Beattie was a murderer. They were undoubtedly influenced by another aspect of George's character – his daydreaming and fantasizing. When he found himself at the centre of the most dramatic event in Carluke's unexceptional history he talked and talked. Eventually, George Beattie was to talk himself into the dock and into prison. He is still there today.

Beattie's problems began on 7 July 1973. It was the day of the major event in Carluke's social calendar, the Carluke Highland Games. Carluke is a sleepy little place, set in lovely Lowland scenery about half an hour's drive from Glasgow. Once a year the pipe bands come from all over the west of Scotland to compete in the modest competition at Carluke. In 1973 many of the competitors and the spectators would have arrived at Carluke station, which lies on the main line from Glasgow. All the regulars would know that the quickest way from the station to the football ground, where the games are held, would be through the Colonel's Glen, a deep valley that runs alongside the railway line. But sometime on that particular Saturday – the police say just before 3 o'clock – the body of a young girl was found halfway down the slope from the railway embankment.

In a small place like Carluke it took no time at all to identify the victim. She was a local girl, Margaret McLaughlin, twenty-three years old, dark-haired and good-looking. She had set off the night before to catch the 8.03 train from Carluke to Glasgow. Her home was in Glenburn Terrace, just over two minutes away from the scene of her murder. Margaret was engaged to be married to a man who was working in South Africa. Her wedding was

Beatties'
house

McLaughlins'
house

UNITAS CRESCENT

GLENBURN TERRACE

Jock's Burn

Position of body

Playground

Carluke
Station

imminent and on the night she was killed she was going to stay with her fiancé's sister to discuss details of the ceremony. She never arrived.

It is very difficult, even with the aid of maps and photographs, to visualize the Colonel's Glen. It is virtually a ravine. It is very difficult terrain to clamber over, particularly if you are in a hurry. The distance from the railway line to the bottom of the cleft where the stream runs through must be approximately 150 yards. Margaret's body was found about halfway down. She was still clothed and there were no definite signs of a sexual assault, although the zip on her trousers had burst open, presumably in the struggle that so obviously had taken place. She lay in the abandoned attitude of death, her head pointing down the slope, her arms stretched out above her head, as though she had been dragged to that final position. Her clothing was crumpled and suggested even more clearly that the body had been pulled through the undergrowth. That undergrowth is still thick today, but back in 1973 it was very heavy indeed. The girl had been stabbed nineteen times. The murder weapon, a knife, must have had a blade about 4½ inches long. The pathologists also found bruises on her face. These could have indicated that she had been punched or that she had hit her face in a fall. Around her body they found bloodstains on the ground and on the leaves of nettles. There seems to have been a trail of blood that led back up from the body to the railway line. The frequent use of the short cut alongside the railway had worn a pathway into the ground, the pathway which the police assumed Margaret had been following when she had been attacked. Just beside the path they found that the grass had been flattened. It looked as though there had been a fight here, prior to the murderer dragging or chasing her down the slope.

It must have been a messy and violent affair. But although the police found blood spots all the way up the bank, they never recorded any footprint evidence. It had been raining all night – Margaret's clothes were wet through – yet whoever had manhandled her down the slope did not seem to have left any footprints.

Near the spot where the grass had been flattened, where the police believed that the initial attack must have taken place, they found three potentially very important clues. Two of them were certainly to prove vital. There had once been a fence running vertically down into the glen. It comprised concrete posts and wire mesh. Remnants of it can still be seen today. On one of the broken posts near the top of the glen the police found some red fibres. These turned out to be the redundant clue of the trio. The police never identified the source of the red fibres. But they also found an item they would later present at the trial as a key clue – a knife. It had been plunged into the earth beside the same broken concrete post. It was roughly the right size to have caused the wounds in the girl's body.

In the grass a few feet from the post the police, who had diligently hacked down all the undergrowth, found a woman's ring. Since her engagement Margaret had been wearing a very fine engagement ring. It was the kind of artefact that would have excited a lot of admiration and comment in a place like Carluke. But this was not the ring that the police found in the undergrowth. The engagement ring was still on the third finger of the girl's left hand when they found the body. The ring in the grass was also Margaret's, but it was a 'pinkie' ring that she wore on the little finger of her right hand.

The police found many other clues. One of them was Margaret's umbrella. It was in the 'down' position and the main shaft was bent, as if she might have used it as a weapon to fend off her attacker.

Some of the evidence on the body itself does not appear to have been fully explored. There were hairs down the front of her clothes and there was blood under her fingernails. There is no record of these clues being analysed and matched to the girl herself or to any third party. The blood under the fingernails obviously implied that she had scratched her attacker and might still have remnants of his blood on her hands and nails. The hairs could have been her own or the attacker's.

Margaret, as we know, was on her way to spend the night with her fiancé's sister in Glasgow. In addition to her handbag (a kind of shoulder bag), she was carrying a suitcase with tartan sides. Both these items were found down at the very bottom of the glen. This was a puzzle that was never explained. There was no evidence that the girl herself had been to the stream at the foot of the glen. There was no reason for the murderer to go there and he could not physically have thrown the suitcase and handbag from the top of the glen or even from the spot where the body was found halfway down. The position of the suitcase and the shoulder bag, beside the burn and about twelve feet apart, suggested a most illogical pattern of events at the time of the attack: Margaret must have been attacked as she walked along the path to the station; she would have dropped her suitcase and shoulder bag in the struggle. She then ran or was dragged halfway down the slope; presumably she was stabbed again and died. The murderer must then have climbed back to the top of the slope, picked up the two bags and carried them back past the body and down to the foot of the glen. Then he would have climbed back up again to make his escape. The contents of the shoulder bag had been strewn around; the contents of the suitcase were still intact and apparently undisturbed, but the catches of the case may have been open.

Despite what seems an abundance of clues, the police actually did not have a great deal to go on. There did not appear to be a motive. They were never to suggest that a sexual assault had taken place. Indeed, they do not seem to have examined the body for signs of sexual assault. Robbery seemed most unlikely: the expensive engagement ring was still on the girl's finger and there was money in her purse. But a couple of items were missing. One of them was a gold charm bracelet which Margaret was wearing that night. It was never found, despite an extensive search.

The most promising clue would seem to be the knife which had been found by the broken concrete post. The police removed it and the section of earth into which it had been plunged. But they found no fingerprints on the handle and no traces of blood either on the knife itself or in the surrounding earth. On that basis they decided that they could hardly claim it was the murder weapon at this point in the investigation. They later found another knife, but that was also eliminated.

To make their problem over motive even more acute the police rapidly discovered that Margaret was a very respectable girl, and much admired in the small community. Nobody could suggest anyone who might have wanted to harm her. The family explained how Margaret had come home that night as usual on the train with one of her sisters. She had changed her clothes and eaten her dinner. It was her main meal of the day, a substantial dinner which she shared with her sister Rosemary at about 6.45 or 7 p.m. She was running late that evening and eventually left the house for the 8.03 p.m. train instead of the earlier one she had originally planned to catch.

So no one could have predicted that she would leave the house at about 7.52 p.m. Either someone had been lurking in the glen waiting to kill whoever came along, or someone had seen her walk into the glen and had decided there and then to murder her. Either theory seemed highly unlikely. And yet she was dead.

As the map shows, Glenburn Terrace, where Margaret lived, forms the south side of a rectangle, which is completed by Unitas Crescent where George Beattie lived. To the north is the flat playground area reached through a corner of Unitas Crescent. The glen is beyond that, leading to the station. So Margaret's route would have taken her along Glenburn Terrace, into Unitas Crescent, heading north, through the little lane and on to the playground.

When the police began their door-to-door inquiries they found several witnesses who had seen Margaret that night, shortly before 8 o'clock on her way down Glenburn Terrace and along Unitas Crescent. It was raining and they remembered that she had her umbrella up.

But the inquiries yielded something distinctly more interesting to the police. A young man volunteered the information that he had been walking through the glen at about the time the girl must have been attacked. His name was George Beattie.

At the time Beattie was working in the steel works in Lanark.

He had been on his way to his night shift job and had set off from home around 8 o'clock on the night of the murder. He walked along Unitas Crescent in a westerly direction and then turned north through the alleyway on to the playground. According to Beattie and his family, he had been watching a television programme called 'Romany Jones' on S.T.V. When that finished, a few minutes before 8 o'clock, he had set off to walk through the glen, past the station and on northwards towards Gorry's Nursery, where he used to buy several pounds of tomatoes to take to his workmates. Earlier that evening George's sister, Ena, had volunteered to get the tomatoes for him. But when she reached Gorry's Nursery it was closed. Mr Gorry was ill and the family had gone to the local hospital, Law Hospital, to visit him.

The police checked Beattie's story. They came across a young lad called Ian Freel who had seen Beattie just north of the station around 8 o'clock or 8.05. He said that George Beattie looked perfectly normal. Further along the route to the nursery another witness who was out cutting his flowers also saw George and talked to him for a few minutes. He too noted nothing odd about him. Several people saw Beattie at Gorry's Nursery around 8.25 or 8.30 p.m. He bought 9 lb tomatoes and went off to his job, stopping for a drink with some of his mates on the way. In other words, Beattie's movements and actions are well documented throughout the evening apart from a few minutes when he passed through the Colonel's Glen, at a time when, as he knew, the police believed Margaret McLaughlin had been killed.

Beattie was first interviewed during the door-to-door inquiries on the Saturday after the murder. The police cannot have regarded him as a particularly important witness since they did not return to him until the following Tuesday afternoon around 4 p.m. By this time they were obviously more aware of how cold the trail had become and they asked Beattie if he had remembered any details to add to his original statement. When he said 'no' the police asked him if he would retrace his steps along Unitas Crescent, through the alleyway and across the glen, in the hopes that this would stimulate his memory. Beattie agreed.

The police returned just before 8 o'clock that night and timed Beattie's walk with a stop-watch. He left his house at 7.55 p.m. and walked along his previous route with a Detective Sergeant and an acting Detective Constable. They timed his walk from home to the railway embankment at four minutes and ten seconds.

At this point it began to rain and one of the policemen went off to pick up his police van. The other officer continued to walk past the scene of the crime with George Beattie. There is no record of their conversation, nor of the things Beattie might have seen on the journey. He would certainly have been able to see the orange ribbons which were used to cordon off important parts of the glen. But suffice it to say that, as the only man who readily admitted to being in the glen that night, he was the only man who was treated to a conducted tour of the scene of the crime.

The following day Beattie was back in the police station. Another Detective Constable had been asked to re-interview him. He was surprised that George Beattie now volunteered further bits of information. Why he did this is, of course, open to a number of interpretations. But one of them must certainly be that Beattie now found himself, for the first time in his life, in an important role. Be that as it may, he now came to the attention of Detective Sergeant Mortimer, who took over the Beattie interview at 9.30 p.m. on the night of Wednesday 11 July. It was to be a vital session.

The interview took place in the back room of Carluke police station. At that time Carluke station was only a front room with the usual counter, a back room for interviews, and two cells. Beattie appeared to know a remarkable amount about the scene of the crime. Detective Sergeant Mortimer had been off duty for three days until 10 July. He was still catching up on the details of the big crime which had happened in his absence. So he was surprised when Beattie told him that he had stumbled over a black collapsible umbrella in the glen on the night of the murder, and even more surprised when Beattie mentioned and described a kind of shoulder bag that he had seen in the glen. Mortimer had never heard of this, so he thought he had better check. He went into the front room of the police station, through which both he and Beattie had entered and there he found two other police officers who were in charge of the productions, the exhibits. Sure enough, the two officers confirmed that there was indeed a shoulder bag of the kind that Beattie had described among their exhibits. Mortimer returned to the interview. Beattie now told him that he had seen blood on the grass at the point where it had been flattened by a struggle. He added that he had seen a red and white or blue and white carrier bag near by. Mortimer went back into the front room. The two exhibits officers agreed that there had been a carrier bag at the scene. They handed it to Detective Sergeant Mortimer. He returned to the interview room and showed it to George Beattie. 'Was it like this?' he asked Beattie. Beattie said: 'It was the very same.'

Detective Sergeant Mortimer asked Beattie if he had seen anything else. George Beattie was becoming expansive. He related that he had seen something blue and something white, something he called a 'goonie', a colloquial expression for a nightgown, and a small tin or bottle of hairspray. Mortimer made his retreat to the front room once more. Yes, all those items were in evidence. But, the officers pointed out to him, they had all been *inside* the girl's suitcase.

The Detective Sergeant went back into the interview room. He asked Beattie if he was quite sure that he had not seen the girl himself that night. Beattie replied: 'Yes, she had an umbrella in her left hand and a suitcase in her right hand.' Mortimer must have sensed the importance of this and he cautioned Beattie. He then recorded that Beattie broke down and sobbed. The story that emerged in the next few minutes was to remain one of the central mysteries of the whole case.

George Beattie told him that he had walked innocently into the glen that night and been seized by three men. He claimed that he had been held by them while three other men attacked the girl. He said the tallest of the men had stabbed the girl repeatedly. He claimed that he had tried to close his eyes but that the men had forced him to watch. Of all the extraordinary claims he made, the most bizarre was that two of the men had been wearing top hats with mirrors on them. Mortimer must have been astonished. Not least because at this point he reported that he thought Beattie was about to have, or indeed was having, an epileptic fit. He said that he was slavering at the mouth, sobbing and shaking.

Four hours after the interrogation began, at 1.30 in the morning, after Beattie had drunk some coffee and calmed down, Detective Sergeant Mortimer charged him with the murder of Margaret McLaughlin. Confronted with the reality of the charge, Beattie stuck to his incredible story: 'I canna say anything more,' he replied, 'I didn't do it – it was they six.'

After the charge had been made at Carluke police station, Beattie was driven to Lanark. On the way in the police car he was still keen to supply further information. In particular he wanted to tell the police where the murderers had put the knife. Detective Sergeant Mortimer told him it was now too dark and that they would have to wait until the morning. Accordingly, at about 5.30 a.m., they all returned to the scene of the crime in the glen. It was just daylight. The man in charge of the investigation, Detective Chief Superintendent William Muncie, and his aide, Detective Chief Inspector William Gold, were now present.

George Beattie was again taken over the scene. He showed the police how the girl had been stabbed halfway up the slope of the glen. He indicated a concrete post where, he said, the murderers had shoved the knife into the ground two or three times in order to clean it. He also told them that the 'gang of six' had thrown the girl's suitcase into the stream at the bottom of the glen.

As in any murder inquiry the police had kept some facts about the murder secret, so that they could eliminate the usual spate of warped individuals who feel the need to confess to any notorious crime. But here they had a man who appeared to have a detailed knowledge of the crime which only someone closely implicated could possibly have. In Detective Sergeant Mortimer's words, they just 'bunged' him back into the car and drove back to Lanark.

On the way back Douglas Mortimer asked him if he had ever been in trouble with the police before. George Beattie said that no he had not, this was his first time, but, he added, with what emphasis we do not know, that this time he had 'hit the jackpot'.

The police now searched Beattie's home. They were still looking for red fibres like the ones they had found on the broken concrete post near the scene of the crime. They found none. They did not believe the knife found by the post was in fact the murder weapon. They searched the Beattie kitchen, and took away a knife. But it, too, was later eliminated. Beattie was closely examined for scratches. Margaret's nails had shown traces of blood and they must have hoped for some incriminating forensic evidence. There was none. In the end the only tiny piece of forensic evidence they could find to corroborate Beattie's story that he had been at the scene while the murder took place was a spot of blood. They found it on one of eight paper handkerchiefs in the pocket of a jacket he had worn throughout his long interrogation at the police station on the night he was charged. The blood spot proved to be group O, Rhesus positive, the same as Margaret McLaughlin's. Beattie's own blood was a group A, Rhesus positive.

The police decided that the spot of blood constituted sufficient corroboration to back up Beattie's 'confession'. They now had a defendant. He was a simple lad; he had been in the right place at the right time; he had been positively garrulous about the details of the crime; he had told a fantastic tale about a *Clockwork Orange* style of gang; and one of his handkerchiefs carried blood which could have come from Margaret McLaughlin.

George Beattie came to trial at the High Court of Judiciary in Glasgow on 2 October 1973.

The Trial of George Beattie

George Beattie's trial lasted just three days. The first two days were strangely inconsequential, until the arrival in the witness box of Detective Sergeant Mortimer. Indeed, in his summing-up the Judge was to say:

> Now, I don't know whether you think this, but you may feel that there was a great deal of evidence in the early part of the case that didn't seem perhaps to be getting very far, and it was perhaps only yesterday [late on the second day] when Detective Sergeant Mortimer was giving his account of what happened during the night of the eleventh and twelfth of July that the case against the accused really seemed to come alive.

So what was going on in the early part of the trial? A great deal of time seemed to be taken up with the geographical details of the site. We have remarked elsewhere that it is a difficult landscape to imagine. The jury and the Judge *did* have the aid of maps and photographs, but these seem to have caused as much confusion as the questions and answers in the Court transcript. In this case we have the advantage of the entire Court transcript. Here is a representative extract from the very first witness. Mrs Jeanie McLaughlin, Margaret's mother, a distressed old lady of sixty-four, was giving her examination-in-chief:

Q.: Can you remember the evening of sixth July this year?
A.: Yes.
Q.: Where were you that evening?
A.: In the house at Thirty Glenburn Terrace.

Q.: Do you know in what direction in relation to the compass Glenburn Terrace runs?

A.: Well, to the right.

Q.: Well, do you know which is north, which is south, which is east or not?

A.: No.

Q.: Is there another street near you called Unitas Crescent?

A.: Yes.

Q.: Does it meet Glenburn Terrace?

A.: Yes.

Q.: Where does it meet Glenburn Terrace?

A.: Just about forty yards from my home.

Q.: Does it meet Glenburn Terrace again at another part?

A.: Yes, at the top end.

Q.: So, are we to picture Glenburn Terrace – is it a straight road?

A.: Yes.

Q.: Does it meet at either end Unitas Crescent, which as its name suggests runs in a shape which can connect with each end of Glenburn Terrace?

A.: Yes.

Q.: Is the centre part of Unitas Crescent parallel with Glenburn Terrace?

A.: Yes, I think it is.

Q.: Is Unitas Crescent in a curve all the way, or does it have a straight part?

A.: It is like a V.

Q.: A curve all the way or a straight part in some part?

A.: It has a straight part, from our place, like *that*, right.

Q.: Is it a straight part in the middle and a curve at each end, which then connects the two arms with either end of Glenburn Terrace?

A.: Yes.

If that seems an inordinately long extract which appears to advance the case for the prosecution not one jot, then that is exactly why it is there. There are literally pages of similar pedantry.

None the less, during the first day of the trial it did gradually emerge that Margaret had come home from Motherwell on the night of the murder at about 6.30 p.m. She had eaten a meal with her sister, Rosemary, and then left the house at about 7.50 to travel back up to Glasgow to spend the night with her future sister-in-law. The important exhibits in the case were fully described and identified by members of Margaret's family. It was stressed by several witnesses that it had been raining when Margaret began her walk to the station and that she naturally had her umbrella up. One witness even described how the wind had blown Margaret's umbrella inside out and she had had to fix it.

Again, the Advocate Depute, Mr Clyde, prosecuting, was very concerned about the geography of the area. While examining Margaret's sister, Rosemary, the jury heard another complicated description, this time of the Colonel's Glen itself.

In the Clarke case, the Velva Liquids site and the various tanks were hard to envisage, so the Judge, the jury and the defendant went to the scene of the crime to see for themselves. It would certainly have saved a vast amount of complicated and stultifying detail if the same procedure had been adopted in the Beattie case.

Before moving on to what the jury heard of Beattie's movements on the night of the murder, it is worth noting one peculiar exchange between the prosecuting counsel and Margaret's mother, Jeanie McLaughlin:

Q.: Were you told the following day [Saturday 7 July] the news of Margaret?
A.: About half past eleven.
Q.: What were you told?
A.: About Margaret being dead.

The police maintained throughout that they had finally located Margaret's body at 2.58 p.m. on the Saturday. So what did Mrs McLaughlin mean? Neither prosecution nor defence ever followed up this strange inconsistency.

George Beattie himself and the members of his family had maintained during the investigation that George had not left home that night until just a few minutes before 8 o'clock, just after the S.T.V. programme 'Romany Jones' had finished. Neither George nor his family were called to testify in Court. Instead, prosecution counsel had the field to himself. He produced several neighbours whose evidence suggested that Beattie had been walking down Unitas Crescent on his way to the glen around 7.40 that night – in other words about ten minutes before Margaret McLaughlin.

In any case, there was no dispute that George Beattie had been in the glen at around the same time as Margaret McLaughlin. He himself had volunteered that information to the police when they were making their house-to-house inquiries. The exact time George Beattie left home was in fact irrelevant to the case. The important timing was the moment that Margaret left home and that seemed to be at or around 7.52. Even if George left shortly after that, the police still argued that he would have had time to commit the murder. But if he left before that, even well before it, he could not have been lying in wait for Margaret, since no one except her close family knew which train she finally elected to go for. The possibility remained that Beattie could have been lying in wait for *anyone*, but that was never seriously canvassed as a theory. In fact no motive for the killing was ever produced.

The first day of the trial also catalogued the grim scene in the glen and the details of Margaret's body lying in the undergrowth, which was described as 'waist-high' in places.

The final witness that day was Ian Freel. He said clearly that he had seen Beattie that night 'round about eight o'clock'. Counsel for the prosecution pressed him:

Q.: Can you be precise about it, or is that a general recollection?
A.: About five past eight; just after eight o'clock.
Q.: Can you be precise about it, or is it in that area?
A.: It would be that time, because I am always down there at that time.

Freel's Friday night job was collecting money for the football coupons, so he was working to a routine and would not be shaken about the time he saw Beattie in West Avenue, the next road up from the station. This would have been the first stage of Beattie's journey on from the glen towards Gorry's Nursery where he was planning to buy the tomatoes. The story clearly gave credence to the idea that he had simply walked through the glen that night without stopping; that he would have had no time to attack Margaret and do all the complicated things that surrounded her death.

Mr MacArthur for the defence had said practically nothing during the trial's first day. Now he intervened to establish that Freel had not seen anything unusual in Beattie's demeanour. He established that Beattie looked normal, not dirty or dishevelled. But Mr MacArthur was clearly working to some other plan, confident that he could allow the main facts of the prosecution case to emerge without serious challenge.

Day two of Beattie's trial began undramatically with another confusing list of photographs, verified and explained at length by the police photographer. The Court then went on to hear further details of Beattie's journey after he left the Colonel's Glen that night. They had already heard Freel testify. Now they heard from Thomas Bryce, the man who had been planting out his dahlias in Stevenston Street. This was Beattie's next point on his way to the nursery. Mr Bryce told the court that George had appeared quite normal and had spoken to him for about five minutes.

James Gorry, the tomato-grower, and his girlfriend testified that they had returned to the nursery about 8.15 p.m. that night, after visiting James's father in the Law Hospital. They too had seen George acting normally, as had another man in the shop, William Knox.

The Court was then asked to consider the evidence of Beattie's workmates. They too seemed to think that he had appeared perfectly normal on the night. But the Advocate Depute for the prosecution made serious efforts to incriminate George out of his own mouth: John McAllister was a workmate of Beattie's. He was asked to repeat what Beattie had said about his various encounters with the police since the murder. Prosecuting counsel wanted to know if McAllister had said anything to Beattie in the week following the crime:

> A.: It was either on the Tuesday or the Wednesday [10 or 11 July]. I said he must have seen something. No, I asked him if he had seen anything – what had he to go back for [i.e. to the police].
>
> Q.: Can you remember what he replied?
>
> A.: He said he couldn't account for three minutes – to the police, like. And I says to him, 'Well, you must have seen something. You must have been there or thereabouts at the time,' and he said, Yes, that he had seen some blood. It was where they skinned rabbits . . .

Later, counsel asked Mr McAllister if he had formed any particular impression about Beattie's frame of mind about the three minutes the police felt he could not account for. He replied, 'No. He didn't seem to be perturbed about it. He seemed to be all right.'

Later still, counsel returned to the same area of questioning:

> Q.: Did you say anything to him about the police investigations?
>
> A.: Yes.
>
> Q.: What did you say?
>
> A.: When he said he couldn't account for three minutes to the policeman I was actually joking with him, you know, and I asked him what he had done with the knife – you know, just kidding, and he replied that he had never had a knife.

McAllister seemed altogether surprised that anyone should seriously be considering Beattie in the role of murderer. He later told us that he remembered George as an inoffensive lad whose greatest sin was fantasizing. 'If you'd drunk five pints, George had drunk ten, and some whiskies – he was always daydreaming.'

Again, Mr MacArthur for the defence did not cross-examine. No doubt he realized that the 'evidence' that George Beattie had said anything out of the ordinary or incriminating to his work-mates was so thin as to be practically non-existent.

The Court now heard how Beattie had volunteered to walk the route he had taken that night while being timed by Detective Sergeant Adam and Detective Constable Waddell. They timed Beattie's walk from his home to the area of the locus (the scene of the crime). It took Beattie four minutes and ten seconds.

Drs Weir and MacLay were now called. They had carried out their post mortem around 6 o'clock on the evening of Saturday 7 July. Dr Weir described the situation of the body and the nature of the wounds:

> ... There were approximately nineteen stab wounds, and these were distributed over the upper arms, the chest, the abdomen and the back and the back of the neck, and these in fact penetrated the lungs, and the ones in the abdomen penetrated the liver, the stomach and the kidney, and associated with that there was a very marked degree of internal haemorrhaging, particularly in the chest.

The pathologists estimated that the girl had been dead 'for something in the region of twenty to twenty-four hours ... it could be in the region of eight o'clock or somewhere in that time' (on the previous evening). They both pointed out that estimation of time of death is an inexact science and they could not be precise.

Evidence was adduced about the blood samples that had been taken from Margaret McLaughlin and George Beattie, but here Mr MacArthur made one of his rare objections. He maintained, in the absence of the jury, that the origin of the sample of blood, which purportedly came from George Beattie, had not been *proved* legally to the Court. After a lengthy legal argument the Judge, Lord Fraser, overruled his objection. So it was subsequently shown in Court that the blood on the paper tissues was blood group O, Rhesus positive, the same as that of Margaret McLaughlin. Beattie's blood group was A, Rhesus positive.

Mr Thorpe, a lecturer in Serology at Glasgow University, was called. He stated: 'Group O, D positive occurs in approximately 43 per cent of the population, and group A, Rhesus D positive in about 30 per cent of the population.'

So far, late into the second day of the trial, Mr MacArthur must have felt fairly pleased. All that the prosecution had been able to show with any certainty was that Beattie had been in the general vicinity around the time the girl was presumed to have died. He had volunteered that information himself. Defence clearly did not regard the fact that a spot of blood, which could have belonged to 43 per cent of the population, was found on Beattie's tissues as particularly damaging. And attempts to incriminate Beattie as a result of his subsequent comments appeared to have failed.

Detective Constable John Semple now took the stand. He recounted how he had been detailed to re-interview Beattie at about 7 o'clock on the Wednesday 11 July. Beattie had clearly been in an expansive, loquacious mood. He began to give much more detail about his trip that night as Semple and Constable Mair questioned him. Detective Sergeant Semple thought he had better tell his superior and he called on Detective Sergeant Mortimer at about 9.30. In Court the Advocate Depute asked Semple:

Q.: What was your state of mind or your impression and opinion of the case as it then stood?

A.: Well I thought that George was just adding pieces to his statement for the sake of talking; either that or he was not really normal.

Q.: Did you take any further part in the matter at that stage, immediately?

A.: No.

Q.: Did you go off to other duties?

A.: Yes.

Q.: Did you return to the station later that night?

A.: The following morning.

Q.: The following morning, yes – about what time?

A.: About one a.m.

Q.: ... And were you present when something happened?

A.: Yes ... When Detective Sergeant Mortimer cautioned and charged George Beattie ... He charged him with the murder of Margaret McLaughlin.

So what had happened in the meantime which had led to the charge? It clearly surprised Detective Constable Semple and it was to convince the jury. It *was* an astonishing tale.

Detective Sergeant Mortimer, you will recall, had been off duty on 7, 8 and 9 July. He knew little about the case and he told the Court that he was unaware that anything had been found in the vicinity of the body. He was detailed to go over the statements that had already been made and decide who should be re-interviewed. He himself went to see a man called Hunter who was a porter at the station. This was on the Wednesday evening. On his way back to Carluke police station he had already decided that he wanted to re-interview Beattie. Hunter had told him that Beattie used to hang around the station precincts. The fact that George was a train-spotter is recorded.

However, when he arrived back at the station about 9.30 he met Detective Constable Semple, who told him he had just been interviewing George Beattie, who 'was making some funny answers'. Semple thought Beattie must be a bit simple. In the previous chapter we have already described Detective Sergeant Mortimer's dramatic few hours with George Beattie. But remember, the jury knew nothing of this and imagine, as details unfold, the effect that Mortimer's testimony must have had on them.

Mortimer told the Court he went in to talk to Beattie in the company of Detective Constable Johnston, in the back room of the police station at Carluke. Beattie was still expanding his story of what had happened to him on his trip through the glen on the night of the murder. Beattie was maintaining that he had hurt his knee in a fall. He said he had tripped over a black collapsible umbrella. So, his testimony continued:

Well, I was wondering at that time had he come on the scene after the thing had happened. Detective Constable MacAllister and Detective Constable McCleary were the men who were handling the productions, and I went to them – they were in the office [the front room, the only other room apart from two small cells] – and I asked them did this umbrella mean anything to them, and they in fact showed me a black collapsible umbrella.

Beattie then described a shoulder bag which he said he had seen. Mortimer went back into the front room. MacAllister and McCleary confirmed that the girl had had a brown suede shoulder bag with her. Mortimer went back to Beattie. Beattie continued to detail exhibits. He described a plastic carrier bag, Mortimer went next door and returned with it:

'Was it a bag like that, George?' asked Mortimer. 'Yes, the very same as that,' replied George.

George now went on to describe the contents of the girl's suitcase. He said he had seen something blue and white which could have been trousers and something he described as a 'goonie', a nightgown. He also said the girl had been carrying a small 'tin or jar or bottle of hairspray' in her suitcase.

When Mortimer went back to the exhibits officers they confirmed that all these items *had* been found, but that they had been inside Margaret's case. This is how Detective Sergeant Mortimer told the Court what happened next:

> I realized then that the only way George could have seen these was if he had seen the case open.
>
> Q.: What did you do?
>
> A.: So I went back in to George and asked him if he was quite sure he hadn't seen Margaret McLaughlin that night ... He then ... he seemed to sort of – he started shaking and sobbing and he said to me, 'I saw her. She had her umbrella in her left hand and her suitcase in her right hand.'

Mortimer decided to caution Beattie. His statement continued:

> He seemed to get even more – he went into a more hysterical state ... he said, 'They telt me they were going to cut me up into sardines if I telt the police ... there were six of them ... Two of them were wearing tall hats with mirrors in them ... The tallest man held her. I felt sick. They poked me with umbrellas and made me watch.' ... He was talking about men grabbing him and three of the men grabbing the girl, and how

she had been stabbed time and time again, and he was in quite a state by this time.

Mortimer told the Court how Beattie was shaking and sobbing now, with his arms around Detective Constable Johnston. They gave him coffee and a towel to dry his face. At around 1.30 in the morning, four hours after the interview session with Mortimer and Johnston began, George Beattie was charged with the murder of Margaret McLaughlin.

The two officers drove Beattie to Lanark. He was still pressing details on them. At 5.30 in the morning they took him to the scene of the crime and he gave them a conducted tour of the site, describing where the body had been, where the knife had been found, where the suitcase had been thrown. Detective Sergeant Mortimer, unaware that Beattie had previously been taken through the scene of the crime, was now totally convinced of Beattie's guilt.

By this stage in the trial, the jury must have been convinced too. After the dull routine that had gone before, this was dramatic indeed!

Mr MacArthur's cross-examination elicited the fact that the policemen thought at the time that Beattie was in Carluke police station he was 'having a mild epileptic fit'. Mr MacArthur also pointed out that Beattie had been in the police station from 7 o'clock in the evening until 1 o'clock in the morning; locked up and then taken to the Colonel's Glen. No one had even suggested that he might see a solicitor, even though it was acknowledged that the lad was 'a bit simple'. The police response was that there was a notice on the cell door at Lanark advising him of his rights.

The second day of Beattie's trial ended with Detective Sergeant Mortimer's testimony under cross-examination:

Q.: I am right in thinking he [Beattie] never at any time admitted to you or any other police officers that he had stabbed this girl?
A.: No, he never did.
Q.: He never admitted that at any time?
A.: No.

On the third and final day of Beattie's trial Detective Chief Superintendent Muncie gave corroborative evidence about the various clues and artefacts found at the scene of the crime. He also described the scene when Beattie took him and other police officers through the glen on the early morning of Thursday 12 July 1973. Under cross-examination, Mr Muncie was asked about the knife. He said that it was tested for fingerprints and found negative. 'But first,' he said, 'the most important thing was blood.' Detective Chief Superintendent Muncie was not clear about whether the police were still looking for a murder weapon on 8 July, the Sunday. Mr MacArthur, for the defence, suggested that it would have been possible for a member of the public, like George Beattie, to have discovered the details of the scene of the crime in the days immediately after the killing. Mr Muncie firmly denied this.

A succession of police witnesses including the two exhibits officers, MacAllister and McCleary, now gave evidence on the various statements and exhibits at the heart of the trial.

Detective Chief Inspector Gold told the Court that from the Monday onwards everybody who used the path beside which the girl had been killed would have their name and address taken by the police. He too seemed to think that no member of the public could have seen the details of the crime that Beattie had described.

A psychiatrist was called. He testified that Beattie's intelligence was 'very, very slightly below average' and that because of his emotional immaturity his responsibility for his actions was somewhat diminished. None the less he regarded him as sane.

That concluded the case for the prosecution.

Mr MacArthur for the defence only called two witnesses: Mr Eynon, a City of Glasgow police forensic scientist, and Ian Crawford Shaw, also a Glasgow police forensic scientist from the Identification Bureau. From them he elicited the fact that apart from the blood spot on the tissues there was absolutely no forensic evidence linking George Beattie with the murder of Margaret McLaughlin, a crime which must have been violent, bloody and dirty.

He then asked to present a motion to the Court in the absence of the jury. This was the culmination of his efforts of the last three days. He had allowed the prosecution to lay out their stall, confident in the knowledge that there was not sufficient evidence on which to convict.

Before the jury withdrew, the Advocate Depute announced that he was removing from the indictment the words 'a bracelet and £15 or thereby of money'. In other words he was no longer trying to attach the charge of theft to Beattie.

Mr MacArthur then addressed the Judge, Lord Fraser, in the absence of the jury: 'The motion quite simply is, my lord, that I would ask your lordship to direct the jury that they would find the accused in this case not guilty as a matter of law, and I do so make the motion because my submission is that there is no sufficient evidence in law to allow the jury to consider the matter at all.'

Mr MacArthur's submission came in two parts. He argued that Beattie's knowledge of the scene of the crime was not 'special'. He pointed out that it was all known to the police and that it could have been observed by a spectator or a passer-by. Secondly, he argued that Beattie's story was not in any case a confession, it was a denial of the murder and there was not sufficient or proper corroboration for it. This is what Mr MacArthur had to say about the blood on the tissue handkerchiefs:

> The thing about the tissues is, of course, that they were only taken possession of from the accused some four days later, from, as I understand it, label No. 70, the jacket; and indeed never once in evidence has it been said that he was wearing that jacket on Friday night, sixth July. All that was said was that at the time he was charged this was the jacket he was wearing, label 70, and at that particular time eight pieces were taken from him, and on one of the tissues there was some blood which belonged to a group that 35 or 40 per cent of the population have ... That might be looked upon as a suspicious circumstance, but it has been said before that a suspicious circumstance is not corroboration.

The Advocate Depute rebutted those submissions, pointing out again the strangeness of Beattie's knowledge of the scene of the crime and maintaining that the blood on the tissues did constitute corroboration.

In the end Lord Fraser elected to dismiss the submission and put the case to the jury. He was clearly in some doubt and admitted that there was considerable force in what Mr MacArthur had said. It can only be a matter of conjecture that he might have imagined that Beattie, left in the hands of the jury, would be found 'Not proven', a verdict available in Scottish Law but not in English Law.

In his summing-up Lord Fraser pointed out that all that Detective Sergeant Mortimer had reported about Beattie: his knowledge of the exhibits; his knowledge of the scene of the crime; his story of the men in the hats, was all to be taken as the evidence of one man – the accused himself. He directed the jury that they must regard it as all one witness's evidence. He continued: 'It is as if the accused had made a confession and had said: "I admit having committed a murder," and gone on repeating it two or three times. You would not be entitled in law to convict him on that confession unless you thought there was some outside corroboration for it.'

In dealing with Mr MacArthur's tactic of stressing that there was no forensic evidence against his client, Lord Fraser did not appear to be over-impressed. Towards the end of his summing-up he said,

Reference was made by Mr MacArthur to the fact that the hair and the fibres examination was negative. Well, that is quite true, it was; but of course that also was based upon information obtained three or four days, at least three or four days, after the events [i.e. like the tissues in the jacket] and you may feel that that was not really very significant beyond the fact that nothing was found at any rate to implicate the accused in the offence. It is for you to weigh that up against the tissues on the other hand.

The Jury retired at 3.45 p.m. Just thirty-five minutes later they returned to find George Beattie guilty by a majority verdict.

Lord Fraser concluded the proceedings: 'George Beattie, the only sentence I can impose, and I do, is that you be imprisoned for life.'

Re-investigation:
The Case of the Missing Meal

What amazed us about the George Beattie case was that at every turn we came across new questions to which we could not get reasonable answers. During the Press publicity after the film had been transmitted we quoted a few of these.

1. Why had crucial evidence at the scene of the crime – such as the victim's umbrella – not been photographed?

2. Why was important evidence, such as the bloodstains on the ground, not photographed in colour? Why was this blood never grouped?

3. Why was the second knife found at the scene of the crime never mentioned during the trial? It could have been the murder weapon just as easily as the first knife.

4. Whose blood did the victim have under her fingernails? (Beattie was unscratched.)

5. Why was there no footprint evidence? It was a wet evening and the path to the station was rough ground. The victim herself wore shoes with heels over an inch high.

6. Why was she not wearing a wristwatch – particularly as she had two trains to catch? If she *was* wearing a wristwatch, where did it go and why did the police not notice that it had gone?

These questions were not the result of months of research. Although we gave them out to the Press after the transmission of the film they were in fact a quote from our original notes on the case after a first reading. After we had researched the Beattie case for nearly a year, made a film about it, and come to the clear conclusion that Beattie was innocent, we realized that none of these first questions had yet been answered.

Our research had actually added more questions to the list, the principal one being: When did the police actually find the victim's body? We did not see how this question could affect the issue of Beattie's guilt or innocence, but it raised issues about the case which disturbed us deeply.

The main evidence of George Beattie's innocence came from the lips of Margaret McLaughlin's sister Rosemary. She testified at Beattie's trial to Margaret's movements on the night of her death.

Q.: After you got home, were you and your sister Margaret in the house for a time?

A.: Yes, about just less than an hour.

Q.: What happened after that?

A.: Well, we had our dinner together, and then I got ready to go back out.

Q.: What time did you leave the house?

A.: It must have been five past seven.

This was crucial evidence, and surprise evidence, from only the second witness in the trial. If it had been followed up during the trial it might have cleared Beattie. But it was not.

Beattie's defence counsel had not been alerted to what Rosemary might say. This is because of a peculiarity of the Scottish legal procedure: depositions, or police statements, are not automatically released to the defence, even if they are judged to be relevant to the accused. Although Beattie's counsel did not have a deposition from Rosemary McLaughlin before him, he held a document which had great relevance to her testimony, and which had greater strength than its equivalent in England. This was the post-mortem report. In England only one pathologist is required to make out a post-mortem report; in Scotland two are required. In fact the post mortem on the body of Margaret McLaughlin was conducted by two of the most eminent pathologists in Scotland – a country famous for its pathologists.

The post-mortem report in the hands of Beattie's counsel made no mention of the contents of Margaret McLaughlin's stomach.

Yet according to her sister Rosemary, Margaret had eaten a meal at about 6.45 p.m. – just over an hour before she was supposed to have died.

When we approached Rosemary during our investigation she confirmed to us that Margaret's last meal had been a substantial one. She could not remember exactly what it had been, though she thought that they had cooked it together. It was however 'the main meal of the day', a 'knife and fork affair', she said. It is scientifically impossible for such a meal to be fully digested in an hour and a quarter.

One of the bibles of pathology – perhaps *the* bible – is *Glaisters Medical Jurisprudence and Toxicology*, originally written by a pioneer in the field, Professor John Glaister of the University of Glasgow. This book has regularly been amended by his disciples – including his son, John, a world-famous pathologist in his own right, and Dr W. D. S. McLay, Chief Medical Officer of the City of Glasgow police. Dr McLay, with another Glaister disciple, Dr Walter Pollock Weir, conducted the post mortem on the body of Margaret McLaughlin. Their 'bible' states:

> *Examination of the stomach.* In all cases, attention should be directed towards the stomach contents. The odour, especially if alcoholic, should be noted ... the stomach contents will give indication of the extent of digestion which has taken place, and, in an approximate manner, the interval of time since the ingestion of the last meal prior to death. An ordinary meal leaves the stomach in about four hours ... A large meal may be retained for five hours and a meal, not necessarily large, but containing a considerable quantity of butter or cream, is retained in the stomach for a longer period.

It is obvious from the post-mortem report that Drs McLay and Weir did not neglect to examine the stomach. They noted 'perforated wounds ... of the stomach'. In Court, Dr Weir stated, 'There were approximately nineteen stab wounds ... the ones in the abdomen penetrated the liver, stomach and kidney.'

In spite of this the pathologists did not note any stomach

contents, nor did they take a sample of stomach contents. Dr McLay consulted his notes for us. They are more extensive than any report we might find. He told us that he had no note of stomach contents whatsoever.

It is not credible that two such eminent pathologists could miss finding stomach contents in the body of a girl who had died only an hour and a quarter after eating a substantial meal. The more so because on this particular case the pathologists had every reason to look for stomach contents. The weather conditions overnight in Carluke had meant that gauging the time of death by the most reliable method – taking the temperature of the body – was not an easy task. At 6.30 p.m. on the Saturday the temperature of Margaret's body was 63 degrees Fahrenheit. During that afternoon the temperature in Carluke had been around 61 degrees Fahrenheit. All pathologists know that when the body approaches the temperature of its surroundings, estimates of time of death by temperature are liable to serious error. So Drs Weir and McLay would not have been happy to estimate the time of Margaret's death solely on temperature. They would have used other means to supplement their estimate. One of those means – indeed the only one at all reliable in the circumstances – would be to look at the contents of the stomach and ask when Margaret had last eaten. Unless, that is, there were no stomach contents to consider.

We considered other possibilities. Had she vomited after being attacked? There was no sign at all of this either in the police reports or in the photographs. We wondered, too, if she could have been stabbed at 8 p.m. yet lived long enough for her stomach to digest the meal fully – perhaps until 10 p.m. The two pathologists ruled this out in their evidence. Dr Weir said that she would have died within 'about ten minutes' of the attack; Dr McLay thought she would have died within 'a few minutes'.

There was only one reasonable explanation to this – Margaret McLaughlin died sometime *after 10 o'clock* on the evening of 6 July 1973 – not at 8 p.m. as alleged by the prosecution. George Beattie had a firm alibi at 10 o'clock – indeed he had one for all but a few minutes around 8 o'clock. He could not have killed

Margaret McLaughlin. Perhaps important evidence was lost because the police never asked where Margaret might have been after 8 p.m.

It is far too late for us to make such an investigation now. It was probably too late even during the trial. But we reasoned that there should be some other indication among the evidence collected by the police that would suggest that Margaret's death had happened later than 8 p.m. We therefore looked for aspects of this evidence that did not fit into the scenario advanced by the police.

It was a pity that footprint evidence was not preserved because that would have shown the direction Margaret was walking when she was attacked. We suspected that if she had died after 10 o'clock she would be walking in the direction of home, not towards the railway station. Her footprints would have shown this. But in spite of the rain on the Friday evening, none appear to have been found.

It was a pity, too, that Margaret's wristwatch was not on her wrist. She had two wristwatches and normally wore one, but it seems that she decided she did not need a watch that evening – although this seems strange because she was going away for the weekend and had several trains to catch. The police have no record of finding a wristwatch – nor do they appear to have looked for one. Considering the fall that Margaret must have taken down the side of the glen, we thought it was possible that her watch had stopped at the time of the attack. But that evidence was not in existence.

There was plenty of evidence, however, that it was raining at 8 o'clock on the Friday evening. Eleven witnesses in all mentioned the rain. It started just before Margaret left home at about 7.55 and ended at about 8.10. When we looked at the bloodstains on the ground and the foliage in the police photographs, we noticed something unexpected. All the blood spots have sharp edges. Rain produces a 'halo' effect on blood spots if it reaches them before the blood coagulates. Although several of these blood spots must have been exposed to the sky, away from the trees in the glen, it seemed that none of them had been wet with rain at the time they were made. This must have been a near-impossibility at 8 o'clock.

Margaret's umbrella was interesting, too. One of the men who first saw it on the Saturday, P.C. Clydesdale, said it was 'badly broken in the folded-down position'. How could it have been in the 'folded-down' position if it had been raining when Margaret was attacked? Margaret would have kept her hair dry for one very good reason – her hair had recently become very frizzy and she wanted it to look nice at her wedding. One of the items found in her suitcase was a very special hair conditioner which her hairdresser had given her to cure frizziness. Having gone to such lengths to groom her hair, would Margaret have folded her umbrella down in the rain? We thought not.

Such evidence, mainly forensic, may seem slight when attempting to prove that a man did not commit a murder. But weighed against the forensic evidence collected from the scene of the crime to incriminate George Beattie, it is a mountain. Indeed, there is no such evidence at all that could implicate Beattie in any way. It is very rare indeed that the police forensic scientists are called exclusively by the defence. But that is what happened in the trial of George Beattie.

As we have outlined earlier, our approach is to look at the forensic evidence first, then the witness evidence. The forensic evidence from the scene of the crime – 'trace evidence' – held nothing that implicated Beattie; neither did witness evidence. If anything, the best witness evidence was alibi evidence in Beattie's favour. Nevertheless, the evidence that persuaded the jury to find Beattie guilty could be split into forensic and witness evidence. There was a blood spot on two tissues found in Beattie's pocket. Then there was Beattie's own statement – not a confession, but the wild story that men in top hats with mirrors had done the murder.

The blood spot was never the best evidence to present against a man accused of a crime as serious as murder. The blood group was acknowledged in Court to be shared by 43 per cent of the population and it is the most common blood group in Scotland.

The tissue handkerchiefs were discovered five days after the murder in the pocket of the jacket of a blue suit which Beattie wore while being questioned. It was never established whether Beattie had worn this suit on the night of the murder. Indeed, witnesses such as Mrs Gorry who had observed him in the queue to buy tomatoes, and Ian Freel who saw him in the street just after 8 o'clock said that he was not wearing a suit, but dark working clothes – perhaps overalls. Mr Bryce, who also saw him in the street, said he was wearing a tweed jacket. The person who came nearest to clothing Beattie in a blue suit jacket that night was Beattie himself. He said he wore 'a blue suit jacket' – but claims it was a different jacket to the one he wore when being questioned by the police.

The incriminating tissues were discovered by Detective Sergeant Mortimer at 2.50 a.m. on the morning of Thursday 12 July. Beattie had been charged, stripped and placed in the cells at Lanark police station. Mortimer took eight tissue handkerchiefs out of the left-hand pocket of Beattie's jacket, then replaced them. No one else at the police station appears to have seen him do this. The jacket was then handed on to the exhibits officers in the case, who rediscovered the tissues in the jacket pocket. They logged and labelled them, then sent them off to the laboratory. The two scientists assigned to the task of investigating this evidence found that two of these tissues had blood on them of human origin. They said it was group O, Rhesus D positive, and told the Court that this was common to 43 per cent of the population.

We wondered how the scientists could be sure that the blood was Rhesus positive. The two small stains were old and on dirty crumpled handkerchiefs which had been used by Beattie, who had Rhesus D positive blood, though in the A group. We wondered because we knew that such stains are extremely difficult to group for a Rhesus factor. *Glaister's Medical Jurisprudence*, for example, states:

> If, however, the stains are very small, old and contaminated it may be very difficult ... we think that the grouping should

always be done by those who have no knowledge of the possible group to which the stain may belong.

Reports have been published of methods to determine the MN and Rh subgroups of stains. We have not found any method which gives sufficiently reliable results for these groups for presentation as evidence in courts of law.

So the leading authority of the day in 1973 said that the scientists working on the stains in the Beattie case were, in effect, 'chancing their arm'. Was that because they knew that Margaret McLaughlin's blood group was O, Rhesus positive, and that some 85 per cent of the population are Rhesus positive anyway?

We calculated that even if they were right about the Rhesus factor, which seemed highly unlikely, their figures for this blood group were wrong.

Official statistics released in 1972 showed that blood group O (both Rhesus positive and Rhesus negative) was common to over 50 per cent of the population in the Glasgow area. In areas closer to the scene of the crime the percentage rose even higher. The nearest large town, Motherwell, where George Beattie's father was born, showed a percentage for group O of 61.57 per cent. The areas of Lanark, Larkhall, Wishaw and Hamilton (which includes the village of Carluke) showed 56.44 per cent, 55 per cent, 58.25 per cent and 57.63 per cent respectively. We visited the Law Hospital where the tests on the tissue handkerchiefs were made. The figures they had for blood in stock and ratio of group O corresponded roughly to the official figures.

Even taking into account the Rhesus factor, which we did not believe reliable, none of these figures was as low as the figure of 43 per cent presented to the Court.

But given that the spot of blood on the tissues in Beattie's pocket could have come from at least half the people in Scotland, but not, apparently, Beattie, how did it come to be there at all? First we tested the blood of every member of the Beattie family who could have come in contact with George during the five days between the murder and the discovery of the tissues. Two of them

– George's father and his brother Tommy – had died since the murder and there was no record of their blood group. The rest had the same blood group as George – A, Rhesus positive.

Then we tried to imagine the circumstances in which blood from Margaret McLaughlin could have got on to Beattie's tissues. Had he wiped it from her body? If he had, we reasoned that there should have been more than just one spot. Had he wiped it from himself after killing Margaret? This indicated that blood had splashed on to him during the attack, yet none was ever found on his clothes.

Perhaps, we thought, he might have wiped his knife on the tissues after the murder. But if he had, there should have been more blood on it than just one small spot. This would also have been so if he had wrapped the knife in the tissues, yet if he had done this, then surely he would have disposed of the tissues when he disposed of the knife?

Another alternative was that he might have partially cleaned the knife at the scene of the crime, then wrapped it in the tissues. But there was no evidence of a knife being cleaned of blood at the scene of the crime – and the tissues had no traces of soil on them which we might have expected if the knife had been wrapped in them.

Perhaps he threw away all the tissues he found in his pocket that were stained with blood, not noticing the spot on the tissues he kept because it was so small? Why should he not throw away *all* the tissues in such circumstances? It was strange that he had not thrown them away anyway – his solicitor noted while viewing the exhibits that the tissues in question were crumpled and dirty from normal use.

There was no reasonable scenario we could imagine in which Beattie could murder Margaret McLaughlin and end up with just one or two small blood spots from her body on his tissue handkerchiefs. Indeed, we wondered about the proof that the tissues actually belonged to Beattie. Tissues normally pick up saliva – and blood groups can be detected in saliva. But no such tests were made on the tissues found in Beattie's pocket, and by the time the defence could see a need for such tests the saliva would probably have been too old for valid testing to be carried out on them.

The evidence that the tissues were in Beattie's jacket pocket came from one man – Detective Sergeant Mortimer. This was six days after the murder and after Beattie had been charged. He did not notice any blood on them. He did not call anyone's attention to them, nor did he mark them in any way for identification. Mortimer's notebook appeared in evidence and we can find no reference in it to him finding these tissues. Detective Constable Johnston, who corroborated Detective Sergeant Mortimer's statements, seems to have seen the tissues only when they were taken out of the pocket (for the second time) by the exhibits officers on the case.

Considering that there was never any proof that Beattie had worn this jacket on the night in question, it seemed to us that whatever proof there was about these tissues and the blood spot, it was becoming extremely thin. We also considered that there was a possibility of contamination. Three policemen at least had touched these tissues on the morning of Thursday 12 July. We do not know the blood groups of these men, nor do we know if they had blood on their hands for any reason. But we do know that about half the men in that area share the blood group of the sample found on the tissues, and that these men not only normally shaved in the morning, but had been rummaging about in the bushes and rubbish of the Colonel's Glen during the previous days.

We also know that samples taken from the glen were still lying around the police station at that time. The tissues, for example, were sent to the laboratory in company with a piece of newspaper picked up from the side of Margaret's body. This newspaper was stained with blood of group O, but although the stains were 'widespread', the Rhesus factor of these stains was not determined – presumably because tests for the Rhesus factor in such stains are unreliable.

At the laboratory the forensic scientists appear to have made no tests on the handkerchief tissues other than a test for blood. But that is hardly surprising because they must have heard by then that Detective Constable John Semple had taken a statement from Beattie early on the Wednesday evening in which Beattie is alleged to have said that he wiped blood on to tissues in his pocket. At the trial Semple stated:

Beattie said, 'I ran to go up the path but I tripped and fell over something. I think it snapped: I don't know. It wasn't wood, I don't know what it was. I picked it up and threw it into the grass. It felt soft. I don't know what colour it was.' (That would be a reply to me asking if he noticed the colour.) 'There was nothing else on the ground. There is some blood. There is often blood on the ground in there.'

I asked him where, and he said, 'Wood,' and I put it in brackets.

'Dogs fighting or somebody skinning a rabbit leaves blood. I ran up the path and I slipped again. I hurted my knee on the fence post. I saw there was blood on my hand, my left one, and I wiped it on the water that was running down the wire of the fence. I dried my hand with a paper hankie. I rolled up the hankie and put it in my left trouser pocket I think, I am not sure.'

George Beattie denies ever having said this. He says that he was talking about 'wood', not 'blood'. It was the police who brought up this subject of blood and tissues and they became confused. Certainly the police had already found tissue handkerchiefs at the scene of the crime. This was perhaps not surprising because the area is something of a local rubbish dump. And certainly there appear to be several points in the above statement where questions have been edited out – one such instance is admitted to within the statement.

Whatever the truth about Beattie's claims, it is perhaps significant that the police never found another tissue handkerchief of the type found in Beattie's pocket – even though they searched the Beatties' house before the Beatties knew of the tissues found in George's pocket.

If the above seems to be the result of an inordinate amount of research spent on one or two small blood spots that could have come from half the population in Scotland, it is worth bearing in mind that the blood spots were the only forensic evidence presented by the prosecution against Beattie.

There should have been more. If George Beattie killed Margaret McLaughlin it is amazing that there was no forensic evidence to prove that he or his clothes had been at the scene of the crime. Imagine the scene as best constructed from the evidence. The murderer grappled with Margaret on the grass of the slope leading up to the railway line. The two of them apparently rolled around on this slope where spots of blood were subsequently found. The murderer should have had blood and grass seeds on his clothes, perhaps blood on the soles of his shoes.

Margaret seems to have hit her attacker with her umbrella, for she had bruises on her left hand consistent with this and the umbrella was bent as if it had hit someone with force. So the murderer should have sustained at least one bruise from it.

The murderer appears to have dragged Margaret's body down the slope of the glen in waist-high grass and nettles. His clothes would pick up more grass seeds and burrs from the underbrush, and his hands may have been stung by nettles. He seems to have dragged her by putting his hands under her armpits, so he could hardly have escaped coming into contact with blood from the wounds in her forearms – defence wounds made during the initial attack. He may have shown other marks on his knuckles, for Dr Weir felt that the blow to Margaret's jaw may well have been a punch – a punch which loosened her front teeth and broke a denture. Her fingernails were found to have blood beneath them: in the vast majority of cases this indicates that the victim has scratched the attacker.

The suitcase was found in the burn, rather than at the top of the glen where Margaret first dropped it on being attacked, so the murderer must have made a second trip up to the top of the glen to get the suitcase and take it down to the bottom. This would increase the likelihood that his clothes would become covered in grass seeds and similar debris. Down by the burn the nettles grow to about face-height so he should have been stung at one time or another.

What evidence did the police find of all this on the man who is still serving his life sentence for the murder of Margaret McLaughlin? None whatsoever.

George Beattie was seen within minutes of 8 o'clock by several people. The light was good, for although it had been raining, it was midsummer. We know of at least nine people who had a good chance to notice any of the possible traces of the struggle on him. None did.

The police saw Beattie on the Saturday, then again on the Tuesday. On the Wednesday at least a dozen policemen saw him and he was examined by Dr McLay on the Thursday. No one noticed anything – no scratches, no bruises, no dirt, no grass seed, no nettle stings, nothing – except the one or two small spots of blood on the tissues taken from his pocket.

Of course, the policemen who saw Beattie on the day after the murder were not looking on him as a suspect. Considering his story, it would have seemed ridiculous to do so. The evidence pointed to someone with motive, or to someone who habitually carried a knife; Beattie fitted neither category.

He did not carry a knife – there are few people who habitually carry a knife large enough to inflict the wounds found on Margaret's body. It would need to be $4\frac{1}{2}$ inches long, possibly longer, because the deepest wound was $5\frac{1}{2}$ inches. The blade would need to have a width of $1\frac{1}{8}$ inches, coming to a point. This would probably rule out a jack knife or a penknife. The weapon used was probably a sheath knife or perhaps a kitchen carving knife. Neither would have fitted easily into a pocket.

Beattie had no reason to carry such a knife on the night in question. He intended simply to pick up the tomatoes from the nursery and then go on to work at the steel works. He could not have taken a knife with him specifically to kill Margaret McLaughlin – no one except the immediate members of her family knew that she would be going to catch the 8.03 p.m. train; indeed, Margaret did not decide to catch this later train until just before 7 o'clock.

George Beattie could not have seen her leave from his own home; his first opportunity to see her would have been as she crossed the end of Unitas Crescent a hundred yards away. He could then have seen her for about ten seconds, and then only if he had been standing at his garden gate. At this point Margaret was about 200 yards from where she was attacked. Beattie would not have had enough time to go back into his house, find a knife, pursue Margaret, catch her up and kill her. He would have needed to run very fast to even attempt it, and there are several witnesses who saw him *walking* along Unitas Crescent that night.

There is only one possible scenario in which Beattie could feature as the murderer: he picked up the knife earlier and went out with the intention of killing someone, though not necessarily Margaret. There is absolutely no evidence to suggest that Beattie is such a pathological killer. In any case, most such murderers in history have laid their plans in advance, not acted on impulse. Until George Beattie's sister Ena came home from work and told him that he would have to go for the tomatoes himself because the Gorry family was out visiting Mr Gorry senior in hospital, George Beattie did not even know he would be going through the glen that night. He normally went to work by bus, and to catch his bus he would have gone in the opposite direction, away from the glen.

So if the policemen who interviewed Beattie during their door-to-door inquiries thought a little about his story, they should have realized that he was not a likely suspect; they did not treat him as one. It would be unethical for the police to take a suspect to the scene of the crime, even give him a 'guided tour' of it, then accuse him of the crime because he seemed to have special knowledge of the scene of crime.

So Beattie was obviously not regarded as a suspect on the Tuesday night after the murder when he was given his 'guided tour' by Detective Sergeant Adam and Detective Constable Waddell. They asked him to reconstruct his walk of the Friday night. Even though he was not a suspect, they decided to time his journey. It took four minutes ten seconds to reach the point at the top of the railway embankment just twenty yards beyond where the attack on Margaret had begun. In Court Detective Sergeant Adam said of this trip: 'I asked him if he reconstructed the walk would that bring anything back to him, anything he may have heard and seen – you know, jolt his memory, maybe give us a lead of some description.'

Later, after giving the timing of the trip, Adam told the Court why the walk had come to an end:

Q.: And then I think you were telling us, the weather was bad?
A.: Yes, it started to come on heavy rain.
Q.: What did you do after that?
A.: I told Constable Waddell to go back and get a police van to pick up George and himself.
Q.: And did he do that?
A.: Yes.

Constable Waddell was also questioned on this matter.

Q.: Why did the exercise end at the point on the embankment which you mentioned?
A.: It started raining after that, and it was raining quite heavily, so we decided to abandon it.

That seemed clear enough – except for the fact that Adam had told a different version of events when he made his pre-cognisance statement to the defence solicitor before the trial. There he had said: 'Unfortunately, heavy rain came on and although Detective Constable Waddell and Beattie carried on past the station, I went back, collected the van and picked them up in Station Road.'

We thought it strange that Detective Sergeant Adam could not remember who had had the job of going back in the rain to the Beattie house to get the car. We thought it odd that the trip was not 'ended' at this point, but 'abandoned'. Where had they intended going if the rain had not begun? If they had timed the rest of Beattie's journey that night they could only have been checking his alibi – the police never suggested that Margaret had got further than the glen. But why should they time Beattie's alibi? He was not a suspect.

We also thought it odd that it should take four minutes ten seconds to make the trip to the glen. We had already timed the journey and agreed with the later police timing made by Detective Constable Richardson that it took about two minutes thirty seconds to get from the Beatties' house to the scene of the crime. Why had Detective Sergeant Adam's trip taken almost twice as long?

We knew that some of the tapes marking the various pieces of evidence at the scene of the crime were still in position on the Tuesday evening. Had the spare two minutes been taken up with innocent questions such as 'Did you see any blood spots on the ground here?' or 'Did you see anything down there where the body was found?' or 'Did you not notice the knife in the ground by this post?'

Such questions, and a dozen others, would have been unethical if Beattie was being treated as a suspect. But, of course, he was not. Since the two policemen were trying to 'jolt his memory', it would have been a perfectly reasonable way of going about it.

Looking back over the episode of the 'guided tour', Detective Sergeant Adam seems to have been somewhat more than embarrassed about having taken it upon himself to suggest it to Beattie. He didn't tell his boss, Detective Chief Inspector Gold, about the trip, nor did he tell Detective Chief Superintendent Muncie, who was running the investigation. And he didn't tell Detective Sergeant Mortimer. Perhaps if he had, Mortimer would have been less surprised, as indeed would the other detectives, when Beattie began to tell them details about the scene of the crime two days later.

Mortimer, who took it upon himself to charge Beattie with the murder, knew less about the crime than any of the other detectives. He had been on holiday and only joined the case on the Tuesday. He had been to the scene of the crime only once, when his inquiries brought him to the name of George Beattie. Mortimer was following up sightings of people seen around the railway station on the night in question and had been told that Beattie was often down there train-spotting.

For some reason which has never been explained, Detective Constable John Semple had also decided to go to interview Beattie. So when Mortimer was on his way to Beattie's home, he heard that his train-spotter was already being interviewed by Semple down at the Carluke police station. Although this evening cannot be judged as Beattie's luckiest – he was later charged with murder – it was a happy accident for him that the police had managed to put two different sets of policemen on to him that particular evening. With Semple was Police Constable Mair and with Mortimer was Detective Constable Johnston. Each of these men gave a precognisance statement to Beattie's solicitor and each gave evidence in Court. We have the luxury of eight versions of what happened in the Carluke police station that night. From these statements we could see how it was possible that Beattie had acquired all the information about Margaret McLaughlin's possessions without being party to the murder. And how Detective Sergeant Mortimer innocently followed a false trail which led to the arrest of the wrong man.

When Semple took Beattie to the police station, they entered by the main door and went into what is called 'the front office'. In that office were Detective Constables McCleary and Mac-Allister, the exhibits officers. There Beattie was checked in. McCleary and MacAllister were in charge of all the exhibits, including those taken from the scene of the crime. Beattie claims that he saw all the objects he later described as he stood by the desk in the front office. He cannot have known who McCleary or MacAllister were because they were based at Hamilton and so were strangers to Carluke. He cannot have known what their job was, yet he described them and their job. He also spoke of a list they were drawing up; they would indeed probably have been drawing up a list at that time, just as he described. They may even have been 'bagging up' exhibits while he waited to be interviewed, for they made a delivery to the laboratory the next morning. So Beattie may have seen all the objects he later described just before he was led into the other room at the police station – the 'muster room'.

After the film of this case was transmitted, Chief Superintendent Muncie, who led the investigation, told a journalist in Glasgow that all the exhibits had been kept in the cells. He knew as well as anyone that they were certainly not in the muster room, and the only other area in the police station, apart from the front office, was the cell area. Rosemary McLaughlin has also stated since the film that when she went into the police station to view the exhibits she was shown into one of the cells where all the articles were laid out. We do not deny any of this, but we cite the evidence from the policemen who were there that at least some of the exhibits were in the front office of the police station on the evening in question. And there is every reason to believe that the list of exhibits that McCleary and MacAllister were drawing up would certainly be there.

By the time the policemen came to Court it was obvious how important this point was, so it is surprising to find no reference to the position of the exhibits in the transcript of the trial. But in their statements to the defence solicitor earlier, Detective Sergeant Mortimer and Detective Constable Johnston made no attempt to hide the facts. Mortimer said of the items of evidence: 'I was unaware of these ever being found and spoke to McCleary and MacAllister. They were actually in the front office of the police station. There is not much room in Carluke police station for any other arrangement and they were looking after the productions.'

Johnston was even more precise: 'I had no knowledge of these items at all which were in the other room in the police station.'

Johnston's statement shows clearly that he knew that there were only two 'rooms' in Carluke police station. Because he had no occasion to see the productions, he also had no occasion to go into the cell area where they normally were kept. If he *had* seen them in the cells, he would have said so: no policemen refers to a cell as a 'room'. There is no reason to suspect that he might be confused about what he said. Like Beattie, he can only have seen the items in question in the front office of the police station.

Neither Johnston nor Mortimer had been in the station when Beattie was brought in at 7.30 p.m. They had both arrived after 9 p.m. when Detective Constable Semple was finishing his interview with Beattie. By that time Beattie had been in the 'muster room' for almost two hours. They had no reason to suspect that he was about to give them an elaborate concoction based on what he had heard and been shown over the past five days, though if they had listened to Semple's last words to them, they might have guessed. For as Semple left he remarked to Mortimer, 'Beattie is making additions to his statement for no obvious reason, for the sake of talking. He's either a bit simple-minded or else he has something more to say.'

Mortimer wrote Beattie's words down in all innocence. He did not know that Beattie had had a 'guided tour' of the scene of the crime. He no doubt assumed that routine procedure had been followed and that the public had been kept away from the glen since the body was discovered; but people had been taking the short cut through to the station since the Monday morning. He no doubt assumed that spectators had been kept away; but we found an aerial photograph taken of the glen on the Sunday in which we could clearly see the police patrolling the south side; however, no one appeared to be guarding the north side. We demonstrated with our cameras that the entire scene of the crime could be observed from the north side. Detective Sergeant Mortimer knew none of this: he had been away on holiday when the glen had been the focus of the investigation. He was naturally surprised by what he was hearing.

If there were any doubts about Beattie's 'revelations' among the policemen who had worked on the case longer than Mortimer, these were no doubt overcome by the fact that Beattie had 'done the trick' twice. The men in the police station, who may have realized that Beattie could have seen the evidence there, would forget their doubts when they heard on the grapevine what Beattie had said in the glen. The men in the glen who might have had doubts about his evidence in their territory (particularly Adam and Waddell) would be reassured to learn that he had shown 'special knowledge' back at the police station.

Such was the surprise, such was the enthusiasm that the case had been solved when it had looked like dragging on for months, that no one thought to examine Beattie's statements for errors. In fact there were nine points where the police could have picked at Beattie's statements and eliminated him. An analysis of his 'special knowledge' shows that it was not special knowledge at all. And where he had the chance to show 'special knowledge', not only did he fail to give it, but the police failed to press him on the matter.

Beattie said there were two carrier bags. One, he said, was lying on the ground; the other he was not specific about. In fact there was only one carrier bag in evidence, and that was inside Margaret's suitcase.

He claimed he had seen the 'men with top hats' take the ring from Margaret's *left* hand, but the ring that was missing from her body probably fell from her hand during the initial scuffle on the ground – and it was from her *right* hand.

The hair conditioner which he referred to as a 'hairspray' had a very distinctive shape. It was sold only to professionals and could not be bought in the shops. Beattie did not know whether this distinctive plastic bottle was a tin, a jar, or a bottle. He described it as all three.

He described Margaret's trousers in the suitcase as being separate from the carrier bag. In fact the trousers he identified were inside the carrier bag, inside the suitcase which had apparently not been disturbed.

Although he mentioned the umbrella three times, he failed to describe its bent and broken state.

When he visited the scene of the crime with the police they were surprised when he could not find the final position of the body. They thought it suspicious that he was moving around halfway down the glen muttering, 'It's here, it's here.' They should have been more surprised if Beattie had gone straight to the place. The real murderer could have done just that. Beattie, who had seen an aerial photograph in the *Daily Record* with an X marking the spot, needed to look for some clue before he pointed to the place.

Also at the scene of the crime he described how the suitcase was thrown down towards the burn. Not only was he describing an impossible throw – because of the topography of the glen, but he failed to mention that the shoulder bag had been thrown with the suitcase.

All of the above could have been overlooked in the heady atmosphere after a suspect has been charged with murder. But two points remain which should have been picked up.

There were only two items of which the murderer alone would have 'special knowledge'. On these Beattie failed to come up with the answers. The first was the gold charm bracelet which Margaret had worn on her left wrist on the night she died. It was never found, and no reasonable explanation was ever given as to why the bracelet should have been stolen and not, for example, her more expensive engagement ring which was on her left hand.

Beattie could not describe the gold bracelet. Chief Superintendent Muncie interviewed him:

MUNCIE: Did you see the girl wearing a charm bracelet?
BEATTIE: One of the men had a gold thing round his wrist.
MUNCIE: Did you see what he did with it?
BEATTIE: I think he threw it down in the tunnel down there.

Beattie was pointing down the glen to the culvert at the bottom. If the bracelet had been thrown in there it would certainly have been recovered. The bed of the burn through the culvert is solid rock. Beattie not only placed the gold bracelet on the wrong wrist – the man's wrist, but he said it was thrown where it was certainly not thrown.

The final and most glaring error in Beattie's statements is the most crucial: he chose the wrong knife as the murder weapon. Beattie described the spot where the 'men with top hats' had cleaned the knife which had been used to kill Margaret. 'He showed us where the knife had been stuck in the ground,' said

Johnston, 'and it looked just like a slit next to an old broken post.'

'It had a wooden handle,' said Beattie to Chief Superintendent Muncie, 'with a funny hook on the end – the handle had the funny kind of hook.'

The knife he was describing was certainly very like Exhibit 4, which most witnesses at the trial referred to as 'the knife'. It had been taken from the ground near the post the previous Saturday by Chief Superintendent Muncie and then for some reason eliminated. Another knife, Exhibit 90, found $1\frac{1}{2}$ yards away from Exhibit 4, had also been eliminated. On the Sunday morning Detective Inspector Kirk was given the task of finding the actual murder weapon. He was not successful. After Beattie had been charged, the police visited the family home and took away a kitchen knife. This too was eliminated.

Now, after Beattie had talked about the knife – Exhibit 4 – having been cleaned in the ground by the post, a sample of the earth around where the knife had been was sent to the forensic laboratory. No blood was found on it. No blood was ever found on the knife Exhibit 4. This was remarkable if the murderer pushed it into the ground as Beattie said. The blood would have been pushed up into the hilt. Yet during the trial everyone seemed to assume that this knife was the murder weapon – though the police never actually claimed it was. In spite of the statements made in the film of this case they have been careful to refrain from making such a statement even today. The only time the claim has ever been made is when Beattie's statements to the police were recited to the Court. Yet it seems with hindsight that the jury who found George Beattie guilty may have walked into the jury room believing that Exhibit 4 was indeed the murder weapon because it had been covered with blood.

When Chief Superintendent Muncie was cross-examined about the knife he trod very carefully. He said as little as he could, yet perhaps too much. When he was asked the crucial question about the fact that he had eliminated this knife from his inquiries on the Saturday night, he made fulsome reference to the Press and inadvertently failed to answer the question that had been put to him. He had no doubt forgotten for the moment that Detective Inspector Kirk had been assigned on the Sunday to look for the murder weapon. Defence counsel was at a great disadvantage during this exchange for, although he had a legal right to have taken a statement from Chief Superintendent Muncie prior to the trial, Mr Muncie had unfortunately been very busy and the interview had never taken place. So defence counsel was perhaps taken by surprise.

The cross-examination of Muncie went as follows:

Q.: The knife, which I think is label 4 perhaps you could look at it. This was discovered on the Saturday sixth July; is that right?

A.: That is correct.

Q.: Now, at that time was there any test made for fingerprints or the like?

A.: Of the knife?

Q.: Yes.

A.: The knife was tested for fingerprints, but first the most important thing was blood.

Q.: Well, I'll come to that in a moment. Do you know if it was tested for fingerprints?

A.: It was tested for fingerprints and it was found negative.

Q.: You had that knife on Saturday sixth; is that right?

A.: That is correct.

Q.: Were you still at or about the seventh or the eighth indicating that you were still looking for a murder weapon?

A.: You mean to the Press?

Q.: Yes.

A.: Well, we have to watch how we handle the Press, and with all due respect to the gentlemen of the Press, by letting things get out it makes it most awkward for us when we are interviewing witnesses or other folk who may be connected with the crime, and there was nothing given to the Press which was to any effect misleading or anything like that at all in connection with a weapon.

Beattie's defence counsel's head must have been reeling at this point. Where was the evidence for the blood on the knife which Chief Superintendent Muncie had mentioned? He had said, 'The most important thing was blood'; did he know something that the defence had not heard of already? If defence went into this, where would it lead? Was it a trap? If he had quickly leafed through the forensic report, he would not have found it there. If he had looked for a precognisance statement from Chief Superintendent Muncie, he would not find that at all. Pressure of police business had taken that legal right away from Beattie.

Because of Chief Superintendent Muncie's unfortunate choice of phrase he was never questioned about blood on the knife. In fact the words 'there was no blood on the knife' were never said during the entire trial. The nearest that was ever reached was the following section of the police forensic scientist's testimony:

> Q.: I think you then deal with a knife, which is labelled as being eighteen inches south side of path at locus, and there was nothing of note on the knife?
> A.: That is so.

As for the sample of soil taken from around where the knife had been stuck into the ground, the evidence was completely confused. One of the policemen said that it had been taken from near the body – that is, some 50 feet from where the knife was found! The forensic scientists mixed it in with two other soil samples that had been taken but not brought into Court as exhibits. Their report made no mention of tests for blood. The soil sample taken from around the knife was said to have been used to try to find a match with soil from the soles of Beattie's shoes. But there was no doubt that Beattie had been in the glen near the broken post where the knife had been. Two policemen had taken him there four days after the murder.

In such circumstances it is hard to blame the jury if they were left with the impression that Beattie had pointed out the murder weapon. But in fact it had been a major error in his story. It led us to wonder, if Beattie were guilty, where could he possibly have hidden the actual murder weapon? George Beattie's movements after 8 o'clock on the Friday night were probably better corroborated than those of any other witness. His journey to work was well known. If he had disposed of the knife along this route it would almost certainly have been found.

The Judge at Beattie's trial also seems to have assumed that the knife was the murder weapon. It is incumbent upon him to mention all the points in favour of the defence in his summary of the case to the jury. He made no reference to the knife at all. When speaking of the negative nature of the forensic evidence, he spoke only of hair and fibres – samples which had also proved nothing against Beattie. If any member of the jury went into the jury room believing that when it came to the knife, 'the most important thing was the blood', then the Judge must share some of the blame for such a gross error.

The police might well have broken down Beattie's story by questioning him further about the knife during the investigation. Certainly they should have got the truth out of him by pressing him for information on the other eight areas where his story did not match the facts. But they did not do so.

Nor did they inquire too deeply into the possible explanation for the story of the men with top hats and mirrors. If they had gone into the local record shop in Lanark that week, or watched 'Top of the Pops' on the day after Beattie was charged, they would have seen the answer staring them in the face.

The pop group Slade was the most successful group of 1973. Throughout the whole of June and July their eighth hit in a row was number one in the pop charts. Their gimmick was mirrors. Noddy Holder, their lead singer, always wore a large top hat with round mirrors stuck to it. Other members of the group often wore similar hats. 'Slade' hats were on sale at all the group's concerts, and many teenagers walked around wearing top hats with mirrors.

But perhaps more important to someone trying to understand the confusion in Beattie's mind as he made his statements, Slade was featured on 'Top of the Pops' on the very Friday night that Margaret McLaughlin died. In fact as George Beattie came downstairs to eat his supper before going to buy the tomatoes, the group, Slade, was on B.B.C.1 in the Beattie sitting room.

The police, who seemed to believe that Beattie had got the image from the horrors of the film *A Clockwork Orange*, were obviously not pop fans.

George Beattie is unlikely to be released from prison before he completes his sentence. The Scots are proud of their legal system and consider it superior to the English one, but the full facts were not brought out at Beattie's trial. In this respect he did not get a fair hearing and he is not likely to get a fair hearing a decade later. No one cares to take up his case because it was Beattie himself who provided the main evidence which seemed to testify to his guilt. But because of inadequate investigation by the police – whose job is to protect the innocent as well as find the guilty – Beattie was denied several legal rights. The blame is not his alone.

A psychiatrist in Court said that Beattie was slightly below average in intellectual capacity, somewhat immature and that his responsibility for his actions was somewhat diminished. This may be why he told the police his wild tale. But there may be another reason.

Detective Sergeant Mortimer, who took the crucial statement from Beattie, said of him, 'He was in a terrible state and almost in a fit. I thought he was taking an epileptic turn. He was slavering with foam at the mouth and was sobbing and shaking.' Beattie was not seen by a doctor until some twenty hours after this incident, yet his words during this period were treated as good evidence.

Beattie's defence counsel made a bad error of judgement which poorly served his client. This is not to say that such an error could have been foreseen at the time. Defence counsel quickly realized that the prosecution case against Beattie was unique in Scottish legal history. Beattie's story was not a confession. He always denied killing Margaret. His statement was an admission that he had witnessed the events.

The prosecution relied on this admission coupled with the evidence of the blood spot on the handkerchiefs as sole proof of

Beattie's guilt. Scots Law requires that a man's confession must be corroborated – but here was a case where there might be corroboration, but no confession.

Defence counsel for Beattie believed that the case would not stand the test of argument before the Judge. A long series of precedents supported his belief. His tactics therefore were to say little, ask few questions and keep the case free of complication. After all, he knew that the police forensic scientists would confirm that there was nothing in the evidence collected at the scene of the crime which incriminated Beattie in any way.

When this point was reached in Beattie's trial, the defence counsel rose and made a most eloquent and deeply researched speech pointing out that the case should not go to the jury as a point of law. The Judge did not agree with him. He decided to let the jury decide whether Beattie's statement was a confession. As a consequence of this carefully laid plan by the defence many questions were not asked. The answers could have been proof of Beattie's innocence.

And yet, even if Beattie's defence counsel had run a different defence and asked these questions, it is not at all certain that he would have got the answers. The investigation had not been thorough enough, and it seems that some parts of the truth were already lost for ever when Beattie's case came to trial.

The question of the victim's stomach contents is one example. Defence had no way of impeaching the evidence of the two pathologists before him. If he had asked them to state what had been in Margaret's stomach, they would have looked up their notes and said they had no note of stomach contents. If pressed to rely upon their memory of the contents, they would have probably truthfully replied that they could not remember. The truth itself had gone. An exhumation and a second post mortem conducted during the trial would only have revealed that, if there had been stomach contents, they had rotted away. Beattie was therefore denied the chance to find the truth of a matter which directly affected the outcome of his trial.

Another similar matter was the question of the blood found

under Margaret McLaughlin's fingernails. Beattie was examined for scratches; but when that proved negative, the blood seems to have been forgotten. The laboratory report merely states that it was of human origin. It does not even state that there was insufficient for grouping. In the vast majority of cases where a girl has been attacked and blood found under her fingernails, the police look to it to give the blood group of her attacker. But if Beattie, or his counsel, had attempted to conduct such tests when they realized that the police scientists had not found a group, they would have been probably unsuccessful. The sample would almost certainly have been too small for *two* such tests, and the Rhesus factor – important in this case – would almost certainly have been lost because of the passage of time.

We do not know from the evidence presented to the Court whether tests for grouping the blood under the victim's fingernails were even made. The question was not asked in Court. But Beattie's counsel would have had to accept whatever answer was given him anyway. The police scientists took two months to prepare their forensic report. Only then could the defence counsel have been alerted that he should conduct tests of his own. But some of the samples were by then destroyed and others too old for proper tests to be made.

Fibres were also found on Margaret's fingernails. Hairs and fibres were also collected from the front of Margaret's jacket and the legs of her trousers. All we can say of these hairs and fibres is that they did not match anything that came from George Beattie. But did they come from Margaret herself, or members of her family? No one seems to have checked this even though it is routine procedure. Of course, they may well have come from her murderer – but if Beattie's counsel had tried to make the necessary eliminations he would not have been able to produce hard evidence. All the clothing in the McLaughlin household would have changed so much that the tests would be invalid. Once again, where police investigation was insufficient, events denied Beattie a chance to get at the truth.

Beattie's lawyers could well feel that they had cause for complaint in being so poorly served by the police. They were feeling sore about the conduct of the case from the first day. It is not normally regarded as necessary to interview a man after he has been charged and before he has had the benefit of legal advice. George Beattie was not only interviewed, he was taken down to the scene of the crime after being charged – passing his solicitor's office on the way!

The easy answer to allegations that Beattie was denied certain rights during the events leading up to his trial is that 'he had his day in Court'. Certainly his counsel had the chance to ask all the questions which remained unanswered from the police investigation. But whether he would have got any answers at all is questionable. As an extremely experienced barrister he was probably well aware that he might appear to be attacking the competence of the police in a desperate effort to save a guilty man. It is not surprising therefore that he chose the tactics that he did.

Later research such as ours was severely hampered by those tactics, but there were also certain incongruities within the evidence not directly concerning Beattie which we found difficult to resolve. The most puzzling of these centred on the question of when Margaret's body was found.

At first it seemed that there was no doubt about this: Margaret was found by Inspector Harry Robson at 2.58 p.m. on the Saturday afternoon. That was the story given in Court and what Harry Robson told us himself. We have no reason to doubt his truthfulness.

But the first witness in the trial, Margaret's mother, seemed to be suggesting something different.

Q.: Were you told the following day the news of Margaret?
A.: About half past eleven.
Q.: What were you told?
A.: About Margaret being dead.

Could that possibly have been at 11.30 on the Saturday night? By then the entire neighbourhood knew of Margaret's death. Her sister and brother had formally identified her body in the mortuary at 7.45 p.m. and the police were already beginning their initial door-to-door inquiries. Margaret's sister Jane also recounted to the Court how she had phoned everyone she could think of in an effort to find her sister. She said: 'In the early morning I phoned a friend of mine ... and between that and the next morning at twelve o'clock it was just a continuous phoning of friends, relations, any possibility of where she could have been.' Did Jane really stop phoning at noon on the Saturday? If so, why? Margaret's body was not found until 2.58 in the afternoon.

We believed that any idea that Margaret's body had actually been found earlier than 2.58 p.m. was highly unlikely. But we made inquiries. The McLaughlins' next-door neighbour remembered very well when she had heard of Margaret's death. She had been about to leave to visit her mother in the neighbouring village of Wishaw where her daughter was staying. She remembered knowing the news when she arrived in Wishaw in the morning. We suggested that the morning in question would be the Sunday morning, but she denied this. On the Sunday she had stayed at home to stop the paper boy delivering the newspapers to the McLaughlin home. She had been asked to do this by Margaret's brother.

We now began to wonder where the reporter had got the information published in the *Glasgow Herald* on the Monday morning, for 'a staff reporter' had written: 'Her body was found by two policemen on Saturday morning'. The *Sunday Mail* had already printed a different version of the story: 'The body was discovered after an all-night search which began on Friday. She was found by a passer-by who was on his way to Carluke station.'

Finally we talked to someone very close to the McLaughlin family who confirmed the story. When he learned that we were making a television film about the case he asked us not to reveal his identity. He is, however, one of the most respected figures in the Carluke area. He told us:

I would suggest that was certainly Saturday morning at half past eleven, because it was around noon that I was down in that area. You know I couldn't actually pinpoint the time, but it was certainly around about twelve o'clock.

Q.: But were you in the [McLaughlin] house round about noon on the Saturday?

A.: I was in the house up to ten times over the week before she was buried.

Q.: But on the Saturday, the first time.

A.: I was certainly in the house.

Q.: And you reckon about noon?

A.: Yes, it was before the Highland Games began, because I remember meeting one of the policemen, just before I met Jane [Margaret's sister] and I said to the policeman, 'Any word about Margaret McLaughlin?' 'Yes,' he said, 'they found her body.'

Q.: Which policeman was this, somebody on the case?

A.: The fellow was called Dunphy.

Q.: And the games, as I recollect, started about one-thirty?

A.: I think they started at either one or one-thirty. There were certainly bands and so on warming up.

This information was doubly strange to us. Not only did it confirm the story that Margaret's body had been found in the morning, but it added the name of a policeman to the case – a policeman who did not appear in the evidence. This would not be so odd if it were later in the police investigation, but few policemen were involved in the initial search for the body and, if the Court evidence was to be believed, we knew the names of all of them.

We eventually traced the Police Constable Dunphy mentioned in the interview. Now in Glasgow, he said: 'I couldn't pinpoint or tell you the time at all. I was engaged actually at the Highland Games that day, and I obviously heard it there.'

At this point we stopped asking when the body of Margaret McLaughlin was actually found. Like so many parts of the case of George Beattie, we do not know what the truth is. But we could not see how the outcome of this line of research could affect the case against Beattie either one way or the other. Perhaps the significant point of the whole exercise is that we became so suspicious of so many parts of this case where routine procedure had not been followed, or routine answers had not been given, that we were willing to follow up the most hare-brained ideas such as this one.

Sceptics about this case claim that the idea that Margaret McLaughlin died at 10 o'clock or later on the night in question is another hare-brained idea. In fact the forensic evidence supports this idea more than the theory that she died at 8 o'clock. That theory is not supported by any forensic evidence. The pathologists gave a range of error in their estimates of several hours. But the question remains – if she died later, where had she been?

We do not know the answer to that question. But we do not believe that simply because no one has come forward and admitted seeing Margaret after 8 o'clock, no one saw her. No investigation was ever made to ascertain Margaret's whereabouts after 8 p.m. on the night she died, so much of the elimination which could have been made was never even begun.

We believe that her whereabouts after 8 p.m. may account for one of the enigmas of the crime. Margaret left her home for the last time with some £35 in her purse – yet the purse found in the glen contained £15. It seems inconceivable that a thief would have taken £20, including all her small change, and left £15 by the body of the girl he had just murdered. It seems more reasonable to assume that Margaret spent the £20 somewhere. But where?

Margaret was a very decent and dependable girl. She obviously missed the train that night, even though she had left home early enough to catch it. In such circumstances she would have probably waited at the station and telephoned home from the phone box near the station, so that her future sister-in-law could be alerted that she would be late. That she did not do so indicates that she must have been somewhere where there was no telephone.

She was attacked in the glen, and there is no indication from the post mortem that she had been attacked or restrained before the attack in the glen. So if she died at 10 o'clock or later she must have been somewhere where she was not in any particular danger. With Margaret, this would mean that she was with someone she knew well. The McLaughlin girls were always very careful and went around in twos whenever possible.

Because the police did not find the bracelet in the glen and because the motive for the attack does not appear to be robbery (her engagement ring was not touched), it is possible that she lost, or gave away the bracelet wherever she was before 10 o'clock. This was perhaps the same place where she spent – or gave away – the £20 from her purse.

Wherever she was, it seems that she was in no danger until she went back home through the glen. At that point a madman took her young life in a most vicious way. That madman is probably still free to kill again, while George Beattie serves his life sentence.

4

The Road to Freedom

Should any of our readers believe that the evidence now available in the cases of Margaret Livesey, Ernie Clarke and George Beattie will ensure their release and that all will be well, let us be the first to disillusion them. The work to bring about their freedom is only just beginning.

The television film of the case is merely the first step of a long journey. The part of television in the investigation and furtherance of the case is over. The research that lies behind the programmes is generally the key evidence which is presented to the Home Office; television itself is too simplistic a medium to make that presentation, and it has other objectives than simply those of righting wrongs. There are further reasons which make it impossible for us to make the main presentation of the case through television. It is a medium with immense power to persuade and its persuasive powers lie ultimately in the emotions and not in reason alone. No matter how hard we attempt to eliminate emotional appeal in the television series, we know that public reaction can be determined by the pictures we use. No better example can be found in our work than that of the pictures of Margaret Livesey. Two distinct types were available to us: family snaps in which she looked relaxed and happy, and press pictures of her during the investigation, in which she looked tense. The first set made her look 'nice'; the second set made her look 'hard'. We knew that whichever pictures we used would determine the attitude of many of our viewers towards her case. In the end we chose photographs from what we thought was the middle of the range in an attempt to remain neutral.

We are fully aware that those who have a vested interest in opposing our cases can always accuse television of unjustly using its influence on the masses to win the argument, and that it weights its evidence by the emotional overtones in its presentation. No matter how hard we try to remain neutral, we can always be accused of bias on these two points because we cannot prove that television has not had such an effect. So it is not the best medium to use in presenting rational argument at the level required to impress the Home Office and the Court of Appeal.

We have already identified one slight emotional reaction against our programmes. Some of the many letters that arrived in our office claimed that we had not presented the prosecution side of the case. This is simply not so. The prosecution case is presented in all our programmes, all the main points are put with what we hope is the full strength of the original argument. We conclude that some members of the public are emotionally reluctant to believe that so many people can be in British jails unjustly; yet we have presented only six cases gathered from the thousands of cases in our courts over the last ten years.

Emotion should never affect arguments such as these. Our work is therefore passed back to the Justice organization which supplied the original research and advice. Its members have immense legal knowledge and the experience of twenty-five years of arguing cases of miscarriages of justice. It is they, often in conjunction with the original trial solicitors and barristers, who present the petitions to the Home Office. Members of Justice deal with Members of Parliament, who raise questions in the Commons about the cases. They argue such points as are necessary along the way – that the original police force should not be used to re-investigate a case, for instance. They produce legal arguments that our evidence is technically 'new' evidence – a requirement of the Court of Appeal. Ultimately, if a petition fails, they consider alternatives, such as taking the case to the European Court, or to the Ombudsman on the grounds that Government departments concerned have been maladministered.

These are all vital parts of a process to which television cannot contribute. As journalists we must earn our living by making other films or researching other stories. We have a natural interest in developments, and a professional interest in our own position, but our active participation declines almost to the role of being witnesses.

The efforts of Justice on behalf of the people who featured in our first series produced impressive results. All of those people are now free. What will happen to those featured in our second series may be judged from the experience of the first series. Tom Sargant, former Secretary of Justice, was responsible for the work and the discussions with the Home Office on those cases; he now explains what happened to them.

Mervyn Russell

The quashing by the Court of Appeal of Mervyn Russell's conviction for the murder of Jane Bigwood was heralded by one of the largest throngs of reporters and cameramen I have seen in Fleet Street. They seemed to have only one thought in mind – to get him to tell them how he felt about his release from prison. They seemed to know or care very little about how such a monstrous travesty of justice had occurred, or about Russell's seven years of torment and unheeded protests, or the amount of work and scheming that had gone into securing his release. All this has now to be told.

On the night of 21 October 1976 at about 8.40 p.m. Jane Bigwood, a young art student at Goldsmith's College, was found stabbed to death in her third floor flat in Speedwell House, a dilapidated block of flats in Deptford, occupied mainly by squatters. She was a gentle loner and, for reasons which could never be established, she had become fearful of an attack on her life. It could be that she had come to know more than she should about drug-trafficking in the flats.

Her killer was disturbed by a friend who called on her and who saw him go into her back room which faced the other three sides of the block. A man who lived in the opposite block saw him sitting astride the window ledge and testified that he was wearing a waistcoat with a shiny back and a buckle. He then dropped 28 feet to the ground below and made off. A cluster of hairs was found in Jane's closed hand, of which four were dark and the rest colourless, which prompted the police to advertise for a man with grey hair. The murder weapon – a $5\frac{1}{2}$-inch sheath knife – was found in the flat and the police distributed posters with a drawing of it.

Jock Russell was a drifter with a record of petty offences who lived in the same block with two friends and two dogs. He recognized the knife as having belonged to him and went to the police to identify it. It had been in his possession on the morning of the murder but he foolishly told the police that he had lost it some days earlier. When the truth came out he could only plead that it was a communal knife and that the murderer must have broken into his flat and taken it. So Russell inevitably became the prime suspect.

Apart from his ownership of the knife and his lie about it, two other matters were held against him. He had been seen in the area of Speedwell House about half an hour before the time of the murder; later this served to confirm his alibi. He had been recounting gory details of Jane's wound which he could have learned about from the sister of a police officer who had been to her flat.

But, far more serious for him, he had been involved on the night before the murder in some horseplay with his two flatmates. One of them had been firing off an air-pistol and to make him keep quiet Russell had poked at him with his knife through his sleeping bag. He did not injure him in any way but the police charged him with attempted wounding and the trial Judge insisted on both charges being tried together.

On the other hand, Russell had what should have been regarded as an unassailable defence not only by the jury but by the trial Judge and even the prosecution. He had an alibi that was without flaw if it had been objectively examined. He had been drinking with his two flatmates at a pub just off Deptford High Street. Just after 8 p.m. one of his dogs had fouled the saloon floor. He apologized to the landlord, left the offending dog with his friends, and took his other dog for a walk. Two girls who had seen him at 8.15 p.m. said that he was watching his dog. He returned to the pub at 8.55 p.m., unruffled and in the same clothes as he had left it. To have been the murderer he would have had to go to his flat, change his clothes, put on a waistcoat he did not possess, commit the murder, go back to his flat, change back into his normal clothes and return to the pub – all in the space of around forty minutes.

There were two other clear pointers to his innocence. A parachute expert gave evidence at the trial that 75 per cent to 80 per cent of his trained men would have been injured by falling from the third-floor window. Russell's ankles had in fact been fractured eighteen months earlier but this could not be adduced in evidence as the hospital records could not be found. But the most disturbing aspect of his conviction was that the Home Office forensic expert, Dr Wilson, gave evidence at his trial that none of the hairs found in Jane Bigwood's hand came from Russell's head. This was to become a dramatic and decisive issue in his final and successful appeal. At his original appeal the Court had found nothing unsafe or unsatisfactory about his conviction. He was not even given leave to appeal.

In the course of his trial Russell had tried without success to point the finger of suspicion at a Hungarian called Michael Molnar. Molnar lived in the flat of two of Russell's friends, Richard Tribe and Norma Fitzgerald. He was a diabetic and had gone off when the police started making inquiries, leaving all his injection equipment behind. On being questioned about him, a police officer told the Court that he had been found dead in the street six months before the trial, but this was all he knew, except that he had grey hair. Russell told the Judge that Molnar wore a waistcoat with a shiny back, but the Judge told the jury that he had produced no evidence to support this. The two men were in fact well acquainted as Molnar had been to Russell's flat to repair his television sets and would have known about the knife.

Russell's plight was first brought to my notice by a member of the Board of Visitors at Wormwood Scrubs, who came and pleaded with me to try to do something about it. This turned out to be a long and difficult process. His solicitor, Michael Burdett, and his junior counsel, Edmund Lawson, were as helpful as they could be, but his appeal had been dismissed and there was no new evidence to put to the Home Office. Russell himself was a bad correspondent and rarely replied to my letters. After a long delay a barrister member of Justice came to my assistance, analysed the whole of counsel's notes and prepared a long memorandum about the case. But this led nowhere except to the conclusion that we had to find out something more about Michael Molnar.

The approximate date of his death was known and a search through the records at Somerset House enabled us to obtain a copy of his death certificate which showed his father to have been an Air Ministry official. Through this I obtained a copy of the coroner's report and of the medical record at the hospital where he had been treated after being picked up in the street in a coma. I also found out details of where he had been buried. None of this was of much help, but I did learn that the police had been less than frank about the circumstances of his death. They had been reported to Scotland Yard and conveyed to his parents.

I wrote twice to Richard Tribe, Molnar's flatmate, at his old address but received no reply. After some further delay I sought the help of the D.H.S.S., which agreed to forward a letter to him. He answered it immediately and at this point Peter Hill came on the scene. He went down to Deptford, found Tribe and his girl-friend, Norma Fitzgerald, and brought them to my office where they both swore affidavits. The main burden of them was that:

Molnar normally wore a waistcoat with a shiny back.
He had greying hair.
They had left him alone in their flat on the night of the murder.
He was a sinister character and gave Norma the creeps.
He claimed to have been a pilot and to have escaped from Hungary in a Russian plane.

Armed with this vital information I drafted a memorandum on the case, had it approved by Edmund Lawson and forwarded it with the affidavits to the Home Office in November 1981. In the meantime Peter Hill had made further extensive inquiries about him and discovered that he had a record of convictions for violence in the Bristol area, and was known to have psychopathic tendencies and to have been picked up three times in the street in a coma.

With my submissions to the Home Office I asked for an exhumation order in respect of Molnar and offered to pay for it. After a long delay I was told that this would not be granted as the hair exhibits had been destroyed. Professor Ralph Turner, one of the foremost forensic scientists in the U.S.A., was in London at the time. Peter Hill brought him to see me and he provided me with an opinion that a useful comparison could be made against Dr Wilson's notes and there was a reasonable chance that Molnar's hair would still be in good condition. To this the Home Office replied that he had been buried in a chipboard coffin and that they had been advised that the hair structure was likely to have been destroyed.

I have already mentioned the question of the fractures in his ankles Russell claimed to have sustained. We had tried very hard to obtain confirmation of this. All that Guy's Hospital could produce was a record of his having attended casualty complaining of tender ankles. They had been bandaged up and he had been given crutches. I questioned him about this and he gave me a detailed account of how he had been taken into the X-ray room by a coloured nurse and had later been told by her that he had a fractured tibia in one ankle and a fractured fibula in the other. These were medical terms which he could not have invented. I put this to the Home Office and they eventually agreed to have Russell X-rayed in Parkhurst Prison hospital. His claim was shown to be well-founded and the Minister agreed to refer his case to the Court of Appeal on the basis of the waistcoat and the fractured ankles, neither of which were guaranteed winners.

Fortunately for Russell, the House of Lords had recently decided that, on a reference by the Home Secretary, any matters relevant to the case could be raised and need not be restricted, as in the past, to the points mentioned in the Letter of Reference. It was this that opened the door to the new evidence about the handful of hairs. Russell was also fortunate in that Michael Burdett and Edmund Lawson were both dedicated to the success of the appeal and that of its own volition the Court appointed George Carman, Q.C., as leading counsel.

The vital break came when Dr Torre, the Home Office pathologist in the case, telephoned Peter Hill to tell him that he had just seen the repeat showing of part of the Russell film and that the evidence about the hair was all wrong. He had not been asked the questions he should have been asked. He was put into touch with Edmund Lawson and gave him the explanation of this, which he was subsequently to give at the Court of Appeal.

As the pathologist, his function was to examine the body and report on the nature of the wound and other relevant matters. He had taken the cluster of hairs out of Jane Bigwood's closed hand with a pair of tweezers and put them carefully into a polythene bag for transmission to the Forensic Science Laboratory. All the roots were aligned and the hairs had clearly been plucked from the head of Jane's killer. He had gone to the trial and given his evidence without having seen Dr Wilson's report or being told what she was going to say. He had not been asked about the alignment of the hairs and when he had given his evidence he was told that he could leave.

An affidavit was taken from him and duly filed with the Court. The investigating officer went to the forensic laboratory and found that the hair exhibits had not in fact been destroyed. The Lord Chief Justice required the Home Office to grant an exhumation order and it was found that Molnar's hairs were still in good condition. They had, however, been dyed black and it was possible only to establish that they had been grey.

While waiting for the appeal to come on, Michael Burdett had arranged for Russell to be examined by Dr Kool, the senior orthopaedic surgeon in the Army Medical Corps. He reported that his ankles had knitted sufficiently to have regained normal strength but he had discovered that Russell had a very rare condition of his right knee (a cyst cavity) which would raise his chance of being injured by the fall to 95 per cent. He gave evidence to this effect at the appeal, but Lord Lane took the strange view that this did not add anything to what had already been pleaded at the trial. He likewise dismissed the waistcoat on the ground that Russell could have had a garment that looked like one and the man who saw it could have been mistaken.

What happened to the polythene bag of hairs after it reached the forensic laboratory can only be a matter for speculation, but it appeared from Dr Wilson's evidence that by the time they reached her they had already been mounted on slides. She knew nothing about the alignment in which they had been found and when, at the trial, she was asked if she could be sure that they had all come from the same head she had in all honesty to say that she could not. This enabled prosecuting counsel to put to the jury the preposterous theory that Jane Bigwood could have scooped them up from the carpet in her dying moments. The Judge did not discourage it and the jury must have swallowed it.

In delivering judgement, Lord Lane went to great pains to dismiss all the other grounds of appeal and to exonerate from blame anyone who had played any part in obtaining the conviction and upholding it. Perhaps with greater justification, he was clearly anxious to avoid pointing a finger of guilt at a dead man. It was not until the last few minutes of a very long judgement that he found that Dr Torre's evidence was true and inescapable and that Russell's conviction must be quashed.

It seemed to many of us that Russell's already overlong torment was being unnecessarily prolonged in order that the image of English justice should not be tarnished. I had myself nourished the hope that the Director of Public Prosecutions, when he was informed of Dr Torre's evidence, would decide that it would be just and humane not to oppose the appeal, but this hope was soon dispelled when prosecuting counsel deployed every argument available to him in his efforts to prove that the conviction was safe and should be upheld.

Justice, however, was ultimately done and Russell found himself a free man once more. For a day he was news, and then he drifted back to the only place he knew – Deptford, where he had been unjustly accused eight years before. A B.B.C. camera team followed him for a few weeks to document his unusual circumstances. The resultant film was somewhat depressing.

In the eight years of his incarceration, Russell had become almost completely institutionalized. He could no longer act without the advice of others.

He had almost no money, no home and few friends. Those who greeted him in the local pubs seemed to expect that he would pay for the drinks. His family in Scotland, whom he had not seen for almost twenty years, now contacted him. They seemed willing to invite him back into the fold, but were somewhat taken aback by his conversation about murderers whom he had met and befriended in prison.

Russell decided in the end that he felt more at home in Deptford. He found a flat and then acquired a girlfriend. Even though he now had a firmer base in the neighbourhood, life was not easy. It was made little easier when he was granted a £15,000 interim payment as compensation for his years of prison. He became a target for all the burglars and con men in the area. He discovered too that he knew nothing of how to manage such a huge sum of money. After eight years in jail he did not know the value of groceries, never mind items such as a car which he had never before dreamed of buying but which now tempted him. He made several injudicious purchases – only to have them stolen by thieves.

In this respect Jock Russell is still awaiting justice, though there is nothing the courts can do about his plight. Prison took away from him the ability to handle his life – and his ability to handle even small amounts of money. He was then thrust back into society, given a huge amount of money and expected to carry on as if nothing had happened. Human beings are, unfortunately perhaps, not as adaptable as that.

John Walters

This was the second case in which almost everyone who had seen the film asked, 'How did it ever come about that he was found guilty?' For the man who had sexually assaulted Roselyne Auffret on a train travelling from Wimbledon to Waterloo in May 1973 was described by her, and by three railway employees who saw him board the train, as between 5 feet 8 inches and 5 feet 9 inches in height, of medium build and wearing a blue denim battledress jacket and jeans. John Walters is 6 feet tall, at the time of the crime he weighed 14½ stone and he did not possess any blue denim clothes.

He was taken in for questioning, despite these glaring anomalies, because he had convictions for exposing himself on trains. This was a weakness for which he was treated with considerable success, and he was working as a clerk in the D.H.S.S. office at Notting Hill Gate. He told the police that he was working there on the afternoon of the assault. His assistant at first confirmed this but later said she had been mistaken, and none of his other colleagues could remember him being there. All he could do was to protest strongly about an incident he recalled and which the B.B.C. were later able to verify.

The absence of a sustainable alibi made things very much easier for the prosecution. Miss Auffret was introduced to an identity parade and, after considerable hesitation, picked out John Walters. It was agreed at the trial that at one point she said, 'I don't know,' and that she had shaken her head three times before saying, 'I think that's him.' She was seen by Peter Hill and Martin Young in the course of their investigations and, although she maintained the genuineness of her identification, she told them that the day before the parade she had been shown a book of mugshots; an officer had later told her that Walters was among them. She also told them that she had recognized him in the parade by his large staring eyes, whereas she had described the eyes of her attacker as small.

Walters also maintained that the parade was unfair because he wore heavy-rimmed spectacles and the other persons on the parade were issued with National Health spectacles.

Of the three railwaymen, only one had said in his statement that he would be able to recognize Miss Auffret's assailant and, according to the Home Office, he had attended a parade on which Walters was standing and failed to pick him out. Walters recalls standing on a second parade but was told that it was in connection with other offences. British Transport police have told the Home Office that the defence was told about the result of this parade, but there is no record of it in the depositions as there should have been, and neither Walters's solicitor nor his counsel can recall it. Whatever the truth of the matter, the jury was kept in ignorance of this important element in Walters's defence.

The three railwaymen's statements were read to the jury, but for obvious reasons they were not called by the prosecution and, for less obvious reasons, were not called for the defence. That this was a grave mistake was made clear by the B.B.C. film, for when two of them were shown photographs of Walters they both emphatically said that he was not the man they had seen board the train, whom one of them described as 'little boy blue'.

Any layman who believes that justice is related to truth would naturally assume that all the above matters, which had not been before the jury, would be regarded as new evidence by the Home Office and put on to the scales; but its strict rules decreed otherwise.

With the identification evidence open to serious doubt and the descriptions greatly in Walters's favour, the prosecution case clearly needed strengthening. The police searched Walters's flat. They could find no jeans but took away a pair of green corduroy trousers and a normal length mauve-blue corduroy jacket. On Miss Auffret's clothes the forensic laboratory found twenty-eight fibres microscopically similar to fibres from Walters's jacket and trousers. This was truly astonishing because Miss Auffret's assailant had indisputably been wearing blue denims. The defence established that there could have been an accidental transfer when the exhibits were being handled and repacked before being sent for testing, but could take it no further. It was admitted that the transfer had only been one way.

Miss Auffret had described the attack on her in horrific terms. Her assailant had forced himself on her and when she resisted and screamed he had choked her with his hands until she passed out. When she came to, he had assaulted her again but stopped short of rape. He had suddenly broken off, told her he was sorry, and jumped off the train as it entered Waterloo Station. Walters had been charged with attempted murder, which was justified on the evidence, but the jury must have had doubts because they found him guilty, by a majority of eleven to one, only of the lesser charge of indecent assault. The trial Judge may also have had doubts, because he gave him a comparatively light sentence of four years.

From the moment of his arrest and after his conviction, Walters had strongly protested his innocence. Both before and after his trial he had tried in vain to obtain confirmation of his activities and the people he had met in the course of the fateful afternoon. Without legal help he sent in lengthy grounds of appeal that were turned down. The Court found nothing strange about the differences in description or the fibres from clothes the assailant could not have worn.

After the dismissal of his appeal he protested even more vehemently. He would not settle down and was moved from prison to prison. While in Reading he was found guilty of assaulting a prison officer, because, he alleged, he was not allowed to call as witnesses other prisoners who could have proved his innocence. Then, on 29 January 1976, he was visited for the second time by a psychiatrist from Broadmoor and committed to that institution as a criminally dangerous person under Section 72 of the Mental Health Act (1959).

Walters first wrote to me while his application for leave to appeal was pending and I found it impossible to give him any effective help. I subsequently obtained copies of his trial documents, and made some abortive inquiries on his behalf. Then, early in 1975, I compiled and submitted to the Home Office a six-page analysis of the evidence with a request for some specific inquiries to be made. In July 1975 the Minister of State, Alex Lyon, admitted in his reply that there was some new evidence, but said that it was not sufficient to justify a reference to the Court of Appeal. When Walters told me about his probable transfer to Broadmoor, I went to see him in Wormwood Scrubs and found him very worried but wholly rational. I could obtain no indication of the reasons for the Section 72 Order and there was no way in which it could be challenged.

In 1978 Walters wrote and told me that the physician in charge of his case (Dr Tidmarsh) was pressing him to admit his guilt and had made it clear to him that he would not be considered fit to be released until he did. I wrote to the physician protesting against this, saying what I have continued to maintain, namely that it was a violation of Walters's integrity to make him admit to a crime he had not committed as the price of his freedom. I received no reply and wrote to the Superintendent, sending him a copy of my memorandum, so that there could be no doubt about the strength of Walters's claim to have been wrongly convicted.

Early in 1980 he was granted a private hearing before a Mental Health Tribunal, at which he was represented by a trainee solicitor, Liz Goldthorpe, and a young barrister, Kevin Rafferty, who had espoused his cause. I was allowed to give evidence as to my belief in Walters's innocence and to say that I thought it was wrong to try to force him to admit his guilt, but I doubt if this made much of an impression on the tribunal. Dr Tidmarsh maintained the correctness of his approach and was helped by the emergence during the hearing of domestic and other difficulties which might be caused by Walters's release. In due course he was informed that the tribunal, which gave no reasons, had refused his application. He then set to work to obtain a public hearing. This took place in April 1981 and I was again allowed to give evidence. His new physician, Dr McGuire, was much tougher than Dr Tidmarsh had been. He invoked minor incidents in Walters's life and prison record as evidence of tendencies to violence and went so far as to say that he regarded him as mad, and therefore not safe to release, because he refused to admit his guilt. This provoked me to go further than I had at the private hearing. I told the tribunal why I believed in Walters's innocence and said that if he was considered mad because he would not admit his guilt, then I was also a candidate for Broadmoor.

An independent psychiatrist had submitted a favourable report and the tribunal was given assurances that a home and employment could be found for him, but this appeal was once again rejected.

When Peter Hill and Martin Young took up Walters's case, they consulted Dr David Crawford, a psychologist who had examined him in Broadmoor. He had put him through all the latest tests, including the viewing of violent and sexually stimulating films and found little evidence that he had interests in sexual violence or was aroused by aggressive sexual behaviour. He concluded that he should never have been convicted in the first place and that there was no evidence to justify his continued detention. My psychiatrist brother, William Sargant, the author of *Battle for the Mind*, has expressed the view that the attempt to force Walters to admit his guilt was not just bad psychiatry but misguided psychiatry.

During and after his trial, Walters had pinned his main hope on obtaining confirmation of an incident which had taken place in the D.H.S.S. office in the middle of the afternoon of the day of the assault. He had been on duty in the inner office when a claimant called Thomas Rochford, accompanied by a social worker, had arrived late for an appointment. The counter assistant refused to deal with his claim; he became furious and began to make a scene. The assistant came into the inner office and asked the supervisor, Graham Heard, to come and quieten him down. Under cross-examination at the trial, Mr Heard had confirmed that Mr Rochford had been late for an appointment, but the Judge had not mentioned this in his summing-up. Walters thought that the social worker came from a unit called the Blenheim Project. He had written to them but they had failed to give him the information for which he had asked.

Peter Hill set to work to trace the social worker, Janet Rose, and succeeded in doing so. She had married and lived in Maidenhead. She remembered having received an inquiry from the Blenheim Project and confirming to them from her diary that she had accompanied a claimant to the D.H.S.S. and that he had made a scene. This was an important breakthrough. Walters had not returned to the office on the following day and it was most unlikely that he could have found out about this from one of his colleagues. So Peter Hill brought Janet Rose into the Justice office to swear an affidavit and this, together with a transcript of the B.B.C. film and accompanying submissions, was duly forwarded to the Home Office.

The B.B.C. film was shown in April 1982 and about six months later a former member of the British Transport police telephoned the Justice office asking if he could come and talk to us about the John Walters case. He said that he had been troubled by the film but because of a drink problem had not been well enough to do anything about it. The story he had to tell was sensational. At the time of the Auffret case he had been a Detective Constable based at Waterloo station and, as he left the office one day, he had been told that the clothes had been rubbed together. He had left the force not long after for personal reasons and had no reason to think that the wrong man had been convicted.

This provided striking confirmation of what had been alleged and in part admitted at the trial, namely that both sets of clothes had been unpacked and repacked in the office by officers who were not wearing gloves and that there could have been an accidental transfer of fibres. It further shed new light on one of the major mysteries of the case, in that it explained how fibres from a mauve corduroy jacket and green corduroy trousers could have become deposited on Miss Auffret's clothes in the course of an attack by a man wearing a blue jacket and jeans. We could see no reason to doubt the truth of this story or the motive of this ex-policeman in coming to see us. I therefore arranged for him to swear an affidavit and forwarded it to the Home Office.

He was in due course called for interview by Chief Superintendent Woodman of the British Transport police. I was worried by this because this was the force that had obtained the conviction and had later reported unfavourably on my earlier representations. I therefore asked to be present at the interview. My fears turned out to be justified because it appeared to me from the outset that Mr Woodman's main concern was to discredit the former Detective Constable's memory of contemporary events and to pinpoint flaws in his character. His memory was faulty as to dates and the exact nature of a statement he had witnessed but he was emphatic that he had been told that the clothes had been rubbed together and that he had no axe to grind. Mr Woodman appeared to be satisfied, but I nevertheless had forebodings about the assessment of his evidence that would be conveyed to the Home Office.

I had further reasons for doubting the objectivity of Mr Woodman's investigations. He had not troubled to interview Walters or any of the three railwaymen or, so far as we knew, Graham Heard, Walters's supervisor; and when Peter Hill telephoned and offered to give him Miss Auffret's address in France, he told him he was not interested because he was satisfied that Walters had been rightly convicted. I was, however, so confident that Janet Rose's affidavit would establish the genuineness of Walters's alibi beyond reasonable doubt that I advised his solicitor not to press for another tribunal hearing for the time being.

I had not, however, reckoned with the ability of the Home Office officials to find reasons for rejecting my submissions. I had expected Mr Woodman to report unfavourably on the former Detective Constable's allegations and to advise generally that there were no grounds for regarding Walters as unsafe, but I was not prepared for the Machiavellian arguments by which Home Office officials were persuaded to regard Janet Rose's evidence as inconclusive.

She had sworn in her affidavit that she had accompanied Mr Rochford to the D.H.S.S. office on 10 May and that having consulted her diary she had confirmed this to her supervisor when she made inquiries of her in 1974 on behalf of John Walters. She also described the disturbance he had created. When, however, she was interviewed by Mr Woodman, she told him that she had not put Mr Rochford's name down. She had taken claimants to the office on two or three occasions and could only say that on at least one of these occasions the claimant had been Mr Rochford. Furthermore, the Minister's letter went on to point out, she had referred to an argument with a male member of staff; Walters to an argument with a female one. This appears to be a valid point. But if Mr Woodman had interviewed Walters and his supervisor, Graham Heard, as in fairness he should have done, he would have found a complete answer to it. Walters's account was that a female counter-clerk had come into the inner office and asked Mr Heard to deal with a claimant who was causing trouble while the social worker was sitting at the back looking amused. Mr Heard went out to deal with the claimant. This was the dispute in which Janet Rose became involved and there was thus no conflict in their stories. Finally, the letter maintained that Walters was in a position to know of Mr Rochford's habitual inability to keep appointments and of frequent altercations between claimants and clerks. This argument takes no account of the fact that Walters worked in the inner office and would normally have no reason to know what went on in the outer office.

The evidence of the former Detective Constable was judged to be 'of not much significance' on the basis of his faulty recollections and the accused officer's emphatic denials. All the other submissions, including the evidence of the railwaymen, were dismissed on the grounds that they were matters which had been decided by the courts or had been raised before.

The Home Office letter was received in April 1983 and I replied to it at length in September protesting strongly against the entrusting of the investigation to the British Transport police and against the spirit in which it had been carried out. I further submitted that any judicial tribunal would inevitably come to the conclusion that Walters and Janet Rose were describing the same happening. By the middle of December 1984 no reply had been received.

After the Home Office letter had been received preparations were put in hand for another application to a Mental Health Tribunal. A wealthy banker who had seen the B.B.C. film was so outraged by it that he offered to pay the fees for a top Q.C. In May 1983 the B.B.C. book *Rough Justice*, which contained a full account of his case, was published and shortly after this news was received that Walters was about to be released. He had been put in the charge of a new physician, who came to the conclusion that Walters was not a patient but a prisoner. This view had been pressed on him by nursing officers who had lived with Walters over the years, had seen the B.B.C. film and were satisfied that he was innocent and thought it was degrading for them to play the role of prison officers.

Walters was told to pack up his belongings and his father was asked to confirm that he was ready to take him into his home. But the decision was almost immediately countermanded by higher authority. At the end of October an independent psychiatrist from Maudsley Hospital was called in for consultation and on 15 November John Walters was unconditionally released. Throughout his stay in Broadmoor he had received no treatment for the alleged violent tendencies which had caused him to be sent there. Either he had never been deluded or within a matter of weeks he had miraculously been restored to sanity.

On his release Walters found it difficult to cope with his freedom in a changed world. His prospects of finding a job were remote, so to regain his social confidence he joined the local bridge club. While in Broadmoor he had kept his sanity by running round the grounds, so he trained for the London Marathon and performed creditably. To his bitter disappointment, his recent application for a computer training course has been turned down because he is too old. He is a free man but the stigma of his conviction has not been removed and he has no immediate prospect of obtaining any compensation.

Michael and Patrick McDonagh

The case of Michael McDonagh and his son Patrick was by no means as straightforward as those of Mervyn Russell and John Walters; nor were their convictions so clearly ill-founded.

The McDonaghs lived in Moss Side, Manchester; the following events took place in early 1973:

After a heavy bout of drinking they had gone with Michael's wife, Rose, to the house of Mr Agbai, where Michael's brother Francis had an upstairs room. Their declared intention was to have it out with Francis over a family fight and a slur which he had cast on Rose's moral behaviour. They all went round to the back door, but Mr Agbai shut them out. Patrick then went round to the front of the house, took a screwdriver from his van and prised open the front door. He rushed upstairs and encountered Francis and his common-law wife, Maureen, who had come out of their room when they heard the commotion outside the back door. He jabbed first at Maureen and then at Francis, drawing blood from his forehead. At this stage, the prosecution alleged, Michael and Rose broke into the house and helped Patrick to drag Francis down the stairs. Michael then stabbed him with a small thin-bladed knife that penetrated the heart wall, causing profuse internal bleeding. Despite this handicap, Francis displayed extraordinary energy. The prosecution said that a frantic fight continued until they got to the bottom of the stairs. Mr Agbai pushed the three McDonaghs out of the front door and Francis, bleeding from the forehead, dashed into a ground-floor room occupied by a coloured man, Jasper Allen, and his girlfriend, Mary Mullen. He rushed straight for the front window, picked up an old television set from a chair that barred his way and threw it on to the bed.

Jasper Allen, angered by this intrusion on his privacy, grabbed Francis by his arms, Mary Mullen ran to the next room and called for another coloured man, Isaac Panton, to come and help. They both fought with Francis and when they left the room he was lying on the floor. Mr Agbai had called the police and when they arrived and searched the house, Francis had disappeared and his body was not discovered until the following day when Sheila Eccleston, Isaac Panton's girlfriend, found it on the roof of an outhouse. To reach this he would have had to crawl up the stairs into the bathroom, climb out of the window and slide down a drainpipe. Dr Alan Bernstein, a consultant physician, told the jury that this would have been possible because the wound was small and would have tended to close up; this would minimize the internal bleeding for a few minutes.

Before the body was found the police treated the matter as a domestic affray, but it had now become a murder. Rose and Patrick had been allowed to go by the police. They had gone off to Birmingham on a business matter and were picked up as they returned to Manchester on the following day. Michael had been arrested outside the house in a drunken state. He appeared at the Magistrates' Court on the following day to answer two minor charges but was re-arrested on his way back to Mr Agbai's house to find out what had happened. Mr Agbai, Jasper Allen and Mary Mullen had told the police that Michael had been involved in the fight and that Isaac Panton and Sheila Eccleston had disappeared.

After they had been questioned, Michael, Patrick and Rose were all charged with murder. When they came to trial in October 1973 Rose's counsel submitted that there was no case to go to the jury and the Judge discharged her. Certainly if she had gone to prison there would have been no one to look after her children. Patrick admitted entering the house and stabbing at Francis's head with the screwdriver, but denied any responsibility for or knowledge of the fatal wounding. Michael vigorously denied that he had ever entered the house and has continued to do so until this day. This made him a very difficult client to defend. No one had actually seen him stab Francis and no knife was found on him or in the house. But, in addition to the evidence of Jasper Allen and Mary Mullen that he was involved in the fight, and appeared to have some kind of weapon, Mr Agbai had told the police that he had cried out at the foot of the stairs, 'Where's my knife,' and he added at the trial that as Francis came down the stairs he had cried out, 'I'm a killed man.' The fact that Michael and Patrick had both been assessed as illiterate dullards with mental ages of eleven made them easy game for the prosecution.

What the police did not realize was that Mr Agbai's house was used for the purposes of prostitution and that its inmates, including Isaac Panton and Sheila Eccleston, would be anxious when it was their turn to be questioned, to protect each other and lay the blame for Francis's death on the intruders. This effectively prevented the emergence before the jury of the scenario which Peter Hill and Martin Young were later able to piece together.

Some pointers to it had emerged before the trial but had been ignored because they did not fit into the prosecution scenario. All three accused said independently that they had seen a coloured man with a knife or weapon of some sort on the ground floor of the house. Rose told her solicitors that she had told the police that a coloured man had struck Francis and knocked him straight down. The police went to elaborate lengths to kill any such story. All the thirteen officers who had been involved in the investigations made statements to the effect that they had heard no mention of a coloured man and a knife.

More significantly, Mary Mullen, the girl living in the front room where the fight with Francis had taken place, had an access of conscience. She had made her statement to the police on 1 March 1973, but early in April she left Manchester and returned to Glasgow where, free from the influence of her Manchester associates, she went to the police and told them that she had heard from Sheila Eccleston that Isaac Panton had confessed to killing Francis. He had come back into Sheila's room after the fight with Francis and said something to the effect that he had just killed a man or just stabbed a man.

Unfortunately for Michael and Patrick, this was inadmissible hearsay unless Sheila Eccleston was willing to confirm it. It was put to her when she gave evidence, but Panton was her man and she had every motive to deny it. The trial Judge brushed aside any suggestion that there was any evidence that pointed to Panton. Michael and Patrick found it impossible to overcome their credibility problem and the jury had no difficulty in finding them both guilty of murder. Their applications for leave to appeal out of time were refused and, with the help of Peter Thompson of the Hulme Civil Rights Group and Mr Robert Lizar, a neighbourhood lawyer, they embarked on a long campaign to prove their innocence.

The basis of the petition that was ultimately to be presented to the Home Secretary was Mary Mullen's statement to the Glasgow police, but two other incidents had occurred that incriminated Panton. A few months after the murder Francis's widow, Maureen, went into a club in Moss Side and saw Isaac Panton standing at the stereo with some coloured friends. She told Peter Thompson that she heard him say, 'It was me that done her man.' She had called the police, but they appear to have taken no action and they later denied any record of the incident. Peter Thompson also learned from Mrs Agbai that when the police had later searched Isaac Panton's room some time after the trial they found a knife with a sharp, thin blade, but again they denied having any record of this. Provided with these denials, the Minister of State at the Home Office, Leon Brittan, could only advise George Morton, the McDonaghs' M.P., that he could find no grounds which would justify the Home Secretary in taking any action.

This was in July 1979. For some time before this I had received distress signals from Long Lartin prison and had been in touch with Robert Lizar but there was nothing I could do to reinforce the submissions. I did, however, ask Sir Brian MacKenna, a retired High Court Judge, to look at the papers then in my possession and he provided me with a helpful note in which he stressed the important part that Mr Agbai's evidence had played in convicting Michael but strongly criticized the reasons for the Home Office's rejection of the evidence that pointed to Isaac Panton.

When, early in 1981, Peter Hill came and asked me to suggest suitable cases for a series of documentary films, the McDonaghs were an obvious first choice. He has told at some length in *Rough*

Justice the story of how he and Martin Young set about their investigations, so I need only summarize them briefly. They first traced Mary Mullen, who confirmed the truth of the statement she had made to the Glasgow police and told them that she had been threatened about it by Isaac Panton and Jasper Allen. Then, after months of frustrating searching, they found Sheila Eccleston, who had moved south, changed her way of life, and borne Isaac Panton a son. She was, however, visiting an aunt in Liverpool and Peter Hill called to see her and took her out to lunch. After he had gained her confidence she told him that on the night of the murder Isaac Panton had joined in the fighting; he then returned to her room and told her that he had stabbed the Irishman in the hall. She added the information that his knife had a white handle. They had then gone off to the house of a girl called Clara Esty.

After going through the story with her again they exchanged addresses. He got in touch with her again in Bristol in January when, after hesitation, she agreed to be interviewed by Martin Young for a B.B.C. film on the understanding that her contribution would not implicate Isaac Panton in the killing of Francis McDonagh. Her account of this was, however, taped and an agreement signed that it would not be disclosed to authority without her consent. It was clear that she was scared of reprisals both from Isaac Panton and the police.

During his talks with Sheila, Martin Young was surprised and excited to learn from her that her friend, Clara Esty, had been visiting her on the night of the murder and was in her room when Isaac Panton was called to help Jasper Allen in his fight with Francis. Sheila provided a clue as to where she might be found and she was eventually traced to Stoke, where she was living with her Jamaican husband. When Peter Hill and Martin Young first called on her and explained the object of their visit, she was reluctant to talk to them, but by the time they returned on the following day she had been advised by her husband to tell them the truth as she had told it to him.

Her story was devastating:

I saw Isaac come into Sheila's room and he had blood over his coat and hands. I'm not quite sure of his words but he was telling his lady that he'd just killed someone outside. Then he just went to pieces and so did she, you know, and she said, 'What can we do? And what are you going to do?' And I sort of said, 'Well, go and wash your hands and take your bloody coat off, like, and you know you can't go on the streets like that.' He looked very frightened and he was shaking. He had blood on his coat and his hands and just a little on his face. I heard him tell Sheila that he had just hurt someone, and he started to panic. Sheila started to panic. I was frightened. He took his coat off, 'cos it's got blood on it, and he put something else on and we went out through Sheila's kitchen, out of the house round to my place.

This was a sensational story and the highlight of the B.B.C. film. It was clearly true because it was essentially the same story that Sheila Eccleston had already told which was attributed in the film to 'another witness'. Moreover there had been no communication between them.

As the result of what Sheila Eccleston had told them, Peter Hill and Martin Young called on Detective Chief Inspector Griffiths, who had been in charge of the case but had since retired. They spent three hours with him and he told them that since the murder he had taken a close interest in Isaac Panton. He had been charged with offences involving a knife and one of his practices, as a pimp, was to hide in a wardrobe while his girl was entertaining a client and to jump out and threaten him with a knife. Mr Griffiths described the knife as a penknife which would have matched the wound in the heart of Francis McDonagh and ended with the words, 'Isaac Panton got away with murder.'

After the interview with Clara Esty, they approached him again and took him and his wife out to dinner. He read the whole transcript of the interview and accepted it as a valid explanation of how Francis McDonagh had met his death. It was made clear to him that there was no suggestion that the police had been at fault because, in order to protect Panton, all the occupants of the house had conspired to give false evidence. On this assurance, he agreed to be interviewed on the following evening, provided his former employers raised no objection. During the day Martin Young had a telephone conversation with Chief Superintendent Forster of the Manchester police, who told him that as Mr Griffiths was retired he was free to say anything he liked about the case.

When, however, the B.B.C. team arrived at his house, he told them that the interview was off and, when pressed, mentioned police pension rights, a Home Office inquiry, possible injunctions and the B.B.C.'s public duty to tell the police everything they knew. He had clearly been warned off.

On the day after the programme was screened it was attacked by the Manchester police. Chief Superintendent Forster issued a long statement to the effect that Clara Esty was not a new witness because she had been interviewed by the police during the investigation and had made a statement which had been forwarded to the Director of Public Prosecutions. He further said he was satisfied that the McDonaghs had been rightly convicted.

Subsequent to this there was a lengthy exchange of letters between the Greater Manchester police and the B.B.C. on some of the points raised in the programme. An impasse was reached and, in an attempt to resolve it, Peter Hill went to see Mr Forster in his personal capacity. It emerged that the crucial information he required was the name of the second witness and the whereabouts of Clara Esty. Peter Hill rightly told him that he could not provide it because of the undertakings he had given. He offered his cooperation but Mr Forster was not interested. He said it was his opinion that the McDonaghs were guilty and that was the end of it.

I must add here that in my view Peter Hill's reactions to Mr Forster's request were wholly correct. In particular, the unscreened interview with Sheila Eccleston posed a difficult problem. It provided vital confirmation of the new evidence obtained from Clara Esty but it laid her open to the charge of having given false or misleading evidence at the trial. In the light of Mr Forster's public attack on the B.B.C. programme I would have expected the Home Office to entrust the investigation to another police force and to enter into negotiations with the McDonagh's solicitor for the granting of immunity to her if she was prepared to come forward and be interviewed.

No such approaches were received and in early July Peter Hill received an agitated telephone call from Sheila Eccleston. It was after midnight and she was scared out of her wits. Some policemen from Manchester had visited her and threatened her with nine years in jail. They had questioned her about her interview with the B.B.C. and mentioned perjury, accessory and conspiracy. He assured her that he had kept to his agreement and told her that if the police returned she should refuse to talk to them.

About a week later he received a telephone call from Clara Esty. She was not as distressed as Sheila Eccleston but she was frightened and worried by the hostility of the Manchester police who had called on her.

In October Peter Hill and I decided to go and see Sheila Eccleston and I took from her an affirmed statement describing her interview with the Manchester police. The substance of it was that the officer in charge had told her that he knew she had committed perjury at the McDonagh's trial and that he could get her nine years' imprisonment unless she went along with him and told him what he wanted her to say for him to put in his report to the Home Office. He had asked her if she was 'the second witness' mentioned in the programme and she told him she wasn't. He then asked her a series of questions about her dealings with Peter Hill in an effort to extract something from her which would discredit him and accused her of conspiring with him. When the officers left they gave her twenty-four hours to think about it but when they returned the next day she refused to see them.

After we had taken this statement Peter Hill had another meeting with her, in the course of which she released him from his undertaking and gave him permission to make use of the transcript of her interview with him. I accordingly sent her statement and the transcript to the Home Office asking that the Manchester police should be taken off the investigation. I further suggested that they were guilty of conspiring to pervert the course of justice and that Sheila Eccleston's statement should be sent to the Director of Public Prosecutions. This met with no response.

Nine months later, in July 1983, I received a long letter from the Minister of State, Patrick Mayhew, turning down our representations. It commenced by explaining that the investigation had been entrusted to the Manchester police because there was no implied criticism of them in the B.B.C. film and that my complaints about the way it had been conducted had been taken into account. It then went on to give reasons why the evidence of the witnesses in the programme had been found unreliable. These I can only summarize briefly together with the refutations I subsequently made to them.

1. Miss Mullen, Jasper Allen and Mr Agbai have re-affirmed the truth of their original statements.

The Manchester police do not appear to have dealt with Mary Mullen's later statement to the Glasgow police.

2. Clara Esty made a statement during the original investigation saying only that Miss Eccleston and Mr Panton had visited her at home.

The making of this statement is disputed and will be dealt with in later paragraphs.

3. Miss Mullen and Mr Allen continue to maintain that Miss Esty was not in the house when the fight took place.

They would not have seen her because when she heard the fight she only went to the door of Sheila Eccleston's room and she had left through Sheila's kitchen at the back of the house.

4. When Miss Esty had been interviewed by Peter Hill and Martin Young she had told them that Mrs Agbai was in the house, whereas she was in Africa at the time.

If the Manchester police had consulted Mr Griffiths during their investigation, as they should have done, he could have provided an explanation. When Peter Hill showed him the transcript of Clara

Esty's interview, he raised this point and said that it would have been very easy for her to mistake Mr Agbai for Mrs Agbai because he was dressed in flowing tribal costume.

5. Sheila Eccleston had not told the police about Panton after the murder and had later told them that she was not the second witness.

After the fight she was understandably loyal to and frightened of Panton and when interviewed at Bristol she was under threat of imprisonment for perjury and conspiracy to pervert the course of justice.

6. Quite clearly, such a knife could not have inflicted the fatal wound.

Sheila Eccleston had described Panton's knife as a small penknife that he usually carried with him. This does present a problem, but Mr Griffiths had told Peter Hill that Panton's knife was a penknife which would have matched the wound in Francis's heart. It is also probable that she wanted to minimize the gravity of Panton's offence: she had been at pains to explain that it was an accident and not a deliberate killing.

7. In an addendum to Sheila Eccleston's affirmed statement, she had described a meeting with Mr Griffiths at Cheetham Hill police station three years after the trial at which he had said to her, 'You knew Isaac Panton had killed Francis, didn't you?' Mr Griffiths has denied this and Cheetham Hill police station had not yet been opened.

Had Mr Griffiths denied having told Peter Hill that Isaac Panton had got away with murder, which was related in 'Rough Justice' and has not been challenged? At the time there were two police stations that served the Cheetham Hill area.

At this point I can only leave it to the reader to assess the objectivity of the Manchester police investigation and their report to the Home Office.

On receipt of the Home Office letter, I decided to go and see Clara Esty and question her about the statement that had been invoked with such effect by the Manchester police. She was quite firm in her belief and memory that she had not made a statement.

Two or three hours after the fight, she had gone back to Mr Agbai's house with Sheila Eccleston and found the police there. The police wanted to know what they were doing and they told them that they had just come from the cinema and that it was the first time that she (Clara Esty) had come to the house. The talk lasted about three minutes and they let her go. She did not see Sheila after that night and after two or three days she left Manchester and went to stay with her parents in Stoke. She returned to Manchester about two months later. Sheila had gone away and Clara stayed with another friend in Longsight. She knew nothing about the murder until Peter Hill told her about it.

When the police came to see her at Stoke they produced what she and her husband both described as a small sheet of paper with some typing on it and her name typed at the bottom. She denied having ever signed such a statement. They said that they would come back the next day with an officer who could prove it, but they never did.

I sent the statement I had taken from her to the Home Office and asked them about the statement she was alleged to have made and they replied that they had seen it in the course of their study of the case. I pointed out that I needed to see a copy of it in order to establish Clara Esty's reliability as a witness and after some delay they obtained a copy from the Manchester police and sent it to me. It was, however, unsigned, the explanation being that the signed copy was not available. It consisted of one and a half pages and I could see no grounds for doubting its authenticity. It had been stamped with a serial number and marked 'omit' to indicate that it was not to be served on the defence. But it told a completely different story from that which had been told me by Clara Esty.

To begin with it was dated nearly six weeks after the murder and gave as her address her house in Manchester which she said she had vacated and given up shortly after the murder. It said that she remembered the man being found dead on the roof and that he had lived in a room she had once occupied. It said that on the day he was found dead she went round to see Sheila Eccleston but there were police officers outside the house who would not let her in. On the previous evening Sheila and Isaac Panton had come to her house because there had been fighting at Mr Agbai's house and she was frightened. Somewhat strangely it did not mention her visit to Mr Agbai's house on the night of the fight and her encounter with the police.

When I took the statement to her and challenged her with it, she denied having made it and both she and her husband said it was nothing like the statement the police had shown her in Stoke. She insisted that she had left Manchester long before the date of the statement and could not understand why the police should have been guarding Sheila's house on the day after the fight.

I duly reported this to the Home Office with the comment that I had not detected any attempt to deceive me. Whatever may be the truth about this statement it could not in my view affect the basic truth of the story that Clara Esty gave to Peter Hill.

In the meantime, and before replying to Patrick Mayhew's letter, I asked Sir Brian MacKenna to study all the available documents and assist me in making further representations. To satisfy himself as to the integrity of their investigations he exhaustively questioned Peter Hill and Martin Young and in a long memorandum he subsequently prepared for the Home Office he expressed the view that they were completely honest.

On the substantive issues of the case he proved beyond reasonable doubt that there had been no possibility of collusion between Sheila Eccleston and Clara Esty, that they had told similar stories and should therefore be believed. He then went on to reconcile their statements with other evidence in the case and to set out a satisfying scenario in relation to the wounds that Francis had received. The post mortem had shown that he had four wounds, viz:

1. A stab wound 6 inches deep in the heart, from which he had died.
2. A slash-type wound, 2½ inches long to the face.
3. and 4. Small slit-type wounds, ¾ inch and ½ inch respectively.

In his view, 3 and 4 must have been caused by Patrick. 2 was probably caused by Michael, despite his denial that he ever entered the house. 1, being the only stab wound, must have been the wound referred to by Panton when he said that he had stabbed or killed a man.

Sir Brian ended his memorandum with a strong plea that something should be done to free Patrick and Michael from the threat that if they became involved in any imprisonable offence they were liable to be recalled to serve their life sentence.

These further representations were delivered to the Home Office in October 1983.

Happily for Michael and Patrick, the Life Review Board took a more enlightened view of the matter and by September 1982, six months after the film had been screened, they had been released on parole, having served only eight years of the life sentences and having strongly protested their innocence throughout that time. A responsible member of the panel which recommended their release told me it had done so because it was satisfied that their protestations of innocence were well founded and that its reasons for believing this would have gone to the Home Secretary. As each panel is presided over by a High Court Judge and their release would have required the approval of the Lord Chief Justice and the trial Judge, it is not unreasonable to say that four members of the judiciary opened their eyes to the light where the Home Office, in deference to the Manchester police, had kept theirs shut.

In November 1983 the Parliamentary Under-Secretary of State, David Mellor, told me that he had been impressed by Sir Brian's memorandum and in January invited us to the Home Office to discuss with him all the issues. He expressed some doubts, which we shared, as to whether the two new witnesses would stand up to cross-examination. He further pointed out that, as Michael and Patrick had indirectly been responsible for Francis's death, it would be difficult for the Home Secretary to grant them a free pardon. He promised to write to us.

At the end of September 1984 we received the welcome news that the Home Secretary had agreed to send the case back to the Court of Appeal.

Miscarriages of Justice

I have been asked by my co-authors to contribute a chapter on the various types and causes of wrong convictions. My qualification for attempting this is that, as Secretary of Justice, I spent some twenty-four years dealing with a constant flow of letters from prisoners complaining that, in whole or in part, they had not committed the offence of which they had been convicted. I investigated a substantial proportion of them in depth and was in the unique position of being able to obtain transcripts and other trial documents, talk to prisoners and their families and consult defence solicitors and counsel. I also had the privilege of taking part in the deliberations of Justice committees composed of some of the most eminent lawyers of the day who critically examined every aspect of our criminal procedures, mainly from their own practical experiences. I can therefore say without hesitation that all the hazards of the accusatorial system I have described below have helped to bring about miscarriages of justice in one form or another and still continue to do so.

Whenever the story of a miscarriage of justice hits the headlines it automatically conjures up a picture of a man who was wrongly identified as a murderer or rapist or armed robber, and has thereby served a sentence of imprisonment for a crime he could not have committed. We are assured by the legal establishment and its supporters that these are exceptional cases and that there is no reason to be seriously concerned about the administration of justice in our criminal courts, or about the ability of the Court of Appeal and Home Office to remedy any mistakes made by the lower courts. This is a gross over-simplification, for miscarriages of justice take many forms and are far more numerous than anyone in authority is prepared to admit, or is in a position to estimate. Furthermore, the proportion of them that is susceptible to remedy by the Court of Appeal is minimal.

I can see no reason to doubt that the majority of them are due to the hazards of the accusatorial system, which does not pretend to be an objective inquiry into the truth. Its sole object is to prove to the satisfaction of the jury by the evidence put before it that the man in the dock has committed the crime of which he is accused. My late Chairman, Sir John Foster, used to describe it as a gladiatorial combat in which, subject to some rules of fair play, counsel on both sides try to outwit or outflank each other by such verbal skills or stratagems as are available to them – the prize being the mind of the jury. In such a combat it is only too easy for the truth to be the main casualty. There is no obligation on either side to produce all the available evidence. Few of the safeguards have statutory force and their observance depends to a great extent on the integrity and right use of discretion on the part of those engaged in the process at every stage.

The more straightforward miscarriages are those in which the accused man has consistently maintained that he was nowhere near the scene of the crime. He has been convicted because he was identified by an honest but mistaken witness or through some irregularity in the conduct of the identification parade. His alibi witnesses have been near relations who can be discredited by prosecuting counsel, or he was in bed with a girlfriend – something he may or may not want to disclose and which, whether true or false, would cut no ice with the jury. One of the more distasteful aspects of the accusatorial system is the way in which counsel and judges assume the right to brand family witnesses as potential liars. There are a number of other factors which may have brought about the downfall of the accused. For example, the police may have decided to bypass the rules and guidelines governing identification cases by refraining from putting him on an identification parade and denying that he asked for one. This enables them to play down the differences in descriptions and to procure or invent some kind of admission. There is then no need to call the eye-witnesses. Their statements only have to be read. The case then ceases to be an identification case and becomes a confession case in which the issue is whether the police evidence about the admission is believed by the jury.

This technique has become more prevalent since, following the report of the Devlin Committee, the Court of Appeal laid down stricter guidelines for trial judges in identification cases. When this report was published I took part in a television programme with the then Chairman of the Criminal Bar Association. I argued strongly in favour of a requirement of corroboration and was greatly embarrassed and puzzled when he opposed it. After the programme, I asked him why he had opposed it and he replied, 'Tom, you are too naive. As things are we stand a chance of challenging unsatisfactory identification evidence, but if there has to be corroboration, the police will invent it and our job will be much more difficult.' He was a good prophet but I doubt if he foresaw the way in which 'confessions' would be used to bypass the Court of Appeal guidelines, as they have in at least three cases in which I have been involved. What, for example, can be said about a case in which, on the strength of a repudiated confession, a giant of 6 feet 8 inches was convicted of raping a young girl. She and a friend who was with her had described the man's height by comparing him with their daddies – about 5 feet $8\frac{1}{2}$ inches. At the Court of Appeal, the confession carried the day. The Presiding Judge thought that it would have been quite easy for the girls to have misjudged the man's height.

Other means employed to secure convictions when the evidence is minimal are to adduce matching fibres or footprints, or to fail to test and report on forensic evidence which might point to someone else's guilt.

Once the jury has accepted and believed the prosecution evidence, there is no remedy for the wrongly convicted unless there have been some material irregularities or misdirections on the part of the Judge, or after an appeal has been dismissed, or it can be proved beyond the shadow of a doubt, by new evidence, that they could not have been at the scene of the crime or that the vital evidence by which they were convicted was false. Examples of this are the Dr Clift cases in which the forensic evidence has been found to be unreliable.

Another category of doubtful cases is where the accused was at or near the scene of the crime and had every opportunity of committing it. Such cases occur under widely differing circumstances. The accused may have found the victim of a murder either inside or outside a house, reported it to the police, and found himself treated as a suspect; or he may have been the last person to see the victim alive. There may be no discoverable motive, but the law does not require a motive. He is questioned under pressure for three or four days. He may be frightened and weak-minded and eventually admit to the crime just to get out of the hands of the police or on a promise that they will not press a charge of murder. Or, among his persistent denials of guilt, some comments he is alleged to have made are interpreted as admissions. Other strategies sometimes used are to attribute to the accused in an interview knowledge of some aspects of the crime which they have in fact told him and this may not emerge later in Court; or to bring to Court another prisoner who, in return for a reduction in his sentence, is willing to testify to an incriminating conversation with the accused; or for a police officer to testify to conversations he has overheard between suspects in adjoining cells.

Another category embraces cases in which it is necessary to prove intent. These include intent to kill or cause grievous bodily harm, intent to defraud and intent permanently to deprive. In the majority of these cases there is very little factual evidence on which a jury can rely. Its members have to put themselves inside the mind of the accused at the time of the offence with the help of reported conversations, equivocal replies to police questions or accounts of the accused's behaviour after the event.

It is inevitable that, from time to time, juries arrive at the wrong verdict. How, for example, can they be sure that the accused intended to fire the fatal shot or knew that the gun was loaded or, in the case of a knifing, that the victim was not the attacker and that the accused did not react in a state of understandable panic, or was goaded to the point at which he lost his self-control. I have studied many cases in which, on an objective view, manslaughter would have been a fairer verdict than murder, and I have a strong impression that since the abolition of capital punishment juries are much less willing to give the accused the benefit of the doubt. Moreover, convictions for murder are now treated with much less seriousness by defending counsel and the Court of Appeal. In the days of capital punishment, the Court would automatically give leave to appeal and leading counsel would 'scrape the barrel' to find some valid grounds. But since it was abolished, unless leading counsel thinks that the summing-up was wholly unfair, the convicted will be left to fend for themselves. This is what happened in the cases of Margaret Livesey and John Walters whose convictions are, at the least, open to serious doubt. Where intent is the main issue, it is quite impossible to quantify the number of wrong verdicts that are reached. If a man protests from the beginning that he had nothing to do with a crime and goes on protesting to the detriment of his prospects of parole by hunger strikes or rooftop demonstrations, then he needs to be taken seriously. He can have no other motive than to prove his innocence, nor is it likely that, as authority is prone to allege, he is deceiving himself or hoping to deceive the Home Office in any subsequent investigation. On the other hand, it is not difficult for a man who had every intention of killing his victim or of causing him grievous bodily harm gradually to persuade himself that he had no such intent.

I must further mention those not uncommon cases in which a valid defence is undermined by overstrict rules of evidence. For example, if a man who has been fatally wounded either names or describes the assailant to those who come to his help, what is called 'a dying declaration' can only be admitted in evidence if it can be shown that the victim had a settled expectation of death. I have been involved in three cases in which a man not so named was convicted of murder. The outstanding one was that of the two

Jamaican brothers, Castin and Leathland Townsend. During a fight at a party they had gatecrashed, one of the guests was fatally stabbed. No one had seen the stabbing, but two guests who drove him to the hospital said that he had described Castin – the tall dark one – and two nurses and the doctor at the hospital made similar statements. Both men were charged with murder and at the trial the younger brother sought leave to call the evidence that clearly pointed to Castin. The Judge asked the doctor if he had told the victim that he was dying, to which he replied in terms, 'Don't be stupid, my Lord. No doctor ever tells a patient that he is dying.' The Judge refused to admit the evidence. Leathland was found guilty of murder and Castin was sentenced to four years imprisonment for causing grievous bodily harm. He later had an access of conscience and made a full sworn confession, first to me and then to Leathland's solicitors. This was sent to the Home Office which decided that a confession to a magistrate and a solicitor was not to be relied upon and insisted that Castin be interviewed by a police officer. As Castin had been released on home leave, I arranged for them both to come to a friendly solicitor's office. But neither of them turned up. I later learned that the officer, a Chief Superintendent from the Crime Squad, had called for Castin and told him that there was no need for him to go through with the confession and that, if he did, he could be charged with perjury at his trial. Despite further representations, Leathland had to serve over seven years before he was released.

A major hazard of the accusatorial system, both in single- and multi-defendant trials, lies in the field of forensic evidence in which the resources of the prosecution far exceed those available to the defence.

The collection and packaging and delivery of specimens and exhibits is entirely in the hands of the police, who hand it over to a Home Office forensic laboratory. In due course the report of the appropriate expert will be delivered to the defence solicitor, who can either accept the findings and conclusions or decide that they should be challenged. If he wants to have independent tests made, he has to find a recognized expert and either obtain authority for the necessary expenditure or take his chance that it will be allowed on taxation. If he does obtain authority, he cannot borrow the exhibits. His expert has to go and carry out his tests at the Home Office laboratory. This inevitably means that a large number of prosecution forensic reports go unchallenged. Apart from the cases in which Dr Clift was involved, there is no reason to think that the findings of the Home Office experts are not honest and reliable. They may, however, be inadequate or incomplete. For example, in the cases of George Beattie and Margaret Livesey, there was no proper examination of and report on the stomach contents, which was of vital importance in the determination of the time of death. In the Livesey case, the defence was not informed of any tests made on three packets of cigarettes and the cigarette stubs found in the room where Alan was killed. These could have pointed to a visit from someone. In the John Walters case, Miss Auffret's assailant was wearing a blue jacket and jeans, but I have been unable to obtain any information from the Home Office as to whether her clothes were tested for blue fibres and, if so, with what result.

In the case of Mervyn Russell the defence was greatly hampered by being unable to take part in testing the forensic evidence. It seems that only Dr Torre knew the hairs had their roots aligned when he took them out of Jane Bigwood's hand. But he did not know what evidence Dr Wilson would give and no one knew how the hairs had been handled on arrival at the laboratory. I was prompted by this, and by the case of John Walters, to recommend to the Home Office that, as a fixed rule, all exhibits should be sealed and handed direct to the forensic expert, and that the reports of the pathologist and forensic expert should be exchanged.

These are not the only hazards presented by police control over the collection and handling of forensic evidence. They can search the houses and cars of suspects and, if they are so minded, can plant what they want to find – especially where drugs are involved. What is perhaps more serious, they are under no statutory duty to look for forensic evidence which might help the defence, for example, fibres, fingerprints, footprints or soil correspondences.

Another general hazard is what are commonly known as 'verbals', i.e. alleged admissions or incriminating statements. Their admission as evidence without some kind of authentication has been condemned by the legal profession and by some members of the judiciary for as long as I can remember. They not only destroy the integrity of criminal trials, but give rise to long and costly Court battles over their validity or admissibility. A retired C.I.D. Inspector once explained to me how easy it was for two dishonest officers to 'stitch up' a suspect. After they had interviewed him, all they had to do was to get together and write up in their notebooks identical accounts of what they wanted to report to the Court. They would then agree in advance that, when they went into the witness box, they would deny that anything else of relevance was said in the course of the interview and thus could not be tripped up under cross-examination.

There are a number of special hazards for an innocent or mainly innocent man, who is arraigned in a joint trial. He may be smeared just by sitting in the dock with a bunch of villains, having been picked up and charged just because he was found to be associating with them. If one of his co-accused is willing to plead guilty, he may be induced to make a statement to the effect that he has played only a minor part and that X was the ringleader. He can no longer make an unsworn statement from the dock, but his statement may be read or the police can give an account of their interview with him. The trial Judge then takes the jury into the land of make-believe, telling them that the statement is not evidence against X and that they must put it out of their minds when weighing the evidence against him. Alternatively an accused pleading guilty may want to give evidence to the effect that X had nothing to do with the crime, but is pressed by the police or his counsel not to do so on the grounds that this could affect his sentence. He should be sentenced before the main trial but some judges decline to do this. If he wants to give evidence after the trial, the Court of Appeal will rule that X's counsel could have called him.

An innocent man can in many cases be safeguarded against conviction by a well-prepared and competent defence but he is quite likely to find himself defended by a counsel whom he sees for the first time on the morning of the trial and who knows very little about the case. He has to depend on counsel's advice as to which witnesses he will call and whether he will go into the witness box. If he is wrongly advised, the Court of Appeal will hold him responsible for his counsel's incompetence or errors of judgement. If the evidence against him appears difficult to rebut – for example, alleged verbal admissions – his counsel may persuade him to plead guilty to avoid publicity or the certainty of conviction on a more serious charge. This happens very frequently in Magistrates' Courts. Furthermore, in these courts it is not uncommon for the police to advise defendants to plead guilty even though they may have valid defences. When I was sitting as a magistrate we had three such cases in one morning.

The final hazard to be overcome is a prosecution-minded judge, who is allowed a very wide degree of licence by the Court of Appeal. He can protect the police from piercing cross-examination or play down any discrepancies in their evidence. He can pontificate about the motives and reliability of defence witnesses. He can make his own views crystal clear and pour scorn on the defence provided he says at suitable intervals, 'but this is a matter for you, members of the jury'.

Nearly all the hazards I have catalogued are inherent in an accusatorial system which is more of a battle than an inquiry into the truth and is operated under wholly inadequate safeguards and controls. They can all lead – and do lead – to miscarriage of justice for which it is very difficult indeed to obtain a remedy.

Remedies

The Court of Appeal

The first remedy available to a man who claims to have been wrongly convicted is an application for leave to appeal to the Criminal Division of the Court of Appeal. To do this with any prospect of success he needs to have the full support of his defence lawyers, who are under a duty to advise him if he has any grounds of appeal and, if they think he has, to provide him with provisional grounds. Counsel can further ask for a transcript of the summing-up to enable him to submit fuller grounds of appeal. If these are rejected by a 'Single Judge' all legal aid ceases. Unless counsel is willing to advise or assist without remuneration, the appellant can only pursue his application to the Full Court with his own native wit and at risk of being ordered to serve extra time. It is entirely a matter of chance whether his papers are read by an open-minded or a hard-line judge.

If he is fortunate enough to be given leave to appeal, or granted counsel to argue his application before the Full Court of three judges, it is again a matter of chance whether he gets a good or bad presiding judge. However the Court may be composed, his counsel will have to battle with it, just as he had to battle in the Court of trial. The judges will have been provided with a summary of the case prepared by a member of the Criminal Appeal Office staff, which the appellant's counsel is not allowed to see. Normally only one of the three judges will have read all the papers and will deliver the judgement.

The obstacles to be overcome are even more formidable than I have indicated in the previous chapter, viz:

1. The Court will only rarely entertain complaints of police perjury or malpractice. These are not investigated until after the appeal has been decided.

2. It will not listen to any evidence or line of defence which could have been adduced at the trial.

3. It is prone to decide that new witnesses will not be credible without allowing them to go into the witness box and have their evidence tested.

4. The Court will not upset the verdict of a jury – provided there was evidence on which a jury could properly convict (and this can consist of one disputed verbal admission) – unless there has been a serious material irregularity or misdirection in law on the part of the trial Judge. Even then it can apply the proviso and refuse to quash the conviction if it believes the appellant to be guilty and that his release would not be conducive to the public good or would be an embarrassment to authority.

In 1967, on the unanimous recommendations of a powerful Justice committee, the Court was empowered to order a new trial on fresh evidence. Nine of its thirteen members wanted it to be given a general power: first to quash the conviction and then to order a new trial. The advantage for the appellant is that it gives him the opportunity of having the new evidence put in its full context. Lord Devlin, in his contribution to Ludovic Kennedy's book on the Luton murder case, *Wicked Beyond Belief*, argued strongly that it was wrong and unfair for the Court, in three successive references, to have considered the new evidence piece-meal. My own comment was that if any jury had heard the evidence of the two uncalled witnesses that pointed to Matthews being the driver of the getaway van, it would never have believed his evidence that secured the conviction of Murphy, Cooper and McMahon.

In the outcome the power has been very rarely used – in the four years since 1978 to 1981 only seven new trials were ordered and in 1982, none. I take the view that this can easily bring about denials of justice. It is surely significant that, in 1982, out of 1,352 appeals to the Court of Appeal only 113 (8 per cent) were allowed, whereas in appeals from Magistrates' Courts to the Crown Court, which are complete rehearings, out of 6,083 appeals 1,696 (27 per cent) were allowed.

The Home Office

The final remedy available to people claiming that they have been wrongly convicted, either on indictment or in a Magistrate's Court, is the Home Secretary, who has the following powers to intervene in cases where a defendant has been convicted of a criminal offence:

1. Under section 17 of the Criminal Appeal Act, 1968, he is empowered where the defendant has been convicted on indictment, to refer the case to the Court of Appeal Criminal Division, for determination as to conviction or sentence or both, as if it were on appeal by the convicted person, or

2. By constitutional convention he is responsible (in England and Wales) for recommending the exercise of the Royal Prerogative of Mercy to grant

(i) A Free Pardon, the effect of which is that a conviction is to be disregarded so that, so far as is possible, the person is relieved of all penalties and other consequences of the conviction, or

(ii) A Conditional Pardon, which excuses or varies the consequences of the conviction subject to conditions. This power has been used primarily to commute a sentence of death to a sentence of life imprisonment, a purpose which it still serves in respect of sentences in the Isle of Man and Jersey, or

(iii) Remission of all or part of the penalty imposed by the Court.

The exercise of the use of the Royal Prerogative is also recommended in cases where mitigation of sentence seems appropriate for reasons not relating to the rightness of the conviction; for example, to reward assistance to the prison authorities or for compassionate reasons.

The above description of the powers of the Home Secretary is taken from the memorandum submitted in evidence by the Home

Affairs Committee of Parliament on the subject of miscarriages of justice. It goes on to point out that by common law and statute the duty of determining individual cases is placed solely on the courts and that persistent intervention by the Home Secretary in the exercise of this duty would run the risk of undermining the distinction between the proper functions of the executive and the judiciary and subjecting the latter to influence and pressures outside the due process of law. Successive Home Secretaries had accordingly held firmly to the principle that it would be wrong for them to intervene in a case on the basis of information which the courts have considered, *whatever their own assessment of that information may be*. This makes it crystal clear that in deference to an unwritten constitutional principle Home Office ministers and officials, even when faced with strong evidence of innocence, may be powerless to do anything about it. There is no doubt at all that in many cases this can lead to a denial of justice because the phrase 'information which the courts have considered' is open to wide interpretation. If, for example, a convicted man, deserted by his trial lawyers, submits lengthy grounds of appeal complaining of malpractice on the part of the prosecution or questionable forensic evidence, or asking to call witnesses whom he wanted to call at his trial, and they are dismissed by the Single Judge, with the comment, 'I can find no reason to give leave to appeal', all his submissions are regarded as information which the courts have considered. This must surely be wrong, because it closes the door to investigation of matters which may have not been considered in the true sense of the word and may conclusively prove innocence.

This can work particularly unfairly in a case where an appellant has been refused leave to call witnesses who, for various reasons, were not called at the trial and the Court has decided without hearing them that they would not be credible. I have submitted a number of such cases to the Home Office asking for inquiries to be made, but invariably the response has been to the effect that the Chief Constable's report does not justify any action being taken.

Difficulty also arises over the definition of new evidence which has genuinely come into the possession of the defence after the dismissal of an appeal. For example, could the defence with due diligence have traced a new witness in time for an appeal? Could it have obtained forensic evidence which rebuts the prosecution evidence or have insisted that it be obtained? Peter Hill discusses this problem in his account of his investigations into the case of Ernest Clarke. In the McDonagh case, the Manchester police claimed that Clara Esty was not a new witness because she made a statement to the police, despite the fact that it was not in the bundle of documents given to the defence.

Even if the evidence is accepted as new, even greater difficulties and potential denials of justice can stem from its evaluation. As the Home Office memorandum to the Home Affairs Committee rightly points out, its officials have to decide whether the new evidence is likely to carry the requisite weight with the Court of Appeal when balanced against evidence that secured the conviction. They do not want to waste the Court's time, or be rebuffed by it, or give the petitioner false hopes. A previous dismissal of an appeal may well act as a deterrent. The evaluation of a new witness may well be difficult, especially when this will normally depend on the report received from the investigating officer. This is surely a matter for an experienced criminal lawyer with no axe to grind rather than for an official of the Home Office with an inbuilt bias in favour of the police and a natural duty to support them.

Special obstacles are met with when a witness wants to go back on the evidence or statement he has made previously. He may be threatened with prosecution for perjury (like Sheila Eccleston in the McDonagh case), or he may just be warned that it will do him no good. I have sometimes taken vital statements from new witnesses, only to be told in due course by the Home Office that they were not prepared to confirm the statement they had made to me. A similar difficulty arises in cases where someone, on an access of conscience, decides to confess to a crime of which somebody else has been convicted. He may either be warned off by the police or, if he gets to the Court of Appeal, will be warned that he need not incriminate himself. It must surely be wrong that while a known criminal can be offered immunity in whole or in part if he is willing to give evidence on behalf of the prosecution, no such immunity can be offered to a man who is anxious to give evidence on behalf of truth and justice.

It is for this reason that Justice made several recommendations to the effect that in default of provision for independent investigations, the interviewing of witnesses should not be entrusted to the police force responsible for obtaining the conviction. The objection to this practice is that it creates a conflict of loyalties which showed itself only too clearly in the cases of John Walters and the McDonaghs.

An outstanding example of this, and of the obduracy of the Home Office, was the case of Anthony Stock, who in 1970 was convicted of taking part in an armed robbery on a Leeds supermarket and sentenced to ten years' imprisonment. The evidence against him was provided by Detective Sergeant Mather, who had charged Stock on a previous occasion without success. Quite irregularly, he brought the store manager to Stock's house for a confrontation. Stock was taken aback by the appearance of his old enemy on his doorstep and shut the door. The jury was not told the reason for this and Mather, supported by his brother officer, attributed his panic to his being confronted by the man he was alleged to have robbed. For good measure, he told the jury that when he took a cup of tea into Stock's cell he had said, 'Whatever happens, my wife will get her share of the swag.' At the time of the robbery he had been at his home in Bradford but his wife's alibi evidence did not help him. His application for leave to appeal was dismissed but, shortly afterwards, his hopes were raised by the news that Mather was facing charges of corruption. He was cleared of these by a jury only to be faced with six disciplinary charges, including two for dishonesty, from which he was again cleared by the Chief Constable of a neighbouring force. I learned that his brother officers were dismayed by this and that he later resigned from the force. It seemed to me quite wrong that Stock's conviction should rest on the word of a discredited officer. I pressed this view vigorously on the then Minister of State but he declined to intervene. Stock's solicitor petitioned the European Commission of Human Rights with a similar result.

Stock served six and half years of his ten-year sentence and on his release moved out of Bradford and built up a successful carpet business. Then, in November 1979, at Maidstone Crown Court, a man named Benenfield pleaded guilty to a number of offences and asked for the Leeds supermarket robbery to be taken into consideration. The police had not thought fit to tell Stock, but an *Evening News* reporter passed the information to the *Yorkshire Post*, which passed it on to Justice. I was able to trace Stock. A Leeds solicitor obtained a copy of Benenfield's statement which named all the men who had taken part in the robbery and asked the Home Office to grant Stock a free pardon and appropriate compensation.

A police inquiry was ordered, but we were disturbed to learn that this was being carried out by a Chief Superintendent of the West Yorkshire force – who was of equal rank to the officer who had supported Mather's version of the confrontation, whose reputation was thereby at risk. It was therefore no surprise when the Home Office rejected Stock's petition, despite the fact, as we later learned, that Benenfield's gang was London-based and that the police had been unable to trace any connection between them and Stock. The reason given was that there was no proof that Benenfield had done the robbery. He had become a Supergrass and was lodged in a police safe house. The Prison Department agreed to pass a message to him. He came to the office and gave me a taped interview in which his description of how the robbery took place was almost identical to that given by the manager of the supermarket. My Chairman made personal representations to William Whitelaw, who was then Home Secretary, and he replied that he was not prepared to give Stock a pardon just on the word of a known criminal. Yet, on the same criminal's word, a number of men had been convicted and sentenced to long terms of imprisonment.

This ruined Anthony Stock's life for the second time. In expectation of having his name cleared, he had agreed to the screening of a documentary film about his case. This alerted his customers and neighbours to his criminal conviction. His business folded and when I last heard from him he was unable to find work.

Prisoners who have been unable to establish the falsity of the prosecution case at their trials frequently resort to a complaint against the police. If an appeal is pending, chief constables normally delay investigation of the complaint until after it has been determined. If, in the opinion of the Chief Constable, the investigation discloses any evidence of a criminal offence on the part of the officer or officers involved, he has to send all the papers to the Director of Public Prosecutions to decide whether or not they should be prosecuted. Knowing from experience how difficult it is to prove deliberate perjury and how reluctant judges and juries are to convict police officers, the Director very rarely prosecutes and the complainant is briefly informed that he has not found sufficient evidence to justify the taking of criminal proceedings. He is not, however, given any information about the factual findings of the investigation, nor any indication whether the police malpractice complained of was responsible for his being wrongly convicted, or whether evidence of innocence had been brought to light – something he desperately wants to know. It is the practice in such situations for a copy of the report to be sent to the Home Office, but the complainant is not informed and it is a strict rule that all police reports and statements taken are confidential. I have always regarded it as quite monstrous that a wrongly convicted man should not be allowed access to evidence which, if pursued, might be strengthened and establish his innocence.

An outstanding example of this was the 'Case of the Clicking Clock', which hit the headlines in 1979. In 1974, on strong circumstantial evidence, Albert Taylor had been convicted of the murder of a young girl. Much depended on the time of death and an alibi that depended on whether or not a station clock clicked on the half-hour. Taylor maintained that he heard it. The prosecution produced evidence that it did not. Taylor complained to the Chief Constable of Huntingdon that the police had brought pressure to bear on witnesses and in January 1977 Chief Superintendent Crust of the Essex force was asked to carry out the investigation. In April 1977 he discovered that when the police made their tests the clicking mechanism was temporarily out of action and in July he visited Taylor and told him that he had uncovered helpful evidence about the clock and the time of the death. At the end of September 1977 Taylor became impatient and his Welfare Officer wrote to Chief Superintendent Crust on his behalf. He replied to the effect that he had expressed the view in his report that the new evidence he had uncovered would have affected the verdict of the jury *and that it should be the subject of examination by an independent body*.

Then, in January 1978, Taylor was informed by the Chief Constable of Huntingdonshire that the Director of Public Prosecutions had decided to take no action and that he did not propose to pursue the matter any further. This prompted me to visit Hull Prison, where the Welfare Officer showed me Chief Superintendent Crust's letter. I arranged for a friendly firm of solicitors to take up the case and they were able to obtain from the Director of Public Prosecutions copies of the report on the clock and medical evidence. We drafted a petition to the Home Office and in December 1978, eighteen months after Chief Superintendent Crust's report had been presented, the Home Secretary referred Taylor's case to the Court of Appeal which three months later quashed his conviction. He was later awarded £20,000 compensation. We were never able to discover if Chief Superintendent Crust's recommendation had been passed to the Home Office and, if it had, at what level it had been considered and shelved.

The level at which cases are considered and the status of officials who man the C5 Department was one of the more important matters on which representatives of the Home Office were questioned by the Home Affairs Committee. It was told that the staff

consisted of one Assistant Secretary (who has other responsi-
bilities), four Principals (one of whom is mainly occupied on other
work), and eight Higher Executive Officers, with appropriate
clerical assistance. None of these was a lawyer. They had to deal
with about 2,600 petitions a year – but the great majority of these
were bread-and-butter cases. The serious cases were first dealt
with by Higher Executive Officers and it was a matter for their
judgement whether they referred a case to a Principal. Cases
would reach the Assistant Secretary only if they raised sufficiently
serious issues, or if there was a serious prospect of taking action
about them. If an M.P. takes up a case, the Minister of State has
to be alerted and sign the letter explaining why no action will be
taken. This is always much fuller than a letter to the petitioner or
his solicitor and the M.P. has the further privilege of seeking an
interview with the Minister.

The extent to which the Minister can study the documents in
a case and master all its implications is highly problematical. He
has inevitably to rely on a summary prepared by his officials and,
when accompanying M.P.s on such interviews, I have invariably
found that the best complexion has been put on the evidence for
the prosecution and worst complexion on the matter raised in the
submissions. On many occasions I have thought that the arguments advanced then, and repeated in a subsequent letter, were
either evasive or Machiavellian. When Miss Alice Bacon was
appointed Minister of State, I asked if I could come and see her
– she had frequently visited a friend who lived in my house. When
I went into her room, she pointed to two piles of case files 18
inches high on her desk and said: 'Tom, I am supposed to read
these and make decisions on them. How can I ever hope to do them
justice? I don't like many of the letters I am asked to sign and have
to send them back.' Who knows how many petitions that merit
top-level attention fail to get it, particularly if they are received
direct from prisoners who are illiterate or have little knowledge
of English. I was once able to secure the release of two Pakistanis,
who had been convicted of murder, only because one of them
happened to be befriended by a prison officer who spoke Urdu.

The level at which a case is first considered is of great importance – if only because of a natural resistance to efforts to get a decision changed. A striking and disgraceful example of this was the case of Roy Binns who, in July 1976, was found guilty of setting fire to a Portacabin outside Scarborough Hospital and sentenced to eighteen months' imprisonment. He and a friend called Wheatley came under suspicion and, after prolonged questioning, they both admitted guilt. At the trial Wheatley pleaded guilty and gave evidence against Binns. Binns, who had a history of psychic disorder, withdrew his confession, maintaining that he had been assaulted and threatened by the police. He was nevertheless found guilty. An unidentified fingerprint was found at the scene, but this was not disclosed to the jury. Binns lodged a complaint against the police, and the Chief Superintendent who investigated it found that the fingerprint was that of a local criminal named Alexandre who admitted responsibility for starting the fire. Wheatley withdrew his confession and admitted giving false evidence against Binns. Early in December 1976 the Chief Superintendent visited Binns and told him that he was recommending a pardon and that he should be out for Christmas.

He could have known little about the ways of authority. His report was sent to the Chief Constable, who in turn sent it to the Director of Public Prosecutions. It was dealt with by an assistant solicitor, who in March 1979 sent a preliminary note to the Home Office saying that he was making further inquiries about Alexandre's confession. So far as Binns was concerned, nothing happened until May, when his solicitors were advised that the Director did not intend to prosecute Alexandre and had not made any recommendation to the Home Office in respect of Binns.

This provoked his counsel to apply for leave to appeal out of time. The Chief Superintendent's report was made available; leave was immediately given; the appeal was heard by a Vacation Court and the prosecution virtually invited it to quash Binns's conviction. He had by then been released on parole.

His solicitors immediately applied for compensation and in December they received a brief reply saying that the law made no provision for payment to persons whose convictions were quashed on appeal and that Binns's case did not justify an exceptional ex gratia payment. This was in clear contradiction to the Home Office memorandum to the Home Affairs Committee which states that an ex gratia payment may also be made where misconduct or default by the police or some other agency of the criminal justice system has been instrumental in the wrongful conviction or charge. For what could be greater misconduct than the suppression of the fingerprint of a man who later confessed to the crime, and the obtaining of a confession by physical pressure from a man with a history of psychiatric disorder? At this point, Binns sought the help of his M.P., Michael Shaw, who in turn asked for the advice and help of Justice. We drafted fully argued submissions, which were strongly supported by the prosecuting solicitor, the senior partner in a private firm, but to no avail. It was clear that once the adverse decision had been made it could not be changed.

I took the view that the case raised an issue of constitutional importance. As justification for its opposition to an independent review tribunal or panel, the Home Office has consistently maintained that it would not be right for the Home Secretary to be advised by anyone but his officials as to the use of his powers of reference or of the Royal Prerogative; in this case his officials appeared to have relied on the advice of an assistant solicitor in the office of the Director of Public Prosecutions.

I accordingly asked Michael Shaw to put this point to the Ombudsman. He found that there had been no maladministration, but his report contained the astonishing disclosure that Binns's case, i.e. the Chief Superintendent's recommendation of a pardon, had been dealt with *at junior management level*. The refusal of compensation to Binns was further shown to have been arbitrary and unjust by a similar case in which I was involved a few months later.

James Stevens had been found guilty of robbery with violence and sentenced to five years' imprisonment on the basis of an alleged verbal admission to a police officer on the night he was arrested. The trial Judge omitted to point out to the jury two important matters, but his counsel had advised against an appeal. Stevens then lodged a complaint and, after a long investigation, the Chief Superintendent who had conducted it told Stevens that although he had been unable to obtain any written confessions, he was satisfied he was innocent and would report accordingly. Moreover, the officer complained of had also visited Stevens and apologized for what he had done.

In the outcome, the Home Office refused to pardon Stevens or to refer his case to the Court of Appeal, saying that it was not prepared to rely solely on the opinion of a police officer. Stevens's M.P. approached Justice and with Binns's case in mind I prevailed upon Stevens's solicitor to apply for leave to appeal out of time and an experienced counsel offered to act pro deo. The Court helped us to obtain access to witnesses and when the appeal came before the Lord Chief Justice, he allowed it after a very brief argument. Despite its refusal in the case of Binns, the Home Office immediately agreed to pay compensation to Stevens and he was awarded £10,000.

The inadequacy of the Home Office procedure and provision for the review of claims of wrong conviction has been authoritatively brought to light by the Ombudsman's report on the cases of the forensic scientist, Dr Clift. As the result of his investigations, no less than sixteen cases have since been referred to the Court of Appeal. These had not all been laid to rest on the shelves of lower management. In one of them I had twice made unsuccessful representations at ministerial level.

If the Home Secretary has doubts about the rightness of a conviction but considers that the evidence which points to it is too old or complex for consideration by the Court of Appeal, he will grant a free pardon only on clear and irrefutable proof of innocence. The burden of proof is reversed. This means that the evidence brought against the petitioner has to be demolished together with any objections by the police, which are not disclosed to him. In the period from 1960 to 1982 I submitted an average of three well-researched and documented petitions a year without securing a single pardon. In the same period only four of my cases were referred to the Court of Appeal – three of them by one Minister of State who had the courage to override his officials.

His final alternative, which is to remit the unserved part of a prisoner's sentence, gives him his freedom but leaves the injustice unremedied. Although there must have been serious doubts about the rightness of his conviction, he is not entitled to any compensation. He does not know if society regards him as innocent or guilty and his conviction remains on police records.

According to the Home Office memorandum I have cited, in the nine years from 1972 to 1981, thirty-four cases involving forty-six defendants were referred to the Court of Appeal, of which twenty-one were allowed. In the period from 1972 to 1980, in respect of convictions on indictment, only nine free pardons were granted and eight sentences remitted.

A number of the failures are attributable to the restrictive terms of the Home Office Letter of Reference. Until the comparatively recent decision of the House of Lords in R *v.* Chard (November 1983), the Court of Appeal took the view that it could only examine and consider the probable effect on the jury of the matters mentioned in the Letter of Reference – unless it was asked to consider the whole case. The Luton murder case provided a striking example of this. The Home Office referred the case of Murphy on the strength of a new alibi witness who had seen him in North London at the time when, according to Matthews, he had been involved in the murder of the postmaster and had been the driver of the getaway van. If the alibi evidence was accepted, it would also discredit Matthews's vital evidence against Cooper and McMahon. I made strong representations to the Home Secretary, Lord Carr, and counsel made representations to the Registrar, that the terms of the letter should be widened to include Cooper and McMahon, but to no avail. After quashing Murphy's conviction the Court went out of its way to say that this did not affect their position. R *v.* Chard allows appellant's counsel full freedom to raise any matter he wishes and it is significant that the Court quashed the conviction of Mervyn Russell on new evidence about the hairs which came to light only a few weeks before the appeal was heard.

In the light of the hazards of the accusatorial system and the obduracy of the Court of Appeal, it is surely beyond argument that the Home Office provides a wholly inadequate last remedy for the wrongly convicted. When the late Lord Brooke was Home Secretary he described the Home Office as a long-stop. But what is the value of a long-stop if he refuses to stop a ball that has passed within the reach of the wicket-keeper? David Mellor, the present Parliamentary Under-Secretary of State, has described it as a safety-net. But what is the use of a safety-net if it covers only a small part of the area into which a trapeze artist can fall?

The Home Office can plead that, because of the number of balls that the wicket-keeper fails to stop, it has been given an impossible task. Similarly, the Court of Appeal can fairly plead that it could not cope with all the hazards of the accusatorial system without the protective wall it has constructed to hold back the flood. But the responsibility for the laws and directives governing criminal procedure has always rested with the Home Office and it has consistently refused to introduce legislation that would effectively prevent or control the abuses of our trial system by substituting statutes for judicial and police discretion.

The other main charge that can be laid against its door is that it takes an unnecessarily restrictive and defensive view of the powers of the Home Secretary, especially in respect of his power to seek independent advice on the use of the Prerogative and the other remedies available to him. In 1968 Justice published a report entitled 'Home Office Reviews of Criminal Convictions'. It was prepared by a committee which included five Q.C.s now serving as judges and was unanimously endorsed by its Council. Its main recommendation was that there should be a panel of experienced barristers and solicitors, appointed by the Attorney-General, to whom, after initial sifting by Home Office officials, cases justifying further investigation could be referred. They would have at their disposal a body of investigators consisting of retired police officers or inquiry agents and make a recommendation to the Home Secretary which he could either accept or reject. Legal advice should be available to petitioning prisoners and reasons for rejections should be communicated to them. The committee further recommended that in the small number of cases which could not be resolved and were unsuitable for reference to the Court of Appeal, a Commissioner of high authority should be appointed with full powers to examine witnesses and call for documents in a search for the truth.

The committee's justification for these recommendations, briefly summarized, were:

1. The hazards of the accusatorial system bring about many wrong convictions which the Court of Appeal is unable to or does not allow itself to remedy.

2. A prisoner without legal aid is in no position to assemble and present the full strength of his case.

3. There is a no man's land between the Court of Appeal and the Home Office in which wounded prisoners lie and call for help in vain.

4. It is basically wrong that the Home Office, which has overall responsibility for the morale and conduct of the police, should be the arbiter in cases where police malpractice is alleged.

Apart from some criticisms of the proposal to appoint a commissioner who would sit in judgement outside the normal appellate procedure, the report met with general approval, but no effective notice of it was taken by authority. The same fate befell Lord Devlin's recommendation, in his report on 'Evidence of Identification' (1976), that the Home Office should study the feasibility of setting up an independent review tribunal by which cases unsuitable for reference to the Court of Appeal could be handled.

Then in 1982, prompted by the 'Rough Justice' cases, the all-party Parliamentary Home Affairs Committee embarked on a study of miscarriages of justice and heard oral evidence from the Home Office, Justice and the Criminal Bar Association. Members of the committee questioned the Home Office strongly and repeatedly as to their reason for rejecting the idea of an independent review body to assist the Home Secretary in determining difficult cases, and effectively deployed all the arguments that had been put forward in the Justice report. But the Home Office took a firm stand on the unwritten constitutional position that the responsibility for deciding whether some form of interference with the normal processes of criminal justice was called for lay with the Home Secretary and the Home Secretary alone. He should retain his full freedom of action and it would be wrong for him to seek advice from anyone outside his department.

This argument, as I later pointed out to the committee, was ill-founded. The late Sir Arthur Dixon, a former Permanent Under-Secretary of State at the Home Office, was a family friend and he told me that when he was head of the Criminal Justice Department and had a difficult case on hand, he frequently asked a leading Q.C. to read the papers and advise him. My own view, for what it is worth, is that the real reason for the Home Office's reluctance to admit outsiders to its inner sanctum is that it might bring to light police malpractice and reveal injustices hitherto kept from the public eye.

The report of the Home Affairs Committee went somewhat further than that of the Justice Committee. It recommended the setting-up of an independent review body with advisory powers, but went on to recommend that the petitioner should not have to prove his innocence. The review body should be empowered to advise the exercise of the Royal Prerogative if its investigation had shown the original verdict of the Court to be unsafe and unsatisfactory.

Despite the weight and cogency of the report, the Government rejected its recommendations out of hand. Its only concession was an undertaking that the Home Office would be more open-minded in its examination of petitions and the Court of Appeal would be more willing to receive fresh evidence. I have as yet seen no sign that this undertaking is being adequately honoured.

A major obstacle facing anyone who wants to help a wrongly convicted prisoner establish his innocence is that he is denied access to unpublished statements, police records and forensic reports. Peter Hill vividly described his difficulties in obtaining such evidence and in securing statements from vital witnesses in his account of his investigations into the cases of Ernest Clarke and George Beattie. The same difficulties face solicitors and a society like Justice, and to them has to be added the prohibitive cost of obtaining transcripts of the evidence of witnesses at the trial. I was repeatedly asked by prisoners for help in obtaining statements taken by the police, but have had to tell them that I had no special power to obtain them. Margaret Livesey told her husband that she had been examined by a psychiatrist who had told her that she could set her mind at rest because she was not a murderer, but the prison authorities refused to give me his name.

The situation is somewhat easier if an application for leave to appeal has been lodged, because the Court can then be asked to order their disclosure. But there is no guarantee that it will do this, and in my experience it will not normally disclose them to the defence counsel unless leave to appeal has been given. To put this briefly, a petitioner or his would-be helper has to go about his task without tools and without the necessary resources to assemble a convincing case. Adequate investigative resources are available only to the media.

In my view the provision of limited legal aid would not always meet the need and in any event would not provide authority to obtain statements and other documents. For this reason I have been attracted over the years by the idea of establishing the office of Public Defender, who could be asked to espouse the cause of persons wishing to pursue their claims to innocence and who appeared to have good grounds for doing so. In New South Wales, the Solicitor-General plays such a role. He collects all the available evidence and presents the petitioner's case to the Court of Appeal. The advantage of having a Public Defender somewhere in the scheme of things is that he would enjoy full authority to obtain documents and be allowed access on a confidential basis to police records and reports. He would not be a substitute for an independent review body but could provide a useful adjunct to it.

I cannot conclude this chapter without calling attention to the report of the Ombudsman, Sir Cecil Clothier, Q.C., on the Home Office handling of the Dr Clift cases, in which he said that a suspected miscarriage of justice was one of the gravest matters that can occupy the attention of a civilized society.

Furthermore, it is not often realized that if the wrong man is convicted, the real criminal remains free to commit further crimes.

Aftermath:
A Chapter of Innocents

In the vast majority of cases where innocent people may have been convicted, the only feasible method of collecting enough evidence to persuade the Home Secretary to order an official investigation is to make television programmes about them. That, unfortunately, is the reality; we are convinced that it is not the best way.

There are many reasons why an official investigative body should be set up to deal with such cases. We are investigators rather than lawyers, and in our eyes one reason carries more weight than the others – the pain that the present system can bring to innocent people.

The investigation of a murder usually leaves a trail of horror and torment behind it. That is readily understood. But the re-investigation of a case of murder recalls all the horror of the original events and re-opens wounds which may have taken years to heal. It is made worse because such re-investigations take much longer than they need and finish in a blaze of publicity. No matter what the justification, it is a nasty and usually thankless task.

The cases in the second 'Rough Justice' series involved convicts who had had little or no previous trouble with the police (Ernie Clarke, you will remember, had been fined for the theft of a Post Office book from his wife). The very thought of crime on the scale of murder entering into the lives of these people was appalling to them. Suddenly their family and neighbours were in the public eye. They became accustomed to being rung up by the Press and being taken down to the police station at all times of the day and night. All would have preferred to live their lives quietly, but suddenly they were notorious.

Re-investigation doubles the horror. Yet we only ever come to such cases because the horror has never really receded. A murder does not stop with the violence done to the victim; it also leaves a wake of destruction far greater than could ever be imagined by the general public. This chain reaction is further aggravated by carelessness.

Did the person who failed to record the Benson and Hedges cigarette pack on the exhibits list in the Livesey case and failed to follow up the forensic clues on the cigarette butts near Alan Livesey's body realize what repercussions this would have in subsequent years?

What of the lawyer who did not call John Kershaw, who would have shown that Mrs Livesey was in the street at the time the jury thought she was stabbing her son? Or the person who persuaded Peter Nightingale to retract his story about the man who left the house after 10 o'clock?

Was it not negligent to omit the records of tank number four from the list of exhibits in the case against Ernie Clarke? And was it not rash to present George Beattie's admission as a confession? Did the person who took that decision realize the consequence of his action?

Innocent people, not solely those inside prison, have been repeatedly reminded of the unhappy events surrounding the murder as a result of such decisions. Whatever one may argue about the faults of our judicial system, our society is such that wherever there is doubt about the justness of a jury's decision there may well be someone who is ready to take up the case again. Someone will rake through the evidence, question the witnesses again, raise the hopes of the convicted person, look around for new witnesses. Someone will keep on asking nasty questions. The corpse of a doubtful verdict does not lie dead in the grave; it rises up to haunt us all.

In many of our interviews, instead of asking the necessary questions, we would much rather have simply said that we were so sorry that such a terrible thing had happened. Sometimes we have wasted our research money because we felt that to go ahead with the investigation at a particular time would cause more grief to other people than we were willing to cause – no matter what the justification.

One of the visits we feel obliged to make is to the family of the victim. It would not be fair to them to produce a television programme without, at the very least, alerting them to what is about to take place. In fact we ask their permission further, for we feel obliged to tell them the basis of our case, our justification for making the programme. We hope that they can be satisfied that we are not simply making a sensational programme.

During the Beattie case we decided that we would have to make this visit early. Carluke is a very small town and it would not take long for the gossip about our inquiries to reach the ears of Margaret's family.

They had all moved house, but we managed to find Margaret's younger sister Rosemary without asking a lot of questions that would have in themselves defeated the object of the exercise. When we located the house we found no one in. So we adopted a technique we had learned well during investigations of fraudsters and the like: we staked the place out.

An hour or so later a woman fitting Rosemary's description turned up, but with a much older lady – too old, we thought, to be her mother. She could have been a friend from work, or a neighbour, but we decided to take no chances. We 'aborted the mission' and went back to London.

We made a second visit, at extra cost, a couple of weeks later and discovered we had been right to be careful. The old lady was indeed Margaret's mother. We met Rosemary and the rest of the McLaughlin family that night and they agreed that the shock would have been too terrible for her. As we thought, they said that they would prefer to break the news to her themselves.

We explained our case to them – such as it was – and discussed it for several hours, trying our best, of course, to refrain from calling Margaret 'the victim' or 'the body' or talking about the blood and wounds. We left with their reluctant approval and the hope that we had not only comforted them in their renewed grief but also that they would be able to shield Margaret's mother from the worst of the effects that the publicity surrounding the programme could bring.

Margaret's mother is just one of the many innocent people who suffer from the repercussions of a miscarriage of justice.

Bob Livesey, the father of Alan and the husband of Margaret Livesey, suffered twofold. He lost not only his son but his wife. After she had made her 'confession' there were attempts to persuade him to divorce her. What this might have achieved is somewhat difficult to understand because he very quickly came to the conclusion that his wife was innocent. But he was even being called as a prosecution witness at one time, until he read a piece of paper he was being asked to sign and realized that it was a waiver, giving up his right as a husband to refuse to give evidence against his wife. This attempt to turn him against his wife embittered him. What has happened since has hurt him even more.

After Margaret Livesey was convicted she suggested to Bob that he contact a woman she knew, an old friend, and ask her to keep house for him. This he did. Then the gossip machine got to work. He was said to be living with a mistress. After four years of this, and the publicity from our film, Bob Livesey finally changed his mind. In spite of believing in Margaret's innocence, he asked for a divorce. Margaret still faces eleven years in jail; she raised no objection. The gossips had had their way. But Bob Livesey was not the only target. Several witnesses were accused of lying and immorality. So, in our turn, were we.

The mother of one of the witnesses came around to her daughter's house in high dudgeon while we were there. She pointed out the twitching curtains across the street and said that the local gossip was that one of us was having an affair with her daughter! It's perhaps just as well that we always go in pairs when we meet such witnesses.

Simply talking to a witness can cause unnecessary grief. They generally wish to know why we have decided to take up a case. The real answer to this question usually lies in the forensic evidence or, more specifically, in the evidence of the post mortem. Unlike the police, we must always justify ourselves. But we try to find an answer which does not go into such terrible details, because most of the witnesses have known the victim.

One of the witnesses in the Livesey case brushed our initial reasons aside. She had been a nurse, she said – so she wanted to know the forensic evidence we were talking about. We warned her that the details were horrific, but she said she was quite used to such things. So we told her – and she fainted. It was a nasty experience, and not one we wish to repeat.

Discussing the remains of Eileen McDougall in detail was absolutely taboo. Even the pathologist on the case was hesitant about going into the details with *us*. We had already debated this matter among ourselves before we ever began to talk to witnesses because there was a point of principle involved which we knew would inevitably arise when it came to writing the script.

The problem was that the only real clues that might point to Eileen's murderer were on what remained of her body. Much could be deduced from it about the circumstances of her death. If we were to go into that evidence, we would have to reveal the details. Although we have discussed some in the film and in this book, we have never publicly revealed the full strength of the evidence because we feel it would cause unnecessary grief to the members of Eileen's family who are trying to live their lives quietly without the notoriety of her death being attached to them.

Eileen's sister Elizabeth suffered terribly during the trial and afterwards because of unnecessary and unsubstantiated stories about her life as a teenager used in evidence against Clarke. We do not believe these stories to be true, and we certainly have no intention of repeating them in detail in these pages because we do not think they had any real bearing on the minds of the jurors at Clarke's trial. Elizabeth vehemently denied the stories at the time, but that did little to stop the gossip-mongers getting to work in South Shields. Because of the controversy that has followed the jury's verdict, Elizabeth, a perfectly respectable married woman, must still suffer the tittle-tattle associated with the murder of her sister more than fifteen years ago.

Eileen's parents have suffered too. They would be the first to admit that they were not the best of parents fourteen years ago. Each of their children left home as soon as possible, and Eileen had run away from home some four times before she finally vanished. The family frequently had arguments, and it was generally agreed that this was because of Mr McDougall's heavy drinking.

But they felt the pain of their daughter's death as deeply as any parents would, perhaps more so than many. Mr McDougall has become a reformed character since Eileen vanished, and this has contributed as much as anything to bringing the McDougall family closer together. Anyone can understand their wish to be allowed to grieve for their daughter in private and not have her picture emblazoned across newspapers and television screens. Yet because of the serious doubts about Clarke's conviction the details of her death have been brought up yet again as a spectre to haunt them.

On the other side of this coin are Ernie Clarke's children. They were infants when Eileen's sister Elizabeth left home, found herself a flat and supplemented her meagre wages by looking after them while their father went to work at Velva Liquids. Today, of course, they are in their late teens.

Four years ago their stable family life was suddenly shattered. Not only was their father arrested, but their stepmother, the only mother they knew, was persuaded to give evidence against him. She had left and divorced Clarke two years earlier and was now re-married, so she was technically free to do so. Her evidence was quite inconsequential; it amounted to a comment that Clarke had hit her with his hand during a domestic argument. The Judge did not even mention it in his summing-up.

But to the Clarke children it was a betrayal. Coupled with the fact that their father had been sent to prison, it devastated them. Suddenly everything that was stable in their lives was gone. They were 'taken into care'. We consider it very much to their credit that they have survived such a disaster.

Since the new evidence about Clarke's case came to light they have become staunch campaigners for their father's cause. As such they are unusual. They were cushioned from the worst of the aftermath. The police did not interview them, the Press did not find them during the trial. They no longer live in South Shields and there is little food for gossips because they cannot possibly have any guilty connection with the murder. They were young at the time, so they bounced back. Most of the people connected with the miscarriages of justice that we investigate do not.

Mrs Beattie, the mother of George Beattie, has now campaigned for ten long years for the freedom of her son. She is worn out with the effort. Along the way she has seen the first re-investigation stopped because someone in the Scottish Crown Office made a simple error in reading the trial transcript so that it was thought one of the main points in Beattie's favour was invalid. She has seen her income to finance her efforts severely diminished as further tragedy hit the Beattie family. First her son Tommy was killed in an accident, then her husband died. She has seen her complaint that her son's defence counsel was negligent turned down by the authorities for reasons she finds hard to believe. Although the defence counsel did not ask many questions which could have persuaded the jury his client was innocent, his tactics were perfectly proper. Perhaps they were ill-chosen in that the Judge did not accept his argument, but mistakes by counsel can never constitute grounds for appeal.

She has now seen a television team take on the case, produce a lot of facts which were never considered by the jury, yet so far achieve nothing.

Throughout all this Mrs Beattie has had to live with the stigma of having reared a murderer. Some former friends no longer talk to her, though oddly enough the victim's mother does. Mrs Beattie is only two thirds of the way through the period of such trial before her son George is likely to come out of jail. What the Court intended as a prison sentence for her son has become for the mother years of complaint, petitions, questions and a search for publicity.

Every year as the Highland Games in Carluke are being organized and publicized, two families suffer. The McLaughlin family mourn the death of Margaret, and the Beattie family think bitterly of the tragedy that took George away from them. In such a close community as Carluke it is inevitable that such mourning extends beyond the family. Everyone – the Beattie family included – mourns the loss of Margaret. She was the 'flower of her year', the most beautiful girl in the town, a model girl and an example to all. She was about to marry a handsome young man who had a good job in South Africa. Margaret's future was something to look forward to and be proud of. Her death robbed the entire community of that pride.

Yet in spite of this, and in spite of the schadenfreude that can be felt in the Beattie neighbourhood, there are many people in Carluke who do not believe George Beattie killed Margaret McLaughlin. Some will not say so outside the privacy of their own homes simply because respect for authority is very strong in a Scottish rural area such as Carluke – and the authorities have said he is guilty. Others, however, are quite open with their views – views based not on evidence, but on their own experience. One solicitor who had not worked on the Beattie case told us he thought George was innocent. When we asked why, he said it was because he had gone to school with George. A neighbour of the Beattie's told us that George was sometimes known as 'Sunshine' because of his cheerful and helpful attitude. 'The big saftie' was another phrase we often heard describing Beattie – and we frequently heard it said that George didn't do the murder because 'he simply hadn't got the guts to do such a thing'.

As a community, Carluke suffers the same conflicts of emotion that Bob Livesey in Bamber Bridge suffers within himself. To help on one side of this conflict can only bring hurt to the other side of it. When there are doubts about the outcome of a trial, such pain is inevitable.

*

The adversarial system in our courts can produce a version of events to persuade the members of a jury, who are pressured into coming to a verdict. But in the days and months after the trial when the pressure has gone, the public at large does not rest easy unless a truth can be discerned beyond the verdict in Court – a truth which answers all the questions about the case. Until the answers to outstanding questions make the verdict 'ring true', the agony continues. Our present system prolongs it.

It is futile to convict Margaret Livesey for the murder of her son if there is no explanation of who caused the 'larking-about' noise in the Liveseys' house around 10 o'clock; who left the house by the back door just after 10; who left the packet of Benson and Hedges cigarettes behind.

It is futile to convict Ernie Clarke for murdering Eileen McDougall if there is no explanation of how she could be hit over the head while in an upright position and yet somehow die without staining her jumper with blood. This was what puzzled people most after the trial.

It is futile to convict George Beattie of the murder of Margaret McLaughlin if there is no explanation of how Scotland's most eminent pathologists failed to list any stomach contents – and if so many other questions about Beattie's story (such as how he came to choose as the murder weapon a knife which the police had already eliminated) remain unanswered.

While such questions persist there is always the chance that someone – a solicitor, a barrister, a journalist, the Justice organization, or even an ordinary member of the public – will sift through the evidence again. When such 'unauthorized' people do the work, it is usually protracted and unnecessarily hurtful. It is often part-time work done without the power of investigation that an official body would have.

But such is the aftermath of doubtful verdicts when the present machinery does not take upon itself the responsibility of answering outstanding questions. The Court of Appeal may be perceived by some as being in existence to weigh up the importance of such points. But no – the ultimate object of the Court is not to answer questions, it is to make judgements on the evidence presented before it that someone else considers relevant. In the future it may deliver judgement on the three cases we covered in the second series of 'Rough Justice', but it will not necessarily answer the outstanding questions. The Court of Appeal may even take the same view of these cases that it previously did – that there is not sufficient new evidence to merit an appeal. 'New' evidence is that which was not available to the defence at the time of the trial, not evidence which, for whatever reason, was not called to the attention of the jury.

The Home Office, or the Crown Office in Scotland, may decide that there is nothing in the evidence discovered by the official re-investigations of the case to merit referring any of them back to the Court of Appeal. No explanation need be given for such a decision. There can be no official appeal against it. The outstanding questions would remain unanswered, so someone will no doubt begin yet another unofficial investigation to try to find the answers.

At the end of all this the convicted person finishes his or her prison sentence, the investigators lose interest because the subject is free at last, the questions remain unanswered and the unpleasant suspicion remains that all is not well with British justice.

When we look at this system from our particular point of view as journalists we find it utterly incredible. Our aim is always to find the truth and then to publish it. When we cannot get at the truth, we tell our viewers why. Perhaps the records are destroyed, perhaps someone is keeping them from us, perhaps we cannot tell whether the evidence of a particular witness is the truth or not. But at least we present as much of the truth as possible to viewers or readers. The official system works in the opposite way. Judgements are delivered from behind a cloak of confidentiality – there, it is said, to protect the innocent; the very people we believe it hurts most.

As journalists our powers are limited, but there is still no official body which can accomplish what we can. The police are sometimes called upon to make further investigations. But they suffer the inevitable handicap of being seen to be 'investigating their own'. We sympathize with them. They can only adopt the same style of investigation technique as the original detectives adopted, 'police style', so they are bound to come to the same dead ends. When they meet witnesses who dislike the police they will meet the same barriers that hindered the original investigation. The tension produced by their uniform of authority may have the same inhibiting effect upon the witnesses that it had during the original investigation. It is like opening with the same gambit when the previous game has been lost.

The Home Office seem to think it is enough. The Parliamentary Under-Secretary of State at the Home Office recently wrote:

> Once an aggrieved person has shown that there is a good prospect of there being evidence which would shed new light on his case, the Home Secretary can, if necessary, ask the police to carry out further inquiries ... In this respect we perform broadly the same role as would the kind of review body proposed by the Home Affairs Committee.

This statement supposes, it seems, that a prisoner in a cell can somehow acquire new evidence about a case. That is virtually impossible. What happens in practice is that a case only gets thoroughly re-investigated when it 'goes commercial'; when a journalist gets involved. From that moment, innocent participants in the case are bound to suffer. But it is now a necessary part of the process if a position is to be reached where 'there is a good prospect of there being evidence which would shed new light on the case'.

It is not the best way. Journalists are not necessarily the best investigators. In the end they will publish the results in a manner designed to sell newspapers or television programmes. There is inevitably an element of sensationalism in what they do. Moreover, when the story is published the journalist is seen to be taking on the courts, the Home Office and the police. An adversarial situation is perceived where none was intended and is exploited by anyone with a will to do so. More heat than light normally comes from such conflicts. Truth and justice are worst served.

There have been many suggestions that the Home Office should create an independent body to review alleged miscarriages of justice. Tom Sargant has already touched on several of the main points of such recommendations in an earlier chapter. We would add one point from our own observations which we believe is often forgotten by lawyers and politicians. There is no point in conducting a full-scale review of a case without first thoroughly re-investigating the evidence. The pronouncement by the Home Office quoted above makes no reference to investigation. That is because the Home Office does not wish to have an investigative body separate from the police. They prefer to 'review' a case and *then* ask the police to make a re-investigation. This is putting the cart before the horse.

There is little alternative within the present system. The police would be severely – and understandably – embarrassed if they were asked to make a re-investigation into areas of a case which they themselves could not account for in their evidence at trial. One can readily understand why the Home Office prefers un-official investigators to present it with a strong case that can overcome any such embarrassment.

But our experience shows that when the review of a case is made official the innocent people whose lives are affected by it are more able to accept the difficulties of the situation. At the moment it is not the review of a case which causes grief – it is the investigation that precedes it. The setting-up of an official re-investigation body would be beneficial in this respect. The people concerned would also be able to trust its findings; they are often not inclined to trust the findings of journalists. It is for this reason that we believe that the work of such a body should be the subject of a detailed annual report, published either openly, or to a committee of the House of Commons.

Re-investigations must not only be properly done, they must be seen to have been done. An official body can achieve this and should prevent much of the anguish caused by the present system.

The process would not take years as it does at the moment. There would be far less publicity involved and no sensationalism at all. The sense of conflict that is inherent in the present system would no longer exist.

Such an innovation would not preclude journalists and other people from taking up cases. Every man should have a right to do that on behalf of his fellow man. But it would take over a large sector of work in the field of investigation which is currently being done by people such as ourselves – not paid by government funds and with inadequate powers for the task.

We investigated the cases of Margaret Livesey, Ernie Clarke and George Beattie because we perceived a need for the work to be done. But we consider that such work is properly the work of good government and not of someone who happens to perceive the need for it. The present system smells of charity.

It would be ridiculous to suggest that police investigations should be financed from commercial funds: we believe that it is also ridiculous to leave the main burden of the investigation of possible miscarriages of justice to an informal system based on the funds of commercial interests. Innocent people suffer unnecessarily.

MORE ABOUT PENGUINS, PELICANS
AND PUFFINS

For further information about books available from Penguins please write to Dept EP, Penguin Books Ltd, Harmondsworth, Middlesex UB7 0DA.

In the U.S.A.: For a complete list of books available from Penguins in the United States write to Dept DG, Penguin Books, 299 Murray Hill Parkway, East Rutherford, New Jersey 07073.

In Canada: For a complete list of books available from Penguins in Canada write to Penguin Books Canada Ltd, 2801 John Street, Markham, Ontario L3R 1B4.

In Australia: For a complete list of books available from Penguins in Australia write to the Marketing Department, Penguin Books Australia Ltd, P.O. Box 257, Ringwood, Victoria 3134.

In New Zealand: For a complete list of books available from Penguins in New Zealand write to the Marketing Department, Penguin Books (N.Z.) Ltd, Private Bag, Takapuna, Auckland 9.

In India: For a complete list of books available from Penguins in India write to Penguin Overseas Ltd, 706 Eros Apartments, 56 Nehru Place, New Delhi 110019.

A CHOICE OF PENGUINS

☐ **The English House Through Seven Centuries**
Olive Cook £10.95

From Norman defensiveness and Tudor flourish to Georgian elegance and Victorian grandeur, this beautiful book records and describes the wealth of domestic architecture in Britain. With photographs by Edwin Smith.

☐ **The Daughters of Karl Marx** £4.95

The letters of Jenny, Laura and Eleanor Marx: 'An enlightening introduction to the preoccupations, political and personal, of the Marx family' – Lionel Kochan. 'The tale they tell is riveting' – *Standard*

☐ **The First Day on the Somme**
Martin Middlebrook £3.95

1 July 1916 was the blackest day of slaughter in the history of the British Army. 'The soldiers receive the best service a historian can provide: their story told in their own words' – *Guardian*

☐ **Lord Hervey's Memoirs** £4.95

As an intimate of the Royal Court – and as a particularly witty and malicious raconteur – Lord Hervey was ideally equipped to write this sparkling account of royal personalities, politics and intrigues, 1727–37.

☐ **Some Lovely Islands** **Leslie Thomas** £5.95

The islands off the coast of Britain, and their islanders, are celebrated in this delightful book by well-known novelist Leslie Thomas. With photographs by Peter Chèze-Brown.

☐ **Harold Nicolson: Diaries and Letters 1930–64** £4.95

A selection of Nicolson's famous diaries and letters. 'A brilliant portrait of English society ... a touching self-portrait of a highly intelligent and civilized man' – Kenneth Clark

A CHOICE OF PENGUINS

☐ **A Colder Eye** **Hugh Kenner** £4.95

A study of the modern Irish writers. 'Anyone interested in language, in theatre history, in, indeed, the great comic literature of Joyce, Beckett and O'Brien will find this a highly enjoyable read' – *Punch*

☐ **The Europeans** **Luigi Barzini** £2.95

Witty, stylish and provocative, this is a veteran journalist's-eye view of the past and present character of the British, French, Germans, Italians and Dutch. 'Fascinating . . . read it immediately' – *The New York Times*

☐ **In Search of Ancient Astronomies** **Ed. E. C. Krupp** £4.95

Forming an introduction to archaeo-astronomy, a series of new essays on the world's most spectacular ancient monuments, from Stonehenge to the pyramids. 'Outstanding . . . accessible even to the beginner' – Patrick Moore

☐ **Clinging to the Wreckage** **John Mortimer** £2.50

The bestselling autobiography by the creator of Rumpole and the playwright author of *A Voyage Round My Father*. 'Enchantingly witty . . . England would be a poor place without Mr Mortimer' – Auberon Waugh

☐ **Chips: The Diaries of Sir Henry Channon** £4.95

'Chips' Channon, M.P., knew everybody that was anybody. Here, from the abdication of Edward VIII to the coronation of Elizabeth II, he serves up history with an irresistible 'H.P.' sauce of gossip and glamour.

☐ **The Miracle of Dunkirk** **Walter Lord** £2.95

'This is contemporary history at its most readable' – *The New York Times*. 'It gives an effective new polish to the golden legend' – *The Times*

A CHOICE OF PENGUINS

☐ *Earth to Earth* **John Cornwell**   £1.95

This Gold Dagger Award-winning recreation of the lives and violent deaths of a Devon farming family is part village history, part enthralling, true detective story and an 'extraordinary tale' – William Trevor

☐ *A History of Venice* **John Julius Norwich**   £8.95

Lord Norwich's loving and scholarly portrayal is now 'the standard Venetian history in English' – *The Times*

☐ *The Pastons*   £3.95

These remarkable letters, linked with a commentary by Richard Barber, constitute a fresh and unforgettable insight into all aspects of the Paston family's life during the Wars of the Roses.

These books should be available at all good bookshops or newsagents, but if you live in the UK or the Republic of Ireland and have difficulty in getting to a bookshop, they can be ordered by post. Please indicate the titles required and fill in the form below.

NAME _____ BLOCK CAPITALS

ADDRESS _____

_____

_____

Enclose a cheque or postal order payable to The Penguin Bookshop to cover the total price of books ordered, plus 50p for postage. Readers in the Republic of Ireland should send £IR equivalent to the sterling prices, plus 67p for postage. Send to: The Penguin Bookshop, 54/56 Bridlesmith Gate, Nottingham, NG1 2GP.

You can also order by phoning (0602) 599295, and quoting your Barclaycard or Access number.

Every effort is made to ensure the accuracy of the price and availability of books at the time of going to press, but it is sometimes necessary to increase prices and in these circumstances retail prices may be shown on the covers of books which may differ from the prices shown in this list or elsewhere. This list is not an offer to supply any book.

This order service is only available to residents in the UK and the Republic of Ireland.